FINDING BLINDNESS

This edited volume explores blindness as a construct with which we the contributors engage as part of our social existence and/or academic research. Irrespective of eye conditions, or the lack thereof, blindness is an understanding at which we have all come to arrive. On the way to this conceptual point, which is in any case unlikely ever to be fixed, we have passed or visited many formative cultural stations.

In the terms of autocritical disability studies (i.e. an explicitly embodied development of critical disability studies), these cultural stations include key moments in education and training; the reflective pursuits of philosophy, aesthetics, and cultural theory; literary works such as autobiography, novels, short stories, drama, and poetry; visual texts ranging from photography to postage stamps; technological developments like television, computer applications, and social media; value systems defined by family and/or religion; and the social phenomenon of hate and war. Each chapter in this volume engages with two of these cultural stations; some ostensibly if not profoundly positive or indeed negative and some that contradict each other within and across chapters.

This book will be of interest to all scholars and students of disability studies, sociology, education, and health.

David Bolt (Professor) is Personal Chair of Disability Studies and Interdisciplinarity at Liverpool Hope University in the United Kingdom. He completed his PhD in 2004 at the University of Staffordshire.

Autocritical Disability Studies

Series Editor: David Bolt,
Liverpool Hope University, UK.

This new book series represents both a contribution to, and a departure from, the academic field of critical disability studies. According to some concerns about that field, disability is the start but never the finish, there is insufficient engagement with the ethical and political issues faced by disabled people, and the work is too insensitive to individual experiences. Such concerns are addressed boldly in the new series via a formal coupling of critical disability studies with the research method of autoethnography.

The qualitative method of autoethnography acknowledges a researcher's individual experience in the most explicit of ways, from the very start of the process to the finished product that reaches publication. Whereas most traditional research methods claim, or at least aspire to, objectivity, autoethnography owns its subjectivity as paramount. This being so, when academic authors/editors have direct or at least intimate individual experience of disability, the subjectivity of their books can predicate a shift in typology from critical disability studies to what the new series terms autocritical disability studies.

In encouraging textual and theoretical work, the series also introduces autocritical discourse analysis and autocritical disability theory to formalise the ethical and epistemological importance of disability experience in many aspects of critical studies. The key point about the books sought for the series, then, is precisely that the individual experience of disability is recognised and positioned as both start and finish.

The book series editor, Professor David Bolt, encourages expressions of interest from potential monograph authors and volume editors.

Finding Blindness
International Constructions and Deconstructions
Edited by David Bolt

For a full list of titles in this series, please visit: www.routledge.com/Autocritical-Disability-Studies/book-series/ASHSERADS

FINDING BLINDNESS

International Constructions and Deconstructions

Edited by David Bolt

Routledge
Taylor & Francis Group

LONDON AND NEW YORK

First published 2023
by Routledge
4 Park Square, Milton Park, Abingdon, Oxon OX14 4RN

and by Routledge
605 Third Avenue, New York, NY 10158

Routledge is an imprint of the Taylor & Francis Group, an informa business

British Library Cataloguing-in-Publication Data
A catalogue record for this book is available from the British Library

ISBN: 978-1-032-22972-0 (hbk)
ISBN: 978-1-032-22992-8 (pbk)
ISBN: 978-1-003-27506-0 (ebk)

DOI: 10.4324/9781003275060

Typeset in Bembo
by Apex CoVantage, LLC

CONTENTS

PART III
**Stage and the Page: Performance, Dramatics,
and Literary Representation**   **127**

CONTRIBUTORS

Talea Anderson is Scholarly Communication Librarian at Washington State University. She completed her MLIS in 2011 at the University of Washington and her MA in 2013 at Central Washington University.

Carlos Ayram is a PhD candidate in Literature at Pontificia Universidad Católica de Chile. He completed his MA in 2018.

Aravinda Bhat (PhD) is an assistant professor in the Department of Languages at Manipal Academy of Higher Education in India. He completed his PhD in 2007 at the English and Foreign Languages University in India.

Mahashewta Bhattacharya is a PhD candidate in Anthropology at the University of British Columbia in Canada. She completed her MPhil in 2021 at Jawaharlal Nehru University in India.

David Bolt (Professor) is Personal Chair of Disability Studies and Interdisciplinarity at Liverpool Hope University in the United Kingdom. He completed his PhD in 2004 at the University of Staffordshire.

Leah Burch (PhD) is Lecturer in Health and Wellbeing at Liverpool Hope University in the United Kingdom. She completed her PhD in 2020 at the University of Leeds.

Marta Pascua Canelo is a PhD candidate in Spanish and Latin American Literature at Universidad de Salamanca in Spain. She completed her MA in 2018.

Lorenzo Dalvit (PhD) is Associate Professor of Digital Media and Cultural Studies at Rhodes University in South Africa. He completed his PhD in 2010.

Kyriakos Demetriou (PhD) is Assistant Professor of Special and Inclusive Education at the University of Nicosia in Cyprus. He completed his PhD in 2013 at the University of Leeds in the United Kingdom.

Monika Dubiel is a PhD candidate in Nature and Culture in the Faculty of Artes Liberales at the University of Warsaw in Poland. She completed her MA in 2017.

Taufiq Effendi is Assistant Professor of Language Teaching and Assessment at Gunadarma University in Indonesia. He completed his MEd in 2015 at the University of New South Wales in Australia.

David Feeney (PhD) is Lecturer in Disability Studies at Liverpool Hope University in the United Kingdom. He completed his PhD in 2004 at Trinity College Dublin in the Republic of Ireland.

Devon Healey (PhD) is Assistant Professor of Disability Studies at the Ontario Institute for Studies in Education, University of Toronto in Canada. She completed her PhD in 2019.

Declan Kavanagh (PhD) is Senior Lecturer in Eighteenth-Century Studies at the University of Kent in the United Kingdom. He completed his PhD in 2013 at Maynooth University in the Republic of Ireland.

Alexis Padilla (PhD) is Director of Research at Disability Policy Consortium, Boston, in the United States. He completed his PhDs at the University of New Mexico in 1995 and 2018.

Ugo Pavan Dalla Torre (PhD) is Teacher of Italian and History at IIS Leonardo da Vinci inm Padova in Italy. He completed his PhD in 2011 at the University of Turin.

Neng Priyanti is a faculty member at Teachers College, University of Pelita Harapan Indonesia. She completed her MA in 2015 at the University of New South Wales in Australia.

Bijendra Singh is a PhD candidate in Sociology at Jawaharlal Nehru University in India. He completed his MA in 2019.

Simoni Symeonidou (PhD) is Associate Professor of Inclusive Education at the University of Cyprus. She completed her PhD in 2005 at the University of Cambridge in the United Kingdom.

Brenda Tyrrell (PhD) is Lecturer in English at Iowa State University in the United States. She completed her PhD in 2021 at Miami University.

ACKNOWLEDGEMENTS

As series and volume editor, I am keen to thank everyone who has made the idea of autocritical disability studies a growing concern, including Routledge, my fellow contributors to this and the previous book, and the undergraduates who opt to do the related course in their third year.

Given the interdisciplinary underpinning of the work, broader thanks are always due to Elizabeth J. Donaldson, Julia Miele Rodas, and all involved with the Palgrave Macmillan/Springer *Literary Disability Studies* book series; as well as to Robert McRuer and everyone who edited or authored material for Bloomsbury's *A Cultural History of Disability*. Similar thanks are due to Liverpool University Press and the list of people who sustain the *Journal of Literary and Cultural Disability Studies*, including Comments Editor Owen Barden, Book Reviews Editor Claire Penketh, the editorial board, the guest editors, the authors, and of course the readers.

As the institutional base of the series and volume, Liverpool Hope University must be credited. Most obviously, I am grateful for the sense of a research community provided by Ella Houston, Erin Pritchard, and all the other core members of the Centre for Culture and Disability Studies, not to mention the fantastic students who have joined us on the disability studies MA across the last 10 years.

On a personal level, special thanks go to my Academic Support Worker, Kay Ross. In Childwall, where I live and work, ongoing thanks for great food and drink are due to Eton Place, Boss Burgers, Zara's Hub, and the Neighbourhood. Personal thanks are also due to my daughter and her partner, Nisha Bolt and Dan Smith; my brother and sister-in-law, Stephen Bolt and Gerry Hickey; and my mum. Work and play are as one to me but I never forget the eternal value of family.

GLOSSARY

Autocritical disability studies   an approach to disability studies that emphasises autobiographical content alongside more traditional academic material.

Autocritical disability theory   an aspect of critical theory that is informed by direct or indirect experience of disability. See also *Autocritical disability studies*.

Autocritical discourse analysis   a hybrid research method that combines autoethnography and Critical Discourse Analysis (CDA). See also *Autocritical disability studies*.

Assumed authority   an elevated subject position that many people snatch in social encounters, based on their exaggerated identification with normative notions and values.

Cultural station   a text, in the broadest sense, that is ascribed formative qualities.

Critical avoidance   the conspicuous lack of academic engagement with disability studies, despite the abundance of representations of disabled people in course reading, case studies, films, and so on.

Disabling dramatics   exaggerated behaviour or representations that obscure the real issues, complexities, subtleties, and joys of disability.

Metanarrative of blindness   the grand story in relation to which people who have visual impairments often find themselves defined – irrespective if not in spite of actual interactions, sexuality, happiness, aesthetics, knowledge, and so on.

Non-normative negativisms   problematic or problematised deviations from socially accepted standards of mind, body, and behaviour. See also *Tripartite model of disability*.

Normative divide   a conceptual distinction between normative and non-normative experience, existence, embodiment, and so on.

Normative positivisms   the dominant and often unnoticed affirmation of socially accepted standards of mind, body, and behaviour. See also *Tripartite model of disability*.

Ocularnormativism   the mass or institutionalised endorsement of visual necessity, whereby other means of perception are rendered wanting.

Residual existence   the notion that when someone becomes disabled, her, his, or their life is a faded echo of the essential past.

Tripartite model of disability   a critical framework used to avoid one-dimensional representations by considering the experience of disability as a combination of indifference, difficulties, and qualities. See also *Normative positivisms*, *Non-normative negativisms*, and *Non-normative positivisms*.

Unforbidden relationship   intimacy between disabled people that, unlike forbidden relationships, does not cross the normative divide but nonetheless shocks as it counters notions of asexuality (not to mention the received incompatibility of happiness and disability).

INTRODUCTION

Cultural Stations of Blindness: From Ignorance to Understandings

David Bolt

Blindness is an understanding at which many of us arrive. If we care not, we may think of it as the complete opposite, ignorance, wherein we find shadowy renderings of unenlightenment, as well as a proliferation of antithetical but contiguous visionary thinkers, lightbulb moments, bright sparks, eye witnesses, long views, profound insights, illuminating ideas, flashes of inspiration, enlightenment, and so on. Although of manifest academic interest, this ocularnormative epistemology also has a very practical relevance, as people who do not perceive by visual means know only too well. If and when push comes to shove, there seems to be an almost irresistible urge for some people to take on the simplistic and superficial mantel of knowledgeability, the sighted supremacy of shared understandings, whereby counterparts outside the visual realm of communication become excluded, controlled, deceived, and diminished if not nullified. With a nod and a wink, a roll of the eyes, a point of a finger, or even a mouthed but crucially unspoken word, silence is weaponised in an anti-disability manoeuvre that places blindness beneath the very need for understanding.

When blindness is found to be a destination rather than a dead end (i.e. conceived of as understandings instead of ignorance), it proves productive to consider our journey, the cultural stations we have visited or passed along the way. While always formative, these cultural stations of blindness take many forms, overtly but not exclusively textual or social, historical or contemporary, local or global, unique or universal, positive or negative, and so on. The salient point is that the cultural stations are always impactful on understandings of blindness; on blindness as understanding.

The most obvious cultural stations of blindness can be found in community. Within academia, for example, we are lucky enough to be able to turn to the work of colleagues who have direct experience from which we can learn. Their writing defies critical avoidance and points us to cultural stations of blindness insofar as it

DOI: 10.4324/9781003275060-1

often explores multiple representations (Kleege, 1999; Thompson, 2017; Kleege, 2018), any of which may prove to be profoundly impactful on a personal level. Moreover, the embodied approach of many such academics means their work may in itself constitute a cultural station of blindness (Hull, 1990; Kuusisto, 1998; Michalko, 1998, 2002; Kuusisto, 2006, 2018; Parrey, 2020), as is demonstrable within multiple chapters of the present volume.

Beyond many privileges of academia, the cultural station of a community connected by blindness is just as impactful but, even in the recent past, has often been haunted by the spectre of institutionalism. In the United Kingdom, for example, it is well within living memory that registration of blindness was typically followed by a few weeks, months, or even years at a residential centre of some kind. I know from personal experience that these stays may have been for the purposes of mobility training, rehabilitation, employment assessment, or further education courses. As such, the activities could involve anything from handling a guide dog to using a long cane; from doing exams to completing vocational qualifications. The wide range of preoccupations notwithstanding, the commonality of blindness and the residential nature of the courses combined to evoke, before and beyond the normative divide, not colleges or even centres but homes for the blind, which thereby resonated with the institutions of the past.

Despite the institutionalised perceptions, for more than half a century one of the most popular rehabilitation centres in the United Kingdom was Manor House. Situated in the English seaside town of Torquay, Devon, Manor House opened as a residential centre in 1941 and went on to provide thousands of registered blind and partially sighted people with skills and strategies related to mobility, touch-typing, braille, low vision aids, computer technology, independent living, crafts, leisure, and so on. In conjunction with the nearby America Lodge, which was originally funded by the United States for civilians blinded in the Second World War (*Conquest of the Dark*, 1955), Manor House had a lasting effect on its residents in terms of reading and writing (Hesketh, 1999), employment and education (*Conquest of the Dark*, 1955; Anon, 2016), and general rehabilitation (Durham, 1992), not to mention friendships and other unforbidden relationships. All this being so, it is surely fair to say that for many people in the latter half of the twentieth century, myself included, Manor House constituted a cultural station of blindness.

As a cultural station, Manor House was impactful but not necessarily in a positive way. According to one personal account (Curtis, 2017), just a couple of weeks on a taster course in 1991 (three years after my own three-month stint in the summer of 1988) was nothing short of torturous, the dominant lasting effect being a fear of all institutionalised living. The bedrooms were like cells; the corridors, a rabbit warren; the residents, in-mates; and the taster course itself, a prison sentence (Curtis, 2017). The various assessments and activities were pointless and demeaning, an annoying waste of time; so much so that the counsellors' recurrent questions about suicide were taken as suggestions with growing appeal (Curtis, 2017). Such was the misery for some people that the only relief came from drinking to desperate excess each and every evening (Curtis, 2017). This being the case, the cultural station of blindness became one from which a rapid exit was desired.

More than being positive or negative, a point to note about cultural stations of blindness is that, even in their reception, they can vary massively from one person to another. Accordingly, in keeping with the criticisms, Manor House was closed in 2004. The RNIB stated that this closure was a difficult decision that nonetheless reflected a fall in the number of service users and the necessity to provide education in mainstream settings (Anon, 2004), as well as a reduction in the donations being left in wills (Sanders, 2004). Importantly, however, if this decision was supported by some people who had direct experience (Curtis, 2017), many were in opposition. Indeed, there was a significant campaign to stop the closure, whereby blind and partially sighted protesters marched to the RNIB's headquarters in London and subsequently gathered for an open forum in Torquay (Anon, 2004); moreover, the matter was even debated in the House of commons (Sanders, 2004). In other words, one person's torture (Curtis, 2017) was another person's escape from such (Durham, 1992); the very same cultural station was transformative for some people but an institutionalised insult to others.

Manor House is one of many cultural stations of blindness considered in this volume, the international discussions of which form three interrelated parts, the first being the critical spaces and events of education. Leah Burch's opening chapter compares and contrasts the prejudice of hateful social encounters and the hopeful possibilities of learning from university classroom dynamics in the United Kingdom. Lorenzo Dalvit's chapter engages with similar dynamics in a South African setting via an enforced but productive technological progression from PowerPoint to Zoom. Simoni Symeonidou and Kyriakos Demetriou ask what we can learn from postage stamps and charity events in Cyprus. Mahashewta Bhattacharya and Bijendra Singh explore the concept of Indianness with reference to ethnography and ontology. Monika Dubiel reflects on two required readings for schools in Poland, Bolesław Prus's short story 'The Barrel Organ' (1880) and Jadwiga Korczakowska's novel *A Meeting by the Sea* (1962). These ten cultural stations of blindness point to understandings broadly if not formally defined as learning, for the communities in question are based in educational institutions.

The second part of the volume explores cultural stations of blindness that relate to the often potent and poignant topics of politics and religion. Ugo Pavan Dalla Torre revisits twentieth-century Italy to venture from world war to social integration. Talea Anderson also goes back to the last century (and earlier) but the geographical location is the United States where Seventh-day Adventist theology contextualises the writings of Ellen G. White and Norma Youngberg's *Jungle Thorn* (1951). Aravinda Bhat focuses on faith healing in India via the cultural stations of family history, and the works of John M. Hull. Neng Priyanti and Taufiq Effendi shift the focus to Indonesian rehabilitation programs and massage parlours. Alexis Padilla provides a diasporic global south Latinx perspective and takes a philosophical route from myth to anti-ableism. Carlos Ayram and Marta Pascua Canelo contextualise their chapter in the Chilean social revolt and identify the literary and photographic cultural stations of Lina Meruane's *Blind Zone* (2021) and Nicole Kramm's *Victims of Ocular Trauma* (2019–2020). From the Great War to one of too many recent conflicts, these 12 cultural stations of blindness define or defy the powers of government and/or God, albeit in different international manifestations.

The third part of the volume finds cultural stations of blindness in and around literary representations. Devon Healey writes from a Canadian perspective about the positive influence of Rod Michalko's work and the disabling dramatics of her acting encounter with a sighted-blindness-consultant. Declan Kavanagh probes the construct of masculinity in the United Kingdom with reference to John M. Hull's memoir *Touching the Rock: An Experience of Blindness* (1990) and Derek Jarman's *Chroma: A Book of Colour* (1994). David Feeney provides a critical engagement with his disciplinary journey from literary studies and aesthetics in the Republic of Ireland to disability studies in the United Kingdom. Brenda Tyrrell contributes a chapter from the United States with a focus on science fiction, namely, H. G. Wells's short story 'The Country of the Blind' (1904) and the character Lieutenant Commander Geordi La Forge from *Star Trek: The Next Generation*. My own chapter turns to Welsh drama and French philosophy, respectively, Dylan Thomas's *Under Milk Wood: A Play for Voices* (1954) and Jacques Derrida's *Memoirs of the Blind: The Self-Portrait and Other ruins* (1993). These ten cultural stations of blindness are largely textual but like the others resonate with lived experience in their selection and discussion.

Given the diversity of the cultural stations identified in this volume, which in itself barely scratches the surface, it follows that the blindness to which they lead differs from time to time, place to place, and person to person. We find blindness in different ways and learn about it from good, bad, or indifferent cultural stations, irrespective of eye condition or injury, direct or indirect experience. This being so, although in the minority, a few of the contributors to this volume do not have a visual impairment of any kind; however, all endorse the reframing of blindness as understandings rather than ignorance. That is to say, each chapter engages with critical concepts that depart from sighted supremacy, such as ocularnormativism, assumed authority, the metanarrative of blindness, the tripartite model of disability, autocritical discourse analysis, and the volume's central concept, cultural stations of blindness.

References

Anon. (2004) Meeting over blind centre closure [online]. *BBC News*. Available from: http://news.bbc.co.uk/1/hi/england/devon/3737667.stm [accessed 14 April 2020].

Anon. (2016) N-vision be inspired: Brian Casey [online]. *N-Vision: Blackpool, Flyde & Wyre Society for the Blind*. Available from: https://nvision-nw.co.uk/about-us/be-inspired/ [accessed 8 April 2021].

Conquest of the Dark. (1955) Film Directed by Douglas Clarke, Associated British Pathé.

Curtis, A. (2017) Dawn Rise behind the home for the blind [online]. *Yes I've Tried Carrots*. Available from: www.ivetriedcarrots.com [accessed 12 July 2022].

Durham, M. (1992) Seaside Centre helps torture victim to health: A blinded Eritrean is being assisted towards recovery at a villa in Torquay [online]. *The Independent*. Available from: www.independent.co.uk/news/uk/seaside-centre-helps-torture-victim-to-health-a-blinded-eritrean-is-being-assisted-towards-recovery-at-a-villa-in-torquay-michael-durham-reports-1539125.html [accessed 4 July 2022].

Hesketh, R. (1999) Reading and Writing Media and Methods Used and Preferred by a Sample of Visually Impaired Adults. *British Journal of Visual Impairment* 17 (1): 17–22.

Hull, J. M. (1990) *Touching the Rock: An Experience of Blindness*, London: SPCK.

Kleege, G. (1999) *Sight Unseen*, London: Yale University Press.

Kleege, G. (2018) *More Than Meets the Eye: What Blindness Brings to Art*, New York: Oxford University Press.

Kuusisto, S. (1998) *Planet of the Blind*, New York: Dial Press.

Kuusisto, S. (2006) *Eavesdropping: A Life by Ear*, New York: W. W. Norton.

Kuusisto, S. (2018) *Have Dog, Will Travel: A Poet's Journey*, New York: Simon and Schuster.

Michalko, R. (1998) *The Two in One: Walking With Smokie, Walking With Blindness*, Philadelphia: Temple University Press.

Michalko, R. (2002) *The Difference That Disability Makes*, Philadelphia: Temple University Press.

Parrey, R. (2020) Embracing disorientation in the disability studies classroom. *Journal of Literary & Cultural Disability Studies* 14 (1): 37–56.

Sanders, A. (2004) Manor house (Torquay) part of the debate in the house of commons [online]. *They work for you*. Available from: www.theyworkforyou.com/debates/?id=2004-04-28.976.1 [accessed 8 April 2021].

Thompson, H. (2017) *Reviewing Blindness in French Fiction, 1789–2013*, London: Palgrave Macmillan.

PART I

The Directions and Redirections of Education

Critical Spaces and Events

1

AFFECTIVE POSSIBILITIES OF EVERYDAY ENCOUNTERS WITH BLINDNESS

Leah Burch

Preliminary Discussion: Social Encounters and Affect Theory

Social encounters have long been a site of sociological fascination (Goffman, 1963). Our encounters shape the very fabric of everyday life. We shape, and are shaped by, our encounters with others, which in turn, are shaped by the kinds of spaces within which we are situated. While we are not able to predict the nuances of social encounters, many of our encounters do abide by particular social norms. For Goffman (1963), these norms constitute our social performances. We interact with the world around us in the ways that are governed by socially accepted routines and structures. Those who abide by these standards are able to pass through social space unnoticed and unmarked. For those who do not neatly pass through these structures, their presence disrupts the rhythm of social space and is met with unease. In the words of Garland-Thompson (1997, 7–8), 'corporeal departures from dominant expectations never go uninterpreted or unpunished . . . those bodies deemed inferior become spectacles of otherness while the unmarked are sheltered in the neutral space of normalcy'. By attending to encounters with blindness, this chapter explores how the rules and rituals of social encounters are disrupted by the presence of visual impairment (Scott, 1991) as a result of the culturally nurtured stories, assumptions, and attitudes surrounding the concept of 'blindness' (Bolt, 2012). These encounters take place within different types of spaces and constitute cultural stations of blindness.

As spaces are organised in categorical and hierarchical ways, it is important to recognise that these social encounters can affect bodies in different ways. Indeed, bodies are moved by these configurations of space, and aligned to or against one another. In this way, space is not only 'a passive container of life, but also an active constituent of social relations' (Kitchin, 1998, 344). Social encounters are affective;

DOI: 10.4324/9781003275060-3

they shape the ways that different bodies are able to be and move within different spaces. Indeed, the presence of visual impairment shapes social encounters in both limiting and productive ways. Engaging with affect theory can therefore help us to recognise the diverse possibilities of disabled people, and, in the context of this chapter, to explore the affective possibility of bodies when blindness enters the room. This approach moves away from the understanding that disabled people are passive (Shakespeare, 1994) and recognises that 'the capacity of a body is never defined by a body alone but is always aided and abetted by, and dovetails with, the field or context of its force-relations' (Seigworth and Gregg, 2010, 3). Indeed, by introducing two cultural stations of blindness, this chapter shows that any single story of blindness is flawed and unable to capture the multiple possibilities of encounters within everyday life. It is only by reflecting upon multiple and often competing stories that we can come to a more nuanced understanding of blindness (and disability more broadly) as a complex, diverse, and multifaceted phenomenon (Shakespeare, 2015). This understanding of blindness recognises moments where affective capacity is limited but is equally attentive to the times where it is enhanced and the possibility of *being* is not limited to the confines of normative social expectations.

In this chapter, I consider two different cultural stations of blindness, each of which constitutes different affective possibilities for moving within social space. The first encounter reflects upon a story shared with me during my research by Shaz. In this encounter, blindness is met with hostility and marked out as 'a presence couched within the understanding of it as the binary opposite of sight' (Michalko, 2001, 356). In turn, this encounter shapes the way in which Shaz is able to move within public space, thus limiting his affective capacity. However, the second encounter considers an alternative understanding of the ways in which blindness can enrich educational encounters. Located within the higher education classroom, this second cultural station demonstrates how blindness can change the way in which classrooms are experienced by those within, which opens up new opportunities for engagement with one another. These opposing cultural stations signify competing constructions of blindness, which in turn, constitute different affective possibilities within encounters of visual impairment.

Everyday Hate and Social Space: Affect in Unsolicited Contact

It is well documented that hate can become an intrusive, yet ordinary part of disabled people's day-to-day lives (Burch, 2021a; EHRC, 2011) particularly as they move within social spaces. Indeed, social spaces can be risky terrain to occupy for disabled people, due to the strict norms and expectations that govern these spaces. During my PhD research, disabled people shared a range of experiences of hate when occupying social space. In one interview, Shaz described a hate incident that occurred while he was walking through his town centre:

> I was actually going independently using my cane in a public space, and somebody, I nearly walked into something. It wasn't until later that somebody

stopped me and said erm, basically it was a group of lads. I was moving using my long cane as you do. I couldn't distinguish people, but I can distinguish light from dark and erm, things suddenly went dark and I ducked because I thought I was going to walk into something. And somebody told me what it was, it was a group of lads walking towards me and one of the lads held his arm out straight as if I'd, so if I didn't move I'd have walked into it. And you just can't understand the, you know, the motivation for that is that the whole thing about wanting to exclude people.

This social encounter creates a space that is characterised by both distance and close proximity between Shaz and the 'group of lads'. The 'group of lads' recognises Shaz's visual impairment through his use of a cane and assume authority (Bolt, 2014a) over the space that is shared between them. Indeed, while the space is shared between both parties, the 'group of lads' takes ownership of the space by making contact with Shaz. In this moment of contact, Shaz is constructed as an Other who is out of place in this space. Indeed, this unsolicited contact is significant in the way in which Shaz is constructed, as the moment disrupts normative urban codes of keeping your distance from others (Tonkiss, 2003) to reinforce his absence from the space. Following what Leder (1990) refers to as 'dys-appearing bodies', we can read this encounter as a cultural station which renders disabled people as both absent and insignificant. Indeed, it is the unsolicited contact with Shaz that renders blindness present within the social encounter and thus, within the surrounding social space. Blindness, as a marker of the inferior Other, is presented to the 'group of lads' through the symbolic signifier of a visual aid and the physical contact that follows. This cultural station of blindness illuminates how 'the norms prescribing respectful distance and mutual inattention between strangers in the public realm are not quite as binding in encounters with those whose appearance diverges from the norm' (Yaron et al., 2018, 748). In doing so, the social space is made in a way that does not accommodate or welcome blindness, and therefore marks Shaz out through unwanted and unanticipated contact.

The moment of contact that is instigated by the 'group of lads' involves a movement towards Shaz in order to create distance from him and ensure the boundaries between them are secure (Ahmed, 2014). Indeed, the physical contact can be read as an expression of hostility that secures the relationship between bodies; it aligns the 'group of lads' together, against Shaz, who is constituted as the 'them' in this encounter (Burch, 2021a). This moment impresses upon the surface of the body and informs future encounters. Indeed, when reflecting upon his experience, Shaz recognised this treatment as a means of excluding him and making him feel like the space is not 'for' disabled people. In this cultural station, then, the architecture of space is not within the material structure but embedded within the way in which social interactions configure the meanings and boundaries of space and the affects that this can have on those who encounter this.

In this encounter, unwanted and unsolicited contact is made as an expression of hostility. There are important parallels here between the reading of disabled people as bodies as inferior Others and as bodies in need of help which can elicit unwanted and improperly performed guiding (Calder-Dawe et al., 2020). Indeed, described by disability activist Dr Amy Kavanagh as 'silent non-consensual touching', it can become a routine feature of day-to-day life to be touched by strangers when occupying social spaces (Kavanagh and Mason-Bish, 2019). Yet these 'unanticipated encounters' are inherently affective, and can undermine 'predictive confidence' within familiar surroundings (Allen, 2004). Indeed, unsolicited contact changes the make-up of an environment for which we are unprepared. While it is possible to become familiar with the physical architecture of space, unwanted contact and the intrusion of space disrupts this. It is also important to recognise the limits imposed upon how people respond to these situations. As Low (2019) has argued, when moments of unsolicited contact are challenged by disabled people, there is a further risk that this will lead to verbal abuse (Low, 2019). Public space can thus *feel* inherently risky for those bodies who are not able to move successfully through space unmarked (Burch, 2021a). Hostile encounters such as the one described earlier can shape the movement of bodies within different spaces; risky spaces come to be known as 'not for them' and avoided. This cultural station therefore demonstrates the way in which social interactions can limit the extent to which people feel they can safely occupy those spaces, and therefore limit their affective capacity to *be* within social spaces in the future.

Higher Education Classroom: Affective Possibilities of Classroom Encounters

The higher education classroom is an interesting space to explore as a cultural station of blindness. In this section, I reflect upon my own higher education classroom while studying for a Masters. The module in question was designed and taught by a person with a visual impairment which shaped the way in which blindness was made present in both limiting and affirmative ways. Like all levels of education, the traditional higher education classroom follows a range of ocularcentric rituals that privilege sight as a form of knowing (Bolt, 2016; Jay, 1994). Indeed, the practices that are ingrained within our previous educational encounters follow us to higher education and shape the way in which we occupy the classroom. These spaces rely upon communication through eye contact and the reading of body language. For example, the act of hand-raising has been culturally implemented as 'the cardinal rule of the classroom decorum' (Kleege, 1999; Michalko, 2001). However, these acts rely on the ocularcentric assumption that everyone in the classroom is able to see through visual means (Michalko, 2001) and, although unintentional, can be read as excluding people with visual impairments. Within this cultural station of blindness, such encounters effectively 'disable' people with visual impairments to denote 'a blind Other, demarcated by an ocularcentric social aesthetic' (Bolt, 2014b, 110). This disabling process may not be intentional, but is embedded within typical classroom practices, as illustrated in the following encounter:

> During a classroom discussion, a student raises their hand to ask a question. The student appears to be confused that their hand has not been recognised.

After a moment of silence, a support tutor tells them to say their name and continue making their contribution. The student appears confused, but continues to engage in discussion.

We can assume that the student in this encounter was following normative classroom rituals. However, in doing so, there is an unintentional ignorance or avoidance of visual impairment which permeates the disabling conventions of confusion, irrationality, and ineptness which are subsequently imposed onto people with visual impairments (Bolt, 2014a; Rodas, 2009). Indeed, this encounter is made in the moment of silence as the student waits for their hand to be acknowledged by the tutor. This silence creates an awkward atmosphere which is felt within the classroom by others who are witnessing the encounter. This encounter creates what Brennan (2004 cited in Åhäll, 2018) refers to as 'affective atmosphere'. This 'affective atmosphere' describes the way in which we sense the moods characterised within the spaces that we enter, and that this mood ultimately influences how we feel and become in that space (Burch, 2021a). As a spectator to this encounter, I felt this affective atmosphere impress upon my own body; my presence in the classroom felt tense and unnerving as I became an unwilling participant in a disabling encounter. I felt stuck within the awkwardness of the encounter, unsure whether to sit within the silence, or to disrupt this and advise the student to say their name.

This encounter illustrates the affectivity of social encounters and the stickiness of emotions as they move to shape those within shared spaces (Ahmed, 2014). Emotions surfaced to create a collective 'us' who, in our shared understanding of the communicative conflicts at play and refusal to disrupt, became unwillingly active in the creation of a disabling social environment. This encounter demonstrates the often unintentional, yet inherently disabling practices that key people with visual impairments to a metanarrative of 'blindness' (Bolt, 2005, 2012). Indeed, while there is an overall shared understanding of more affirmative classroom practices, the collective ignorance and awkwardness of these marks out visual impairment as an Other figure that does not align to the normative higher education classroom. In this encounter, then, the higher education classroom as a cultural station becomes a space that is limiting. Similar to the first encounter experienced by Shaz, blindness is constructed as an Other to the normative configuration of social space.

While we must continue to draw attention to, and reflect upon, moments of awkwardness and oppression, we must also be attentive to 'how people make sense of their circumstances and negotiate and initiate patterns of activity in concert with others' (Wetherell et al., 2020, 18). Importantly then, paying attention to affective capacity opens up a space to recognise the ways that the navigation of everyday space represents a unique and embodied way of knowing and being in the world – that is, affective possibility (Burch, 2021b). Attending to what Wetherell et al. (2020) term as 'acts of quiet resistance', it is possible to consider the different ways that disabled people come to negotiate the spaces around them. Such an approach takes into account the ways in which we are affected by, and go on to affect, our surrounding worlds. In doing so, it is possible to ask questions about our affective capacity to address and combat the harsh realities of oppressive environments by drawing attention to the strategies that we develop. Indeed, the higher education classroom is not solely a disabling cultural station, but one of affective possibility and opportunity enriched by blindness. As Scott suggests, 'the norms governing ordinary personal interactions cannot, as a rule, be applied when one of the actors is unable to see' (1991, 25). Thus, in order to overcome the exclusionary conventions of ocularcentric classroom practices, the tutor invited us to communicate with him and one another in different ways:

> During the first taught session, the tutor asks students not to raise their hands when responding to questions. Instead, he invites students to say their name before continuing to make a contribution to discussion.

The presence of visual impairment within the classroom invited students to engage in different ways with each other and the tutor. Importantly, a shift from hand-raising to verbal identification changed the way in which 'visual impairment' and 'blindness' are marked by the social encounter as it enabled the visual to become present through means other than sight (Michalko, 1999). Indeed, by moving away from a reliance upon the visual means of sight, deviance is no longer problematised and typical barriers are alleviated (Mallett and Runswick-Cole, 2014; Corker and Shakespeare, 2002). That is, the construct and assumptions of 'blindness' are no longer imposed upon people with visual impairments, as the setting no longer requires the ability to communicate through visual means (Bolt, 2014a). Knowledge and experience of oppression can therefore pave the way for new ways of interacting with what would typically be a disabling environment. It encourages different ways of *being* and *doing* within surrounding space based upon the unique knowledge of disabled people.

This encounter demonstrates a small shift that can change the way in which the higher education classroom is experienced, and the way in which blindness becomes part of that space. While the previous encounters have constructed blindness as Other, this encounter welcomes blindness as an opportunity to engage with one another in different ways. Indeed, while the shift away from hand-raising removes a barrier to communicating within the classroom, it constituted a range of affective possibilities for those in the room. Asking students to say their name as opposed to hand-raising invited alternative ways of being *in* and engaging with the classroom environment and with one another. As a change to established educational norms, social encounters that encourage self-identification are established as 'oral events which are interpretively transformed into the communication event' (Michalko, 2001, 352). This small change helped to create a space that was inclusive, open and welcoming to all (Bolt, 2016; Oliver, 2004). Indeed, saying our names as a means of making ourselves present and offering our contribution helped to create a more interactive classroom environment. As someone who has to be reminded of someone's name several times before remembering it, I found this shift in classroom practice dispelled the usual awkwardness I feel when meeting new people. The onus was not on me to ask what people's names were and remember them for the first time, as I was continually reminded of names as different students engaged with the discussion. This practice gave us the time and space to get to know one each other and changed the rhythm of the classroom. Indeed, as noted earlier, hand-raising is a classroom practice that informs power relations; it is a form of classroom management whereby the tutor controls the flow and direction of discussion. This one-directional power relation can create jolted discussion practices and can impede the flow of conversation. On the contrary, by no longer watching for visual cues, we were able to just *be* in open dialogue and discussion. In this way, moving away from normative classroom behaviours offered alternative and more comfortable ways of being and participating in the classroom.

Concluding Discussion: Affective Possibilities of Blindness

In this chapter, I engage with the theoretical framework of affect theory to explore two cultural stations of blindness. Affect theory helps to move beyond the mere shaping of bodies according to social space and instead attends to how the existence and interaction of those bodies shape the space around them (Burch, 2021a). Moving away from thinking about the body as a singular entity, affect theory considers 'how bodies are always thoroughly entangled processes, and [are] defined by their capacities to affect and be affected' (Blackman and Venn, 2010, 9). By engaging with affect theory, then, we are asked to think about the way that bodies (both human and non-human) interact with one another, which is also shaped by the characteristics of the space that we are in. Affect theory asks questions about affectivity within the context of our everyday encounters, spaces, and lives (Jóhannsdóttir et al., 2020; Wetherell, 2015). It considers how feelings and movements are negotiated in the public sphere which come to be experienced through the body (Gorton, 2007). Indeed, the way that we are moved by these feelings can shape how we interact with those around us and how we situate ourselves within particular social spaces. This diversity of affects is explored throughout this chapter, both by attending to how cultural stations of blindness can be limiting and enhancing.

Cultural station one 'everyday hate' explores hostility within the context of everyday social space, and the making of blindness as both absent and present. In this encounter, Shaz is marked out as a blind person, as the 'group of lads' physically interfere with the space around him. The encounter treats Shaz as an absent presence; absent from the space while simultaneously present through the marker of blindness. The unsolicited contact is an affirmation of boundaries between Shaz and the 'group of lads' which constructs a space that is 'not for' people with visual impairments. Indeed, social spaces that are known as 'hot spots' for hate encounters are made sense of as inherently risky and thus constructed as spaces to avoid. This sense of space and marginalisation can impress upon the bodies of disabled people and limit their affective futures. The boundaries that are constructed between non-disabled and disabled people within social encounters are felt under the skin, shaping the extent to which people feel free to move through and between different spaces (Burch, 2021b). Such encounters can therefore constitute a disabling cultural station of blindness which imposes limits upon the affective capacity of individuals and shapes how they interact with social spaces in the future.

Cultural station two 'the higher education classroom' is more attentive to the affective possibilities of blindness and the ability of disabled people to disrupt normative standards and expectations. While the normative conventions of classroom practice can continue to mark out blindness as Other, there is an opportunity to transcend these standards and offer alternative ways of being in the classroom. Due to the requirement of many disabled people in navigating an inaccessible social world, disability is considered to be a body of knowledge (Siebers, 2014), within which disabled people 'embrace complex embodiment as a means to take on unsuspected forms and to hold them in memory for the possession and use of the disability community (Siebers, 2015, 244). Indeed, it is through 'their unique navigation of, and movement within, society (physically and symbolically), disabled people generate deep understandings of their surrounding world, which can come to critically inform future encounters' (Burch, 2021b, 86). From this perspective, visual impairment and blindness 'emerge not just as the Other side of the oppression coin but also as a resistant alternative' (Goodley and Runswick-Cole, 2016, 4). Indeed, cultural station two shows how the presence of visual impairment within the classroom created a space that was not limited by or tied to conventional classroom rituals, but was more free, welcoming, and participatory. That is, space does not determine the capacity of bodies entirely, but can be shaped by the interactions that take place within them. This cultural station of blindness thereby demonstrates the ways in which visual impairment shapes surrounding space and creates the possibility for more inclusive affective futures. Encounters with blindness are affective, and these affects are long-lasting.

To quote Ahmed (2014, 39) 'the impressions we have of others, and the impressions left by others are shaped by histories that stick, at the same time as they generate the surfaces and boundaries that allow bodies to appear in the present. The impressions left by others should impress us for sure; it is here, on the skin surface, that histories are made'.

As a non-disabled person who does not have a visual impairment, I am a spectator in the different encounters shared in this chapter, but all have had a lasting impression upon me. Indeed, the cultural stations that I share reflect encounters that have resonated with me and encouraged me to think about the affective possibilities of blindness. These encounters ask questions about the ways in which the architecture of space is not limited to physical characteristics, but to the way in which bodies interact and engage with one another. Being attentive to these interactions, reflecting upon how they make us feel, *be*, and think is important. We learn about ourselves and the world around us by reflecting upon social encounters. The cultural stations of blindness shared in this chapter therefore offer an important learning opportunity, to ask ourselves about our own experiences with, and perceptions of, blindness.

References

Åhäll, L. (2018) Affect as methodology: Feminism and the politics of emotion. *International Political Sociology* 12 (1): 36–52.

Ahmed, S. (2014) *The Cultural Politics of Emotion*, Edinburgh: Edinburgh University Press.

Allen, C. (2004) Merleau-Ponty's phenomenology and the body-in-space encounters of visually impaired children. *Environment and Planning D: Society and Space* 22 (5): 719–735.

Blackman, L. and Venn, C. (2010) Affect. *Body & Society* 16 (1): 7–28.

Bolt, D. (2005) From blindness to visual impairment: Terminological typology and the social model of disability. *Disability & Society* 20 (5): 539–552.

Bolt, D. (2012) Social encounters, cultural representation and critical avoidance, in T. Watson, A. Roulstone, and C. Thomas, C. (eds.) *Routledge Handbook of Disability Studies*, Abingdon: Routledge.

Bolt, D. (2014a) *The Metanarrative of Blindness: A Re-Reading of Twentieth Century Anglophone Writing*, Ann Arbor: The University of Michigan Press.

Bolt, D. (2014b) An advertising aesthetic: Real beauty and visual impairment. *The British Journal of Visual Impairment* 32 (1): 25–32.

Bolt, D. (2016) Enabling the classroom and the curriculum: Higher education, literary studies and disability. *Journal of Further and Higher Education* 41 (4): 556–565.

Burch, L. (2021a) *Understanding Disability and Everyday Hate*, London: Palgrave Macmillan.

Burch, L. (2021b) Everyday hate and affective possibility: Disabled people's negotiations of space, place and identity. *International Journal of Disability and Social Justice* 1 (1): 73–94.

Calder-Dawe, O., Witten, K. and Carroll, P. (2020) Being the body in question: Young people's accounts of everyday ableism, visibility and disability. *Disability & Society* 35 (1): 132–155.

Corker, M. and Shakespeare, T. (2002) *Disability/Postmodernity: Embodying Disability Theory*, London: Continuum.

Equality and Human Rights Commission (EHRC). (2011) *Hidden in Plain Sight: Inquiry Into Disability-Related Harassment*, Manchester: Equality and Human Rights Commission.

Garland-Thompson, R. (1997) *Extraordinary Bodies: Figuring Physical Disability in American Culture and Literature*, New York: Columbia University Press.

Goffman, I. (1963) *Stigma: Notes on the Management of Spoiled Identity*, London: Penguin.

Goodley, D. and Runswick-Cole, K. (2016) Becoming dishuman: Thinking about the human through dis/ability. *Discourse: Studies in the Cultural Politics of Education* 37 (1): 1–15.

Gorton, K. (2007) Theorising emotion and affect. *Feminist Theory* 8 (3): 1464–7001.

Jay, M. (1994) *Downcast Eyes: The Denigration of Vision in Twentieth-Century French Thought*, Berkeley: University of California Press.

Jóhannsdóttir, A., Egilson, S. and Gibson, B. (2020) What's shame got to do with it? The importance of affect in critical disability studies. *Disability & Society* 36 (3): 342–357.

Kavanagh, A. and Mason-Bish, H. (2019) As a disabled woman, I'm harassed on the street daily – where's my #metoo movement? [online]. *Huffington Post*. Available from: www.huffingtonpost.co.uk/entry/disabled-woman-me-too_uk_5d3eaee2e4b0db8affaadf12?guccounter=1&guce_referrer=aHR0cHM6Ly90LmNvL0plWVJSZmFiZG8&guce_referrer_sig=AQAAAHtHiVhyU6mEDWmpvq32f_u90gPTFD_GH4rzNF4Y6_9cdDqAR66AqYHFjdy8gNdUfbMULvTlPEprDA2Vjx_PEQatvZ-mkzRMx2_-SjYAzRM4jIANBOqeXm3lE_8MemRGJ0s9xllXl3a55VaNPPJ-QDixn5T79pzKA4Sme9I1VxyF [accessed 25 May 2022].

Kitchin, R. (1998) 'Out of place', 'knowing one's place': Space, power and the exclusion of disabled people. *Disability & Society* 13 (3): 343–356.

Kleege, G. (1999) *Sight Unseen*, New Haven: Yale University Press.

Leder, D. (1990) *The Absent Body*, Chicago: University of Chicago Press.

Low, H. (2019) Spikes – and other ways disabled people combat unwanted touching [online]. *BBC*. Available from: www.bbc.co.uk/news/disability-49584591 [accessed 25 May 2022].

Mallett, R. and Runswick-Cole, K. (2014) *Approaching Disability: Critical Issues and Perspectives*, London: Routledge.

Michalko, R. (1999) *The Two in One: Walking With Smokie, Walking With Blindness*, Philadelphia: Temple University Press.

Michalko, R. (2001) Blindness enters the classroom. *Disability & Society* 16 (3): 349–359.

Oliver, M. (2004) The social model in action: If I had a hammer, in C. Barnes and G. Mercer (eds.) *Implementing the Social Model of Disability: Theory and Research*, Leeds: The Disability Press.

Rodas, J. (2009) On blindness. *Journal of Literary & Cultural Disability Studies* 3 (2): 115–130.

Scott, R. (1991) *The Making of Blind Men: A Study of Adult Socialization*, New Brunswick: Transaction Publishers.

Seigworth, G. and Gregg, M. (2010) An inventory of shimmers, in G. Seigworth and M. Gregg (eds.) *The Affect Theory Reader*, Durham: Duke University Press.

Shakespeare, T. (1994) Cultural representation of disabled people: Dustbins for disavowal? *Disability & Society* 9 (3): 283–299.

Shakespeare, T. (2015) *Disability Research Today: International Perspectives*, London: Routledge.

Siebers, T. (2014) *Returning the Social to the Social Model, Non-Normative Positivisms: Towards a Methodology of Critical Embodiment*, Minneapolis.

Siebers, T. (2015) Introduction: Disability and visual culture. *Journal of Literary & Cultural Disability Studies* 9 (3): 239–246.

Tonkiss, F. (2003) The ethics of indifference: Community and solitude in the city. *International Journal of Cultural Studies* 6 (3): 297–311.

Wetherell, M. (2015) Trends in the turn to affect: A social psychological critique. *Body & Society* 21 (2): 139–166.

Wetherell, M., McConville, A. and McCreanor, T. (2020) Defrosting the freezer and other acts of quiet resistance: Affective practice theory, everyday activism and affective dilemmas. *Qualitative Research in Psychology* 17 (1): 13–35.

Yaron, G., Meershoek, A., Widdershoven, G. and Slatman, J. (2018) Recognizing difference: In/visibility in the everyday life of individuals with facial limb absence. *Disability & Society* 33 (5): 743–762.

2

FROM POWERPOINT TO ZOOM

Interrogating the Gaze in Teaching at a Small South African University

Lorenzo Dalvit

Preliminary Discussion: The Power of the Gaze

I teach Media and Cultural Studies at a small residential university in South Africa. Rhodes University is a historically white institution located in Makhanda/ Grahamstown, a small town in the predominantly rural Eastern Cape province. While the demographic composition of the university community still reflects, to some extent, the legacy of apartheid's institutionalised racial segregation, our campus attracts students from different socioeconomic and cultural backgrounds and from all parts of South Africa and sub-Saharan Africa. As is the case with other universities in the country, Rhodes is under pressure to decolonise and transformation is recognised as a priority (Makgakge, 2020; Dalvit, 2021a; see also Bosch, 2020). The School of Journalism and Media Studies, where I have worked since 2011, consistently ranks among the top ones in the discipline on the African continent and prides itself on a strong critical orientation. I have developed and taught courses at undergraduate and postgraduate levels with a particular focus on digital media, introducing and reflecting on several pedagogical innovations (Dalvit, 2014a, 2014b, 2015, 2016, 2018). Classes vary in size between approximately 100 students in my third-year course on 'Radical online discourses and the South African digital public sphere' and, depending on the year, anything between 4 and 12 students in the module 'Critical Media studies and Social Theory' in the Master programme. The format of lectures varies from frontal lessons for the former to small group seminars for the latter. After an emergency shift to remote teaching and communication due to COVID-19 restrictions, at the time of writing, we are in the process of returning to in-person or, whenever this is not possible, hybrid teaching. In Dalvit (2021b), I critically reflect on my own experience of remote teaching and communication, including some initial considerations which are further developed in the present chapter.

DOI: 10.4324/9781003275060-4

Due to retinal degeneration, during my academic career, I had to move progressively away from paper documents and increasingly rely on electronic tools and resources as well as a student assistant. When I started teaching digital media, I had sufficient residual vision to navigate familiar surroundings independently and operate a computer by using magnified fonts and high contrast themes. Over the span of a decade, however, my eyesight deteriorated to almost complete blindness. I currently rely entirely on screen readers to operate ICT devices and I recently acquired a guide dog to move around with some independence at home and in the workplace. My employer has been very supportive (e.g. by allowing the use of research funds to pay for an accompanying person when attending conferences or during field trips, excusing me from tasks such as exam invigilation, and allocating a dedicated graduate assistant to me). My colleagues and students have proven very accommodating and understanding, consistent with the collegial culture of our department and institution. Such adjustments remain premised on the assumed authority of those who can see and, as such, they are not meant to challenge dominant ocularnormative hierarchies (Bolt, 2021). My experience is comparable to that of other visually impaired academics in South Africa in terms of a fragile sense of inclusion, an effort to overcompensate for my limitations, and a feeling of disability as a lesser category of diversity (Lourens, 2021).

In this chapter, I draw on the concept of the gaze as understood within the critical tradition to reflect on my journey as an academic with a specific focus on teaching. The concept of the gaze has been used extensively by critical scholars across fields and areas of interest (Koch, 1985; Thomas, 1991; Groys, 2012). The power of the male gaze, the white gaze, and so on, has long been explored in relation to media representations (Cuklanz, 2013; Griffin, 2014; Laurent, 2021). Zuboff (2015) argues that the pervasiveness of digital media under a condition of surveillance capitalism makes it almost impossible to escape the power of the disciplining gaze envisaged in the panopticon (i.e. a spatial design privileging a single point of observation). As members of other subaltern groups, people with disabilities are subject to the able body-mind's gaze both online and offline. For the blind and visually impaired, living in a Global South context, the oppressive power of such a gaze adds to the frustrations of living in a world designed by and for someone else (see Padilla, 2021).

The gaze is central to the power dynamics enacted in the classroom. Based on the seminal work by scholars like Freire or Gramsci (Fischman and McLaren, 2005), critical pedagogy problematises a view of education purely as an opportunity for personal empowerment and social transformation. On the contrary, the dynamics enacted in the classroom as a site of struggle either challenge or reproduce hegemony and oppression. The authority of the teacher or lecturer, who embodies dominant values and worldviews, is supported by spatial arrangements and visual clues. In most teaching venues, from primary school classrooms to university auditoria, the teacher or lecturer is the natural focus of the students' gaze, but students cannot look at each other without attracting negative attention. Furthermore, particularly in large venues, physical distance makes it difficult for individual students to know if the lecturer is looking at them specifically. This situation is airily reminiscent of the panopticon (Landahl, 2013). One could go as far as noticing that while the lower (and most vulnerable) part of the lecturer's body is usually hidden behind a desk and thus protected, this is seldom the case for students. Furthermore, a common setup places the lecturer close to the entrance door, thus forcing latecomers to pass next to or in front of her/him/them and be 'seen'. The above scenario describes the venue where I teach my undergraduate course, where the classroom power distance is arguably greater. Postgraduate seminar venues tend to reflect a more egalitarian setup (e.g. with desks arranged in a 'U' shape) although the lecturer still occupies a prominent position.

The gaze in the classroom can be a double-edged sword, particularly when technology use is concerned. Fear of appearing incompetent, unprepared or inept in full view of one's students is one of the key barriers to the adoption of ICT in Education by those who teach, be it in marginalised rural schools or at universities (Gunzo, 2020; Gunga and Ricketts, 2007). While the disempowering and alienating potential of technology use during lectures for South African university students who are visually impaired is well documented (Lourens, 2015), relatively little is known about the experience of lecturers. For such academics, common classroom setups potentially reverse the power of the gaze by subjecting a blind or visually impaired lecturer to the inescapable gaze of sighted students. Assistive technologies such as screen readers are impractical when not impossible to use, as these would monopolise the only sense (i.e. hearing) one could rely on to manage the classroom or maintain the correct orientation. My only experience of presenting while using a screen reader in combination with Bluetooth headphones resulted in me slowly facing away from the audience and ending up facing the wall. The way the introduction of technological innovations in the classroom affects power relationships between lecturers and students is worth exploring through the lens of cultural constructions of blindness and visual impairment. Through an (auto)critical somatographic approach (see Lourens, 2021; Padilla, 2021), in the following two sections, I reflect on how my own understanding and experiences of blindness have changed over the span of a decade working as an academic in a specific Global South context. The departing and arrival stations of the journey discussed here are PowerPoint presentations (which students have come to expect as part of a lecture) and Zoom meetings (which have become part of our new normal as a result of emergency remote teaching).

PowerPoint: All Eyes Are on You

Since the late 1990s, PowerPoint has accounted for 95% of all presentation software. It was initially released by Forethought in 1987 and acquired by Microsoft soon afterwards. The name was a last-minute change from the original *Presenter* (which had already been registered) and was specifically chosen with reference to the empowerment of individual speakers. The use of PowerPoint expanded from business communication to a wide range of other domains, including education. The use of PowerPoint in the classroom has been extensively problematised. A comprehensive review of research over the past two decades suggests that, as a teaching and learning tool, it does not seem to increase tertiary students' understanding (Baker et al., 2018). Roberts (2018) contextualises the use of PowerPoint in academia within a generational shift towards (digital) visual representation in general and visual learning in particular. He notes the incongruity of some academics holding on to a text-centric use of this most visual teaching tool and emphasises the cognitive advantages of using a combination of both images and words. Blind and visually impaired students, however, are inevitably left behind in this visual shift. The use of PowerPoint during lectures is recognised as alienating (see Lourens, 2015).

In my own experience as a university student in the late 1990s and early 2000s, first in Italy (with some exchange experiences in Norway and Finland) and then in South Africa, whiteboards and transparent slides were still the main visual aids in university lectures. By the time I took an extra credit in computer science in 2005, PowerPoint slides had become an integral component of university teaching, at least in that discipline. My own initial teaching experiences in African Languages and Education between 2007 and 2011 coincided with increased expectations of PowerPoint use, particularly in relatively large classes. By 2012, when I taught my first course in New Media to a small group of Masters' students in Journalism and Media Studies, I felt compelled to use PowerPoint slides for my initial lecture and justify my preference to limit their use afterwards. When I first taught my third-year course in 2015, I felt compelled to go back to using PowerPoint, despite the challenges this posed to me as a lecturer with a visual impairment. It is interesting to note that expectations concerning the use of presentations are implicit. I have not come across any prescription or even recommendation at the institutional, departmental, or programme level. In an attempt to meet perceived ocularnormative expectations, however, I made sure to use PowerPoint slides at least in my undergraduate lessons.

PowerPoint use entails a considerable amount of extra effort on my side. First of all, I need to prepare the slides well ahead of time so my sighted assistant can check and format them. Second, I attempt to memorise the whole presentation (sometimes for a double period) so I can recite it point by point while complementing it with explanations. Third, I coordinate with my assistant who moves to the next slide, reminds me of the next point or alerts me of questions as needed. My presentations' layout and appearance tend to be very basic, with only three or four bullet points with a short phrase each per slide. For the benefit of sighted students, I occasionally make use of photos to illustrate particular points. Rather than empowering me as the focal point of attention, using PowerPoint in my undergraduate teaching puts my dependency on another person and my need to overcompensate by memorising entire lessons on full display.

As a teaching aid, PowerPoint can entrench the power of the gaze in the classroom in two ways. First, it removes the need for a lecturer to turn their back on students to write on a whiteboard or to look downwards to arrange transparent slides. The most common setup enables the speaker to keep the audience in their sight at all times, thus removing any moment of distraction. Second, students are prompted to look at the slide show while remaining exposed to the authoritative gaze of their lecturer. For a visually impaired academic like myself, however, the use of PowerPoint represents at best a distraction and at worst an extra source of pressure. Under the gaze of my students, not only must I make sense of what I am teaching, but also ensure a flawless performance with a technology I cannot control. The lockdown measures in response to the COVID-19 pandemic and the subsequent shift to remote teaching and learning removed me from this 'reverse panopticon'. For the first time in my teaching career, I experienced teaching free from the gaze of my students and realised the additional pressure this brings. For the first virtual iteration of my third-year course, I pre-recorded my presentations as slides and audio clips. Doing this in advance freed me from the pressure of memorising a whole lesson and enabled me to re-record when I made mistakes. This resulted in much better teaching material available to students as both preparation and follow-up to lessons as part of a flipped-classroom approach (Tucker, 2012).

Zoom: Levelling the Playing Field

Zoom is a videoconferencing application. Originally intended for corporate use, during the COVID-19 pandemic its use increased to over 300 million daily meetings. Accessibility features such as (autogenerated) captions, adjustable font size or screen reader integration were introduced in September 2020. In August 2021, Zoom focus was launched for digital classrooms. It enables teachers to see everybody's screens but prevents students from seeing each other, thus reproducing the panopticon setup. Privacy and security are key concerns on Zoom. On the one hand, the application has the potential for unauthorised surveillance and invasion of students' private space through the camera (Moses, 2020). On the other hand, lessons are exposed to the risk of Zoom bombing (see Minhas et al., 2021), a form of protest consisting of disrupting a session by multiple users unmuting themselves and making noise. In early 2021, my own university experienced such disruptions as part of student protests (Dalvit, 2021a). This problem can be addressed by requiring registration and/or authentication for Zoom meetings. Camera use and (self)monitoring are recognised as contributing to a more stressful experience while using Zoom (Ngien and Hogan, 2022). As a result of its extensive use during lockdown, students and academics allegedly experienced Zoom fatigue (Morris, 2020; Toney et al., 2021), resulting in calls for a return to in-person contact. However, going back to normal has been problematised as potentially exclusionary and alienating, particularly for those who represent different categories of diversity (Hodges, 2022).

Unlike most (or perhaps just the most vocal) of my colleagues, the experience of teaching via Zoom has been liberating for me. I deliberately refer to liberation as a radical shift implying a new point of departure, as opposed to emancipation which entails different degrees of success in filling the gap (see Dalvit, in press). Although South Africa boasts one of the highest Internet penetrations on the African continent, the shift to remote learning highlighted profound digital inequalities in our university community. Due to bandwidth constraints, virtual lectures via Zoom are audio-only. With a slight sense of guilt, I must confess that I experienced removing the visual component from my teaching as a welcome fresh start, levelling or even subverting the playing field. While lack of visual feedback seemed to be stressful and challenging for my colleagues, I felt my condition prepared me for that. I use the Zoom app on an iPhone in combination with a screen reader. For the first time, while teaching a large class, I was able to know when students raised their hands as I received a voice notification. I could also identify students by associating their voices to their names, which the screen reader voiced out for me. I was also notified of people joining or leaving and could access a full list of those in attendance. Teaching remotely via Zoom enabled me to mute all the background noise which represents such a distraction in face-to-face lessons. I could even read my own notes using headphones on another device, without having to memorise the whole lesson beforehand. My teaching assistant was ready at hand in case of emergency (e.g. if I got disconnected or in case of Zoom bombing), but his intervention was never actually required.

As a teaching tool, Zoom can either reinforce or subvert the power of the gaze in the classroom. If the goal is to try and recreate the traditional setup, an audiovisual application like Zoom lends itself to monitoring students. For example, the lecturer can escape the students' gaze by sharing their screen while inviting students to keep their cameras on. The impossibility for students to see or communicate with each other completes the panopticon scenario. If, on the other hand, Zoom is employed to rethink teaching and learning, several possibilities emerge. Zoom can be used as part of a flipped-classroom approach. As mentioned in the previous section, recorded presentations for my third-year course were made available to students before class. Lecture time via Zoom was reserved for questions and discussion of the topics presented, with which students were already familiar. Recordings of such interactions were made available to students through a zero-rated e-learning platform. While students did not have to pay for data to access either the presentations or the recorded Zoom sessions, they had to use a portion of the data supplied by the University as a contingency measure to participate in class discussions. This constraint played to my own advantage by limiting interactions to audio or text and encouraging students to make the most of our time together by preparing for class. To my surprise, both attendance and quality of the assignments submitted were comparable, if not better than pre-pandemic ones.

Concluding Discussion: A Different Normal

The emphasis on power and control might give the reader the impression that this is a personal obsession of mine. In actual fact, rather the opposite is the case. My own experience as a university student in Europe before coming to Rhodes has been one of almost complete freedom and flexibility. Within the old Italian system

(Vecchio ordinamento) which remained in place until 2001, attendance was not mandatory, very few if any coursework assignments existed, and most exams were oral. Many of the constraints a blind or visually impaired student would face in my course (e.g. having to be present in class, interacting with the e-learning management system, writing exams in a dedicated venue and, most importantly for the present work, accessing PowerPoint slides) would not have arisen. Conversely, online resources and screen reader technology were not sufficiently popular or developed to support a person with my current eyesight trying to cope with university studies. I feel my rather unique epistemological vantage point as both the product of a very different higher education system and a person with progressive visual impairment enables me to critique the status quo and imagine alternative possibilities. In other words, my personal experience (of which blindness is an important component) may enable me to see power relationships which are invisible to others.

As a result of the visual turn epitomised by PowerPoint, until recently my understanding of blindness was one of loss, suffering, and defeat. During the span of my teaching career, my students relied more and more on sight, the very sense I progressively lost. The emotional suffering which accompanied such loss was accompanied by physical suffering as I strained my eyes more and more to make the most of my residual eyesight, resulting in frequent migraines and additional stress. Paradoxically, reaching complete blindness brought some relief as I was forced to accept that no matter how much effort I put I would always lag behind my sighted colleagues and that my teaching material would have to be the result of a compromise. In my relatively small master's classes, I devised coping strategies to help me identify students and familiarise myself with their voices, such as starting seminars with an activity requiring each student to say something (Dalvit, 2014a). Besides fostering some pedagogical innovations, I feel that my blindness enforces a culture of silent listening in my courses, as background noise is particularly distractive to me. The shift to remote virtual teaching changed my perspective of blindness to one of advanced training, resilience, and equality or even advantage. For example, the lack of visual feedback from students, which was so taxing for others, is normal for me. Partly because of the subjects I teach, I was already familiar with the technologies we had to rely on. Such technologies gave me a level of control in the classroom I no longer had during face-to-face teaching. I must recognise that my positive experience was due in no small measure to the fact that I spent lockdown in a comfortable and spacious home with reliable Internet connectivity and a loving and supportive family. Course evaluations and informal communications reveal that this was not the case for many of my students and some of my colleagues, who apparently could not wait to return to campus and face-to-face teaching. As for me, I was reminded of the feeling I got at the end of a 'dinner in the dark', an event during which sighted guests experience eating without being able to see. While this may be regarded as enlightening for some and mildly intimidating for others, it made me realise that real blindness starts when the lights come back on.

References

Baker, J. P., Goodboy, A. K., Bowman, N. D. and Wright, A. A. (2018) Does teaching with PowerPoint increase students' learning? A meta-analysis. *Computers & Education* 126: 376–387.

Bolt, D. (2021) *Metanarratives of Disability: Culture, Assumed Authority, and the Normative Social Order*, Abingdon: Routledge.

Bosch, T. E. (2020) *Social Media and Everyday Life in South Africa*, London: Routledge.

Cuklanz, L. M. (2013) Mass media representation of gendered violence, in C. Carter, L. Steiner, and L. McLaughlin (eds.) *The Routledge Companion to Media & Gender*, London: Routledge.

Dalvit, L. (2014a) Tech stories': A pedagogical innovation for new media and mobile communication courses. *Proceedings of the International Association for Media and Communication Research (IAMCR) Conference*, 15–19 July 2014, Hyderabad, India.

Dalvit, L. (2014b) Knowledge and external influence in journalism education: Reflections on a master course in new media at a South African University. *Proceedings of the International Association for Media and Communication Research (IAMCR) Conference*, 15–19 July 2014, Hyderabad, India.

Dalvit, L. (2015) *Beyond m-Learning: Mobile Video Narratives for Teaching, Research and Community Engagement at a South African University* [Paper presentation] Mobile Innovation Networks Australasia (MINA) Conference, 19 November, Melbourne, Australia.

Dalvit, L. (2016) *A Heutagogical Approach to Digital Media Teaching and Learning: The Case of a Master Course at a South African University* [Paper presentation] International Media Education Summit, 4–5 November, Rome, Italy.

Dalvit, L. (2018) *Critical Pedagogy 2.0: Reflections on Teaching Digital Media and Education at a South African University* [Paper presentation] 12th International Technology, Education and Development Conference, 5–7 March, Valencia, Spain.

Dalvit, L. (2021a, June 24–26) *Problematising Networked Spatialities and Temporalities: New Inclusions and Exclusions at South African Universities* [Paper presentation] The Network Society: Re-evaluation and Applications of a Concept Conference Event, Virtual Event.

Dalvit, L. (2021b) Back to whose "normal"? Personal reflections of a visually-impaired academic at a small South African University. *Communication, Culture & Critique* 14 (2): 328–331.

Dalvit, L. (in press) Differently included: A decolonial perspective on disability and digital media in South Africa, in P. Tsatsou (ed.) *Vulnerable People and Digital Inclusion: Theoretical and Applied Perspectives*, London: Palgrave Macmillan.

Fischman, G. E. and McLaren, P. (2005) Rethinking critical pedagogy and the Gramscian and Freirean legacies: From organic to committed intellectuals or critical pedagogy, commitment, and praxis. *Cultural Studies, Critical Methodologies* 5 (4): 425–446.

Griffin, R. A. (2014) Pushing into precious: Black women, media representation, and the glare of the White supremacist capitalist patriarchal gaze. *Critical Studies in Media Communication* 31 (3): 182–197.

Groys, B. (2012) Under the Gaze of Theory [online]. *e-flux Journal* 35. Available from: http://worker01.e-flux.com/pdf/article_8953828.pdf [accessed 6 July 2022].

Gunga, S. O. and Ricketts, I. W. (2007) Facing the challenges of e-learning initiatives in African universities. *British Journal of Educational Technology* 38 (5): 896–906.

Gunzo, F. T. (2020) *Teachers' Perceptions, Experiences and Challenges Related to Using ICTs in Teaching Social Sciences in Marginalised Classrooms in the Eastern Cape Province, South Africa* [Doctoral dissertation]. Rhodes University, Makhanda, South Africa.

Hodges, D. Z. (2022) Higher education cannot return to normal. *Dean and Provost* 23 (7): 3–7.

Koch, G. (1985) Ex-changing the gaze: Re-visioning feminist film theory. *New German Critique* (34): 139–153.

Landahl, J. (2013) The eye of power (-lessness): On the emergence of the panoptical and synoptical classroom. *History of Education* 42 (6): 803–821.

Laurent, G. (2021) *Media Matters: A Critical Analysis of Black Panther's Role in the Pursuit of Cultural and Racial Media Representation* [Research paper]. University of Ottawa, Ottawa, Canada.

Lourens, H. (2015) *The Lived Experiences of Higher Education for Students With a Visual Impairment: A Phenomenological Study at Two Universities in the Western Cape, South Africa* [Doctoral dissertation]. Stellenbosch University, Stellenbosch, South Africa.

Lourens, H. (2021) Supercripping the academy: The different narrative of a disabled academic. *Disability & Society* 36 (8): 1205–1220.

Makgakge, R. D. (2020) *A Comparison of Representations of the Imperative of Higher Education Change as Transformation Versus Decolonisation in South African Public Discourse* [Doctoral dissertation]. Rhodes University, Makhanda, South Africa.

Minhas, S., Hussain, T., Ghani, A., Sajid, K. and Pakistan, L. (2021) Exploring students online learning: A study of zoom application. *Gazi University Journal of Science* 34 (2): 171–178.

Morris, B. (2020) Why does Zoom exhaust you? Science has an answer. *Wall Street Journal*, 27 May. Available from: www.wsj.com/articles/why-does-zoom-exhaust-you-science-has-an-answer-11590600269 [accessed 6 July 2022].

Moses, T. (2020) 5 reasons to let students keep their cameras off during Zoom classes. *The Conversation*, 17 August. Available from: https://theconversation.com/5-reasons-to-let-students-keep-their-cameras-off-during-zoom-classes-144111 [accessed 6 July 2022].

Ngien, A. and Hogan, B. (2022) The relationship between Zoom use with the camera on and Zoom fatigue: Considering self-monitoring and social interaction anxiety. *Information, Communication & Society*. Available from: https://doi.org/10.1080/13691 18X.2022.2065214 [accessed 6 July 2022].

Padilla, A. (2021) The metanarrative of blindness in the Global South, in D. Bolt (ed.) *Metanarratives of Disability: Culture, Assumed Authority, and the Normative Social Order*, Abingdon: Routledge.

Roberts, D. (2018) The engagement agenda, multimedia learning and the use of images in higher education lecturing: Or, how to end death by PowerPoint. *Journal of Further and Higher Education* 42 (7): 969–985.

Thomas, N. (1991) The curiosity of the gaze: Imperial and Anthropological Postmodernism. Social analysis. *The International Journal of Social and Cultural Practice* 30: 20–31.

Toney, S., Light, J. and Urbaczewski, A. (2021) Fighting zoom fatigue: Keeping the zombies at bay. *Communications of the Association for Information Systems* 48 (1): 40–46.

Tucker, B. (2012) The flipped classroom. *Education Next* 12 (1): 82–83.

Zuboff, S. (2015) Big other: Surveillance capitalism and the prospects of an information civilization. *Journal of Information Technology* 30 (1): 75–89.

3

BLINDNESS AS A SOCIAL CONSTRUCT IN CYPRUS

What Can We Learn From Cultural Events and Artefacts Aiming to Claim Rights, Celebrate, or Prevent Blindness?

Simoni Symeonidou and Kyriakos Demetriou

Preliminary Discussion: Blindness and Its Educational Connotations

Cultural contexts, among other parameters, shape the understanding of blindness as a medical issue and negatively impact on the personal experiences of blindness. The endorsement and superiority of visual perception, known as ocularnormativity (Bolt, 2019), is one common aspect among Global North cultures (Padilla, 2021). Visual perception is considered the norm and everything (e.g. environment, buildings, services, products, websites, TV shows, and novels) privileges people who do not have visual impairments. People with visual impairments increasingly expose such superficial understandings of blindness, offering the counter position that the experience of blindness is a complex human experience that needs to be understood as such, rather than being narrowed down to the opposite of sightedness (Healey and Michalko, 2021).

The conversations about blindness are on parallel tracks with the conversations held about disability. Ableist thinking is dominant in cultures that consider non-disabled people as superior, and thus, they consider it natural to 'serve' the norm, rather than everyone. Ableist thinking is evident in policies, processes, and structures, such as the development of general policies for education and separate policies for disabled children; the former are supposed to serve the 'able', 'competent', and 'independent' children, and the latter are for the 'unable', 'incompetent', and 'dependent' children who need special rather than mainstream education, therapies rather than education, pull-out programmes rather than inclusive learning experiences (Symeonidou and Mavrou, 2020; Tomlinson, 2017). The unfair treatment towards disabled people is known as disablism. Ableist thinking and its consequences are disabling, albeit they are not easily recognised by the different stakeholders (e.g. policy makers and professionals). Deal (2007) refers to 'aversive disablism',

DOI: 10.4324/9781003275060-5

as the actions or rhetoric expressed by stakeholders. For example, non-disabled politicians often consider that they recognise disablism (e.g. violation of rights), but at the same time, they are themselves prejudiced and guided by ableist thinking. Bolt's (2019) tripartite model views ableism as normative positivisms, which privilege non-disabled people, and disablism as non-normative negativisms, which expose unequal treatment. He suggests a third component, the non-normative positivisms, being the 'affirmed deviations that depart from the social norms of ableism and disablism' (Bolt, 2019, 5). Arguably, non-normative positivisms see the experience of disability as valuable and disabled people as valued humans who need to be respected and appreciated as an integral, rather than a separate, part of their culture (Bolt, 2019; Goodley, 2021).

In this chapter, we explore blindness as a cultural construct in Cyprus. In particular, we examine the language, assumptions, and social understandings embedded in two cultural stations of blindness: postage stamps and the annual event 'Walk – Claim with the Blind'. We used artefacts and quotes from these, which we translated from the Greek language, except for one quote that was originally in English. In some instances, we did not agree with some terms (e.g. the blind, handicap) but we kept them as part of the original quotes which reflect dominant ableist language. The autocritical analysis approach we followed entailed employing our experiences and knowledge in the analysis of discourses and portrayals of blindness (Bolt, 2021). Even though we do not have the experience of blindness, we share some experiences that helped us rethink and refine our understanding of disability issues over the years. To begin with, we both grew up in the Cypriot culture, in which blindness is considered a devastating condition and people who have visual impairments are believed to be pitiful. As university students, we followed similar education paths, in different time periods, and we gradually confronted our own stereotypes and misconceptions about disability. We are now based in two different universities in Cyprus, where we have the roles of the researcher and teacher educator in inclusive education. We are concerned with the way blindness is presented as a medical issue our culture. In our university teaching and research work, we expose the oppressive pedagogies followed in Cypriot schools (Symeonidou and Chrysostomou, 2019; Demetriou, 2021), where being a disabled child is equated with inability and dependency. We also have close links with students and activists who have visual impairments with whom we discuss their understandings of how blindness, and disability issues in general, are perceived in our culture. On a parallel track, one of us is a philatelist; the other often writes to the press to criticise charity events for disabled people or comment on education policy developments in relation to disabled children. Our profiles influenced the selection and analysis of the selected cultural stations.

Postage Stamps: Preventing or Celebrating Blindness?

Postage stamps, either directly or indirectly, unveil political and cultural values, and have the power to affect the everyday lives of people who either collect them or not (Ogletree et al., 1994). The examination of postage stamps as a cultural medium may reveal the cultural representations of disability of a nation at a particular time (Swan et al., 2006). In our effort to interpret Cypriot stamps highlighting issues associated with blindness, we recognised the importance of investigating the context, the background story, as well as associated texts. Thus, after selecting the stamps related to blindness issued from 1960s onwards (the year that Cyprus became an independent republic), we searched for relevant publications issued by the Cyprus post (i.e. two volumes of the Philatelic Encyclopedia and brochures following each series of stamps).

In 1976, the Cyprus Post, followed the example of many other countries, and issued a commemorative postage stamp on the occasion of the World Health Day (Figure 3.1). The chosen theme was the prevention of blindness, and the stamp illustration showed two hands holding an eye. The accompanying motto was 'Foresight prevents blindness' and was written both in Greek and in English. The body was eliminated in an eye and two hands, substituting the person. This is common on other stamps seeking to represent issues related to visual impairments, issued in different countries and time periods (Demetriou and Symeonidou, 2021). In this particular stamp, the two hands protected and defended the eye from vision loss, and warned the audience that their vision was endangered.

The significance of preventing vision loss is confirmed in the explanatory text that accompanies the stamp in the Philatelic Encyclopaedia issued by Cyprus Post (2005a). It is mentioned that eye-related diseases, such as cataracts and trachoma, are common causes of blindness, even though they are treatable.

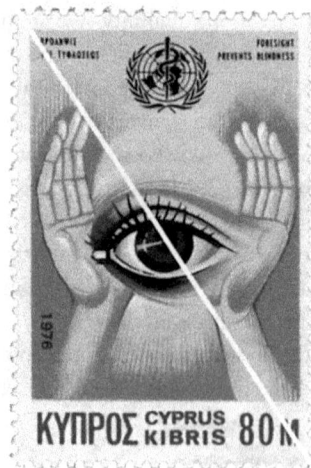

FIGURE 3.1   Foresight prevents blindness (1976)

Source: Cyprus Post

The brief text found in the Philatelic Encyclopaedia, explaining the intended messages of the stamp, starts like this: 'The loss of any of our senses can have a serious impact on the quality of our lives' (Cyprus Post, 2005a, 160). It sounds like a simple warning, but it could also be interpreted as an attempt to intimidate that the loss of any of our senses will affect life to such an extent that it amounts to disaster. This is not clear here, but it is clearer in the statement: 'Blindness and the lack of the sense of sight deprive perhaps the most wonderful sense of God's creation and immerse us in a life full of darkness'. Here the sense of sight is praised as the sense of the senses. It is presented as a wonderful divine creation but woe to those who may lose it. Loss of sight is seen as synonymous to a curse, as a life doomed to live in utter darkness. There are three aspects to be noted in this sentence. First, loss of vision is equated with loss of health. As a result, disability is medicalised and is perceived as something that must be prevented and cured, otherwise disabled people's lives are less worthy. The medicalisation of losing sight is clearer in the epilogue of the text: 'the main goal of the World Health Organization is to achieve the highest possible level of health for all people'. Second, being healthy and able-bodied are deemed gifts from God while their loss can be seen as a life-changing punishment. This reflects a religious stereotype in the Cypriot culture where impairment is considered as part of God's design, a destiny, punishment or affliction for those who experience it and their families (Symeonidou, 2009). Third, there is an impression that people who were born blind or acquired visual impairments during their lifetime are cursed to always live in darkness and misery. This is a stereotype among people who do not have visual impairments and believe in the authoritative figure of sight. They are influenced by what they experience in simulations of blindness (i.e. occluding sight) that blindness is synonymous to absence of sight, or seeing in the dark (Symeonidou and Chrysostomou, 2019; Titchkosky et al., 2019). The stereotype that people who have visual impairments are dependent on others is also highlighted: 'People with visual impairments . . . necessarily need our help, which we must generously provide to them'. This attitude reflects a prevalent assumption in cultures where the charity model of disability still flourishes. The majority of Cypriots were taught to show compassion, sympathy and pity towards disabled people (Demetriou, 2020; Symeonidou, 2009).

Another stamp worthy of comment is the one issued in 2005 to honour Carolina Pelendritou, a Paralympic swimmer who has visual impairment (Figure 3.2). Pelendritou won her first gold medal at the Athens 2004 Summer Paralympic Games, competing in the 100 m breaststroke S13, achieving a Paralympic record. This gold medal was the first Olympic medal ever awarded to an athlete from Cyprus. The stamp depicts a smiling portrait of the athlete, with the coat of arms on her chest, proudly holding her gold medal which is worn around her neck. It is without a doubt a beautiful picture taken of an important event for the sports history of Cyprus. It is important to note that Pelendritou was the first living person to ever appear on a Cypriot stamp, following her achievement.

FIGURE 3.2 Carolina Pelendritou (2005)

Source: Cyprus Post

The following commentary appears in the Cyprus Post brochure that accompanies the stamp. It was written in English, and used terms that were not challenged at the time, such as 'handicap' and 'handicapped persons':

> The willpower: With this stamp, the Cyprus Post honours handicapped Persons all those who set high goals, who continue to fight, overcoming internal and external barriers, mental and natural obstacles, taboos and prejudices, providing that they can offer and become creative members of society presupposing that society gives the opportunity, accepting them as its equal members. A brilliant example is the career of the athlete Carolina Pelendritou from Limassol, who won the gold medal in swimming 100 metres stroke in Athens Para Olympic Games 2004. Due to her will power she overcame successfully the increasing problems of diminishing eyesight. Overcoming tremendous difficulties relating to her handicap she came first making proud all her Cypriot compatriots.
>
> *(Cyprus Post, 2005b, English text in the original)*

On the one hand, Pelendritou is presented as a role model and a source of inspiration, proving how one can achieve high goals with hard work, dedication, and above all strong will. On the other hand, the text attempts to elevate society – and consequently the state – which cares for all citizens and gives equal opportunities to those who stereotypically cannot achieve their goals on their own. Pelendritou is presented here as a person who, despite the difficulties caused by her impairment, can be a productive citizen. There is an attempt to honour the 'superhuman' achievements of the athlete who managed to succeed and triumph in activities and sports regularly associated with the so-called 'normal' despite the limitations caused by her impairment (Demetriou and Symeonidou, 2021). She is presented as 'supercrip' or 'spectacular disabled' (Swan et al., 2006, 231) who makes us proud because she succeeded thanks to her strong will and the contributions of the society – including the state – that gives opportunities to and accepts disabled people.

Nevertheless, there is an oxymoron between the 'success' story narrated by the state and experienced by Pelendritou. In an interview published in a daily newspaper in 2009, the athlete stated that she felt abandoned by the state and her fellow athletes: 'All these years I have been swimming and I have competed at the highest sport events, but I have not been given any reward by the state' (Alexandrou, 2009, 11 December). She also stated that before joining the Paralympic team, she forced herself to hide the fact that she had impaired vision, and she competed with non-disabled athletes. When she decided to start competing with athletes who had the same impairment, she came under fire from various directions and was accused of lying (Petri, 2021, 30 September). It needs to be highlighted that even if the state recognised Pelendritou's great achievement in rhetoric and celebrated it with an honorary stamp, in practice it has not contributed to her success. In various press articles published from 2005 onwards and more recently, after Pelendritou's achievements in the Tokyo 2020 Paralympics (gold and bronze medal), she stated that she continues to finance her preparation without state support.

'Walk – Claim with the Blind': Is Claiming Rights a Matter for People Who Have Visual Impairments?

This section draws on the annual event 'Walk – Claim with the Blind' to examine the cultural representations of blindness in the social media. This is a popular event organised by the Pancyprian Organisation of the Blind (POB), an organisation of people who have visual impairments. A thorough examination of materials related to the event from 2010 to date (i.e. published invitations to the event, press articles that follow the event, and the way it is covered in TV reportages) shows that the aim to inform society about the inequalities and unfair treatment experienced by people who have visual impairments coexists with a dominant ableist perception of blindness.

The cultural representations of blindness in the social media rely on the cultural binary dividing people into those who are 'normal' and those who deviate from the norm (Bolt, 2021). This binary is realised through the invitations published on social media to advertise the event, which are prepared by people who have visual impairments seeking to reach people who do not have visual impairments. Despite the language that intends to show the need to join forces (e.g. 'travel-companions', 'together we open pathways, together we achieve a lot' ('We walk . . .', 2019, 28 March, n.p.), people who do not have visual impairments is the actual target group. It could be argued that this is justified, since people who have visual impairments are committed to a 'genuine' and 'difficult struggle' (ibid.) to achieve equal rights and participation. Thus, they view this event as a means to achieve their goals. According to the invitations, the 'friends of the Blind' are invited to support them in claiming their rights and contribute in the removal of 'barriers in attitudes, environmental attitudes which prevent full and effective participation on equal terms with others, and secure equal opportunities, equal treatment and social recognition'. However, the binary thinking which is embedded in the Cypriot culture entails reducing people who have visual impairments to individuals with one single attribute, instead of viewing them as complex persons. Further, the understanding that they are merely people who are unable to see is reflected in the photos that accompany the invitations. The photos are chosen by the journalists, and they usually feature the legs of a blind man holding a white cane, walking through tactile paving or trying to cross the road. Such photos indicate that the dominant view is that the main 'challenge' faced by people with visual impairments is walking independently.

The superiority of people who have visual impairments, granted with the attribute of the politician or the philanthropist, pervades in the published invitations. The organisers (POB) assume that people who do not have visual impairments are more likely to encourage the coverage of the event by the media, and at the same time, form close bonds with them. According to the invitations, a key-male policy figure takes the event under his auspices and leads the walk (e.g. the president of the Republic, the President of the Houses of Parliament, the Minister of Education, and the Mayor of the city). The invitations also list the organisations which support the event, and are known for their charity actions in Cyprus; for example, the Youth Department of the Red Cross, the Scout Association, and bikers associations ('I walk . . .', 2017, 20 April). The key-policy figure and the representatives of the organisations listed earlier, are asked to greet the event. The TV reportages and the online articles that cover the event ensure that the superior guests shadow the voice of the organisers. For example, a 3-minute video shows the head of the POB saying some incoherent phrases as they are cut from different parts of the greeting, whereas the guests representing the supporting organisations say one or two complete sentences (FamagustaNews, 2018, 15 April). Similarly, online articles that report the event begin by quoting parts of the guests' greetings and end with a quote from the POB's head greeting.

Aversive disablism flourishes, as depicted in the following quote by the secretary general of the Board of Ministers, Theodosis Tsiolas:

> It's a fact that the President of Cyprus and the whole society appreciate the work of the POB, and we recognise that we need to help and support every attempt aiming to alleviate and reinforce our fellow human beings who are in need of our support. . ... For forty years now, the POB is a pioneer with notable work in providing support services, education, employment and entertainment to a great number of blind people. . . . Each one of us needs to promote the implementation of a quality social support system with modern structures and services, so that blind people have a safe, decent, quality living and equal treatment and they are able to use their abilities and fulfil their expectations. . . . . It is worth praising all those who voluntarily show solidarity and participate in every effort to support blind people, and they complement the help provided by the state.
>
> (Cyprus News Agency, *2019, 7 April, n.p.*)

Tsiolas appears to understand what needs to be done, without realising that the government he represents is part of the problem. He takes for granted that voluntary work needs to continue. He also considers that the government provides 'help' which can be complimented by volunteers. In his opening speech to the event of the same year, the head of the POB, Christakis Nikolaides, referred to the ongoing violation of rights of people who have visual impairments in Cyprus which 'forced the Organisation [POB] to reconsider its goals and priorities, turning it many decades back' (Cyprus News Agency, 2019, 8 April, n.p.). Nikolaides concludes that 'each subsequent government doesn't hesitate to punish those who claim their intrinsic and evident human rights, and violates their right to decide about their future, to become equal citizens, and to have an equal and decent place in the community' (ibid.).

When non-disabled politicians stand side by side with people who have visual impairments, more than being part of the problem because they do not take action, they make efforts to suggest solutions that would help them solve any technical problems they may have. In his greeting in 2018, the former head of the Parliament, Dimitris Sillouris, characterised the event a 'remarkable initiative' which helps us cultivate empathy and build a more humane society, and he highlighted the view that 'other skills they [people who have visual impairments] develop, can be useful to the society in multiple ways' (Cyprus News Agency, 2018, 22 April, n.p.). He referred to an 'innovative programme' in Germany which aims at turning 'blind women's strong sense of touch into a specialised tool for detecting breast cancer'. Inherent in this greeting were ableist questions, such as: How can they find a job if they cannot see? How best can they use their sense of touch? How can they be useful to the society? Blindness is limited to a technical issue that needs to be solved.

Aversive disablism is also combined with celebrating independent disabled people, who managed to achieve their goals despite their impairment. The former head of the Parliament, Giannakis Omirou, started his greeting in 2015 by saying that in the past month, one blind student participated in the students' national parade for the first time in Cyprus, and 'he led the parade with the eyes of his soul, giving everybody the moral lesson that where there is a will, the barriers are overcome and the goals are achieved' (Omirou, 2015, 4 April, n.p.). The barriers became an individual matter, the student overcame them because he is independent, and he 'led the parade with the eyes of his soul' because he might have a visual impairment, but he has a good heart. In the rest of his greeting, Omirou stated that the Parliament will support them to secure a better quality of life and equal opportunities. Without realising the Parliament's responsibility and his role as the head of the Parliament, he highlighted the need to implement the UN Convention on the Rights of Persons with Disabilities ratified in Cyprus since 2011.

The April Fair is an event that takes place immediately after the end of the walk, in the gardens of the School for the Blind. This is a one- or two-day event which is not advertised as a charity event, but it contains all the elements that make it one. According to the annual invitations, the wife of the president of Cyprus opens the Fair, a common practice in other charity events in Cyprus. The gardens of the School for the Blind turn into a place for entertainment, where different items and snacks are sold, together with arts and crafts made by people who have visual impairments and work in sheltered employment:

> It is an event that gives carelessness and relaxation, and it is worth visiting. The income from the event finances actions for the well-being of blind people, the treatment and prevention of blindness, and their smooth and uneventful integration to the society.
>
> (Pancyprian Organisation of the Blind, *2015, 4 April, n.p.*)

Clearly, the invitations target people who do not have visual impairments, and highlight the argument that they will all enjoy the event, and at the same time, contribute to the well-being of people who have visual impairments.

Concluding Discussion: Drawing the Links Between Blindness as a Social Construct and Education

The rationale, the organisation, the implementation, and the social media coverage of issues related to blindness indicate that normative positivisms and non–normative negativisms act as two sides of the same coin. The dominant ableist ideology considers it natural to live in a society that favours people who do not have visual impairments. In this context, people who have visual impairments are believed to be unfortunate and pitiful for not being able to operate in the society. This understanding justifies the belief that people who do not have visual impairments are expected to do their best to 'help'. Disabling thinking and practices are hard to identify, because the way 'barriers', 'participation', and 'equal opportunities' are understood is linked with the inability to see, and not with the 'inequity of the normative social order' which is 'divisive and profound' (Bolt, 2021, xvi). This is reflected in other actions that take place in the Cypriot culture, that aim to cultivate 'empathy' towards people who have visual impairments, such as covering one's eyes and trying to move around or even play blind football in order to feel/understand the difficulties faced by people who have visual impairments (Symeonidou and Chrysostomou, 2019).

The narratives of people who do not have visual impairments dominate in both cultural stations presented in this chapter, and gradually build the 'metanarrative of blindness' which does not reflect the narratives of people who have visual impairments (Bolt, 2021, xvii). Not only that, but a venue for 'aversive disablism' is established, in which politicians and the social media 'recognise that disablism is bad but do not recognise that they themselves are prejudiced' (Deal, 2007, 93). This is reflected in the state's response to Pelendritou's gold Paralympic medal: an honorary stamp was issued, her achievement was praised, but no financial reward was allocated because she won a Paralympic and not an Olympic gold medal. Similarly, politicians who participate in the event 'Walk – Claim with the Blind' state their commitment to equal opportunities for people who have visual impairments, but at the same time, they thank the volunteers for 'helping', and they try to see what is positive in this 'negative' situation (e.g. a blind student was capable enough to overcome his difficulties and lead the parade). Aversive disablism is often combined with treating visual impairment 'as a technical problem in need of technical solutions' (Healey and Michalko, 2021, 9). Thus, preventing blindness is an important solution, but in case it is not prevented, there are other solutions. According to the politicians, blind students or athletes can overcome their 'problems' if they have the will power, blind women can use their sense of touch to participate in cancer detection programmes, and blind people can be employed in sheltered workshops. Not only blindness is limited to a technical issue, but conceptualising it as such reveals an authoritative division of citizens into two groups, the Self and the Other, where the Self is the norm and the Others are those who need to surpass any problems they face so that they secure a place close to the norm and become integrated in the society.

As teacher educators and researchers, we strongly feel that student teachers, who are an integral part of Cypriot society, have difficulties in looking for hidden meanings in multimodal texts, such as the ones presented in this chapter. Student teachers often accept what is presented on social media as valid. It will require an approach that combines theory, research, and cultural examples related to disability to encourage them to appreciate the value of deconstructing ableist ideas about disability related issues. Often, asking student teachers to appreciate artefacts from the past, such as postage stamps and accompanying position texts, press releases/ articles published by different stakeholders, news videos, and so on, is quite difficult, as they enter their studies with the expectation to learn how to 'treat' children with disabilities. Our effort needs to be focused on critically engaging them with cultural stations of disability and equip them with the tools to detect ableist messages and symbolisms.

References

Alexandrou, P. (2009) I feel abandoned from the society. *Simerini Newspaper*, 11 December. Available from: https://bit.ly/3ILpUlg [accessed 15 March 2022].

Bolt, D. (2019) *Cultural Disability Studies in Education: Interdisciplinary Navigations of the Normative Divide*, London: Routledge.

Bolt, D. (2021) Introduction, in D. Bolt (ed.) *Metanarratives of Disability: Culture, Assumed Authority, and the Normative Social Order*, London: Routledge.

Cyprus News Agency. (2018) People with visual impairments are an integral part of the society. Greeting of the president of the parliament for the opening of the event 'Walk – Claim with the Blind' in Nicosia, 22 April. *Kathimerini*. Available from: https://bit.ly/3sQ9LFu [accessed 15 March 2022].

Cyprus News Agency. (2019) Tsiolas: People with visual impairments should have equal treatment, Cytoday, 7 April. Available from: https://bit.ly/3tyxCc1 [accessed 15 March 2022].

Cyprus News Agency. (2019) POB: The Cypriot society came back with policies adopting the anachronistic philosophy of pity, Cyprustimes, 8 April. Available from: https://bit.ly/3Kncooh [accessed 15 March 2022].

Cyprus Post. (2005a) *Philatelic Encyclopedia: Cyprus Stamps-History and Culture, 1880–2004*, Nicosia: Ministry of Transport, Communications and Works, Department of Postal Services.

Cyprus Post. (2005b) *Philatelic Information Brochure for Commemorative Issues, Issue Date: 3 March 2005*, Nicosia: Ministry of Transport, Communications and Works, Stamp and Philatelic Service of the Department of Postal Services.

Deal, M. (2007) Aversive disablism: Subtle prejudice toward disabled people. *Disability & Society* 22 (1): 93–107.

Demetriou, K. (2020) Do you want to play with me? Acceptance and preference dilemmas in choosing playmates with physical disability. *Early Child Development and Care* 192 (6): 947–963.

Demetriou, K. (2021) Intentions of children without disabilities to form friendship with peers with physical disability: A small scale study. *Early Child Development and Care* 191 (13): 2141–2157.

Demetriou, K. and Symeonidou, S. (2021) Stamped allegories of disability: Representations of the disabled body on postage stamps. *Disability & Society*. DOI: 10.1080/09687599.2021.1983417.

FamagustaNews. (2018) Walk-claim with the blind. *Paralimni*, April 15. Available from: www.youtube.com/watch?v=QV_5oHeGK98 [accessed 15 March 2022].

Goodley, D. (2021) *Disability and Other Human Questions*, Bingley: Emerald.

Healey, D. and Michalko, R. (2021) The metanarrative of blindness in North America: Meaning, feeling and feel, in D. Bolt (ed.) *Metanarratives of Disability: Culture, Assumed Authority and The Normative Social Order*, London: Routledge.

I walk with the blind on the 23rd of April. (2017) *Politis News*, 20 April. Available from: https://bit.ly/3hPLV6s [accessed 15 March 2022].

Ogletree, S. M., Merritt, S. and Roberts, J. (1994) Female/male portrayals on US postage stamps of the twentieth century. *Communication Research Reports* 11 (1): 77–85.

Omirou, G. (2015) Greeting of the president of the house of representatives for the opening of the march 'Walk – Claim with the Blind', 4 April. Available from: https://bit.ly/3pK7I42 [accessed 15 March 2022].

Padilla, A. (2021) The metanarrative of blindness in the global South: A LatDisCrit counterstory to the bittersweet mythology of blindness as giftedness, in D. Bolt (ed.) *Metanarratives of Disability, Culture, Assumed Authority and the Normative Social Order*, London: Routledge.

Pancyprian Organisation of the Blind. (2015) Events on the occasion of 'Walk – Claim with the Blind' and "April Fair". *Pancyprian Organisation of the Blind Facebook* Page, 4 April. Available from: https://bit.ly/3KmFc0b [accessed 15 March 2022].

Petri, P. (2021) 'They said that I don't have a problem, that I tried to deceive them, and I remembered it out of the blue . . . I was hurt'. *Omada Reporter*, 30 September. Available from: https://bit.ly/373fD5T [accessed 15 March 2022].

Swan, G., Meade, T., Klein, J. and Serlin, D. (2006) Licking disability: Reflections on the politics of postage stamps. *Radical History Review* 94: 228–232.

Symeonidou, S. (2009) Trapped in our past: The price we have to pay for our cultural disability inheritance. *International Journal of Inclusive Education* 13 (6): 565–579.

Symeonidou, S. and Chrysostomou, M. (2019) 'I got to see the other side of the coin': Teachers' understandings of disability-focused oppressive and anti-oppressive pedagogies. *International Journal of Educational Research* 98 (2019): 356–365.

Symeonidou, S. and Mavrou, K. (2020) Problematising disabling discourses on the assessment and placement of learners with disabilities: Can interdependence inform an alternative narrative for inclusion? *European Journal of Special Needs Education* 35 (1): 70–84.

Titchkosky, T., Healey, D. and Michalko, R. (2019) Blindness simulation and the culture of sight. *Journal of Literary & Cultural Disability Studies* 13 (2): 123–139.

Tomlinson, S. (2017) *A Sociology of Special and Inclusive Education*, London and New York: Routledge.

We walk with the blind in Nicosia, Limassol and Famagusta. (2019) *Check in Cyprus*, 28 March. Available from: https://bit.ly/3tElWoa [accessed 15 March 2022].

4

THE FLAG, A RAP, AND THE ETHNOGRAPHER

Looking for 'Indianness' Within Visual Impairment

Mahashewta Bhattacharya and Bijendra Singh

Preliminary Discussion: Unlearning in an Indian University

This chapter arises out of the two years we spent around and among the blind students at Jawaharlal Nehru University (JNU) in New Delhi, from a situatedness as sighted individuals amidst yet apart from blindnesses as ways of being. The two cultural stations of blindness that we are working with are ethnography as a method and understanding the metaphors of nationalism. We were trying to understand the category of imagination sans the image, how visually impaired persons imagine, articulate, and express the abstract idea of 'Indianness' through a cultural vocabulary specific to their ontology. We were interested in alternate affordances of the category of imagination understood to be critical for the consolidation of a nationwide community without or with varied notions of an image or visual metaphors. With this, we traced a journey across a symbolic universe of objects, arts, and performances that our respondents were kind enough to take us through, to arrive at their imagined communities, their imagined Indianness. JNU as an institutional space was the most conducive for such an overarching question because of its wide representation of people from the length and breadth of the nation, and beyond, as we see in the case of one of our respondents who hails from Nepal. Our data is based on a case study of eight visually impaired students, four men and four women. Some names have been changed for the maintenance of confidentiality while others have been retained with consent. Our second station is found at the interface between sighted and non-sighted ontologies established for an ethnographic exercise and looks critically at the methodological orientations assumed through the process. It examines the very practices and sensibilities that constitute the ocularnormative discipline of sociocultural anthropology. Defined as the mass or institutionalised endorsement of visual necessity (Bolt,

DOI: 10.4324/9781003275060-6

2014), ocularnormativism is a bane of the ethnographic orientation and, being its practitioners, we subject ourselves to the criticality as much as the discipline and its methods. In ways, therefore, this chapter is a back-and-forth between analytics, temporalities, spaces, and social locations; between reflexivities and reflections, acquired sensations and discarded sensitivities; and between progressions that propel us forward and regressive methods that tie us back.

Ajit was ordering the quintessential cup of overly sweetened chai at the School of International Studies canteen when I, having recognised him by his impairment, broke my stupor of introversion to interrupt him. I put on my unusual sales pitch voice and introduced myself as a sociologist who wanted to do 'some research' on 'something' related to blindness[1]. He readily agreed, with a warm smile that immediately put me at ease and we shared contact details and a promise to meet later that week. When I went to meet him in the hostel, it was shortly before dinner and the Delhi autumn was beginning to rob the day of any and every remnant bit of sun. I was there to interview him and his roommate who was blind as well.[2] I hesitated for a minute before asking him if I could turn on the lights, to which he laughed – a laughter which denoted no mockery or ridicule but sheer acceptance of my presence as a person disabled by darkness. While my own visual imperative always kept me from attaining any appreciable degree of immersion into the blind ways of being, I was shown these ways nonetheless in the friendliest of nudges, laughter's and corrections for which I am immensely grateful. The more time I have spent with people with visual impairments, the more I felt the powerlessness of the very difference on which I had based my entire universe of assumptions. I found acceptance in their laughter and was enabled to laugh with them, echoing a language of reaction that was inherently visceral. This laughter thus resounds through the course of our interviews and therefore this chapter – in responses, corrections and filling pauses thus assumes power in itself.

Ethnographically Seeing, Sensing, and Being: Destabilising Observation

Gaurav and Ajit speak to us against the backdrop of the busiest *dhaba* in JNU. Each of the pink cement roundtables around us houses a cacophony of voices speaking different tongues in a characteristic early evening glee and loudness. The man behind the Nilgiri Cafe counter has to shout over the youthful voices to announce orders that are ready for grabs. Our recording begins with the announcement of '*one masala omelette*' before they take turns to help us get rid of our many ableist biases. I motion to Biju to begin, a gesture that goes unnoticed by our respondents. The noises in the background immediately dim for Biju and I, as we try to hook on to every word they speak, jotting furiously and thinking through their words. Ajit stops suddenly, a pause uncharacteristic of his eloquence and appears unsettled. We worry and ask him what happened. '*Kuttey*' (dogs), he says with unconcealed dejection. 'Must have attacked somebody', I say, generalising stray dog behaviour.

'More like a terrorist attack', Ajit says with a chuckle. 'They should bite one or two (people), only then some action can be taken against them', adds Gaurav. They spend a minute lamenting how the campus dogs are a massive hazard for the VI students, many of whom have been attacked in the past, and that the most vociferous of dog lovers gang up against them whenever they have tried to pass a petition for their removal. As a mode of enquiry that is fundamentally premised upon a holistic reading of the respondent – from the contents of their speech to the changes in their disposition, very little should ideally escape the hawk eye of a good ethnographer. Smiles, nods, frowns, hand gestures, and tapping of the feet and laughter – each of these culturally defined sets of expressions and bodily dispositions are often the first things we try to familiarise ourselves with and the first set of responses we jot down in our notebooks.

One of our many ethnographic unlearnings therefore was to decentralise this discourse of reading face and body. Alongside the space of 'seeing', there is the space of 'not seeing' that constitutes ethnography. This could be the much lamented missing of events happening in the field while the ethnographer is absent or busy jotting down notes. Alternatively, it is the intentional act of looking away – the moral imperative to turn one's gaze away from a site of occurrence to maintain human dignity or respect cultural codes. We could no longer employ the same cultural vocabularies with which we would read a twitch, a frown or general face-work in a social interaction (Goffman, 1955), yet acknowledge that they could mean something. Thus we were left to propose that an ethnography of and with blindness by a sighted individual requires a much more nuanced and multi-sensory vocabulary of reading bodies and faces that is adequately triangulated and substantiated by the narratives of respondents instead of being mostly reliant on visual cues. Similarly for questioning, when Gaurav and Ajit pause confusedly before answering a question, or when Sylvia would speak over Ritu, we realised it was our fallacy of using 'you' over specific names. While this seemed to be a practical challenge at first where we were limited by our ocularcentrism, we found ourselves picking up more holistic modes of operating in a face-to-face interaction as we progressed through the course of our research. From loosening up from a position of hypersensitivity to practising sonic modes of being present cognitively, our initial behavioural inconsistencies soon gave way to a more effective multisensory (Pink, 2009) pattern of 'being with' sightless persons visually.

Amidst the processes of holding gaze, maintaining eye contact or lowering the gaze, the third trope of visuality which complicates the balance between seeing and not seeing is the reverse gaze or 'being seen'. As much as the respondent readies himself for the interaction through a preconfigured line of facework, the same holds true for the ethnographer. While ethnographers observe the community that they set out to study, they at once open themselves up to the very vulnerability of being observed by the community, which ultimately decides how they are to fare within the field. We fared rather poorly, only visually imperceptibly. In measured doses of hand gestures, eye movements and shaking of heads, Biju and I developed a secret code of communicating that spoke over, under and around the voices of

our informants. Effectively an interface of bodies, ethnography as it is conventionally taught, practised and internalised, presupposes visually co-constitutive phe-
nomenologies of bodies being set in motion through the modality of observation.
In the following section, we aim to destabilise this settled interrelation of bodies as
being constituted on a singular sensory plane through co-presence in the context
of qualitative research and insert into it the polemic of transgressions that are made
possible through a supposed invisibility.

It had been a long day after which we had gone to speak to Chunnu in his
room. Biju seated himself on the bed next to Chunnu, while I sat down on the
floor, already announcing a stance of comfort within the space. As we mechani-
cally fired our set of questions at him, he took us through a detailed description
of how he lost his vision as a child and continues living in the hope and nostalgia
of regaining back his sight to this day, an optimism that he admitted had suffered a
few dents and fractures in the way in disproportion to his faith in scientific progress.
The interview was long, and we were grateful for his readiness to share his story
with us. But the time impressed itself upon my body. I began sitting cross-legged
on the floor. Within a few minutes, I had stretched my legs in front of me and
frequently stretched my hands as well. I twisted and turned, careful not to crack a
bone and made an occasional jotting in my notebook about things that appeared
to excite him that showed in his voice or in the otherwise unchanging stance
he had assumed throughout while being potentially observed simultaneously by
two ethnographers. Having been fully sighted till the age of 6, he may have felt
more conscious than the others who had not a memory of watching people being
watched. On the other hand, I felt liberated in my invisibility. I thought I could
conduct my body in whichever way I was most comfortable, as long as my bodily
transgressions and 'ethnographic slack' were sufficiently masked by the words of
affirmation and encouragement I spoke and my tone that suggested a keen audience with undivided attention. I assumed my sonic compensation to be a good
enough placeholder for not conducting my body in an 'ethnographerly' manner.
I went as far as allowing myself a soft yawn and stretched further onto the floor,
almost reclining against my hands. Biju smiled at me half compassionately and half
in understanding of what I was experimenting with.

These multifaceted corporeal transgressions that I would take the liberty of
allowing myself would be recurrent through the course of our research conscious-
ness. At every point, the liberty of not being watched would push us into breaking,
playing with or remodelling the very structures of expected corporeal conduct
signifying ethnographic diligence. From animated expressions of surprise, wonder, and confusion thrown at each other to using hasty signs to suggest changing
the course of the conversation, we would often be communicating parallel to the
interview. There was the possibility of our transgressions to be 'felt', a feeling to
be a composite of the sum total of all the other senses that supposedly rush in
to take the place of an impaired sense, but the absolution of invisibility within a
tightly visual discourse of observation in qualitative research was something we
were quite intrigued to experience. For instance, in anthropology, we take our eye

contact very seriously. We are taught that nothing conveys genuine interest and presence more effectively than looking one in the eye, holding the gaze (Emerson et al., 2011) and nodding, smiling and sending out these subtle waves of commonly understood energies. The eye's dual role as a physiological apparatus and a social organ is strongly felt through this act of being together in discourse. We had to learn quickly to replace that with verbal expressions of listening, in voicing a smile (Hull, 2017) or humming a nod. Invisibility was an affordance to be experimented with and silence was a liminality to be replaced and compensated with audible affirmations.

What came out of this encounter was thus a reconfigured space of sensing, not-sensing, and being sensed in lieu of the conventional seeing, not-seeing, and being seen mode of observations. In not being subject to visual scrutiny we were at once liberated as well as constricted in our conduct. We were left more aware of ourselves and our bodies as sensory openings that had at once the ability to affect and be affected (Spinoza, 1667) by the real material presence of our respondents. In trying to theorise this space of encounter and resonance, we are attempting to contain a certain rush of energy (Durkheim, 1961) that is always already in motion, captured like a snapshot, a spatiotemporally dissonant slice cut off from a flow. This rush, always already present, would be intensified with and within us in moments when we would be asking a question, to be shifted with and within the respondents as they shared with us their gifts of time, patience and information. While they were left acutely aware of the sensory vulnerability of our gaze resting upon them, moving them and nudging them into a corporeal self-consciousness, we were similarly made conscious of the violence of this gaze, alongside our 'other-sensory conduct' and modes of affecting. This multi-sensory co-presence and multimodality brought to life the Deleuzian being that is alive and one through its various ways of being – through bodies reacting differently together. Together we constituted, continued, and complemented one another in ways that precluded language, description, and theory.

What enters into this play of intensities within the affective atmosphere as something felt yet ambiguous (Anderson, 2009) in the ethnographic exchange is the sheer materiality of the space where the exchange would take place. Due to the assumed affordance of invisibility, the room itself, as an extension of its inhabitants, often became an object of scrutiny. We would look past our respondents at the arrangement of things and scrutinise the curatory logics that would inform such an arrangement. Now none of these stealthy gazes are unheard of, yet doing so, in pulling in the object universe into the discourse of a violent unrequited gaze and compelling its participation in the discourse of ethnographic enquiry, seemed unethical. With our visual lifestyle vocabularies that inform reading space, certain objects would cause a stir within us and cause us to focus ourselves away from the conversation, while still maintaining the sonic compensation, towards the new-found focus of intensity[3]. The not seeing by looking away described earlier suitably also includes an avoidance of explicitly looking at the objects arranged in the living spaces of the people to whom we are speaking. We do not go into somebody's house staring at the things that line the walls or are scattered around. In most cases, doing this requires looking past them in their presence or taking a quick stock of things around in their absence. We see things that are shown and only glance at others that catch our attention. Graduating from this stealthy glance to an unabashed gaze that involves reflection, recognition, and resonance (Mazzarella, 2017) therefore brings in this extended materiality into the atmosphere of affecting and being affected. The 'irresistible and magnificent presence' of the objects (Dufrenne, 2005) thus perpetually form and deform the said atmosphere, appearing and disappearing, as bodies enter into relation with one another in their presence.

Picturing *Bharat Mata*: A Nation Mapped, Rapped, and Imagined

Ajit encountered 'India' for the first time around the same time that he started losing his vision. He was five years old. India was at war with Pakistan at the Kargil border and his father was in the army. He remembers his absence during the state of unrest in the house as doctors gave them ultimatums and prescribed immediate intervention to save his sight. They wanted to wait for his father's return, but the wait was indefinite. His blindness intensified against the backdrop of one of the most intensive wars in the recent political history of the nation as television media defined the contours of the nation against its constructed neighbourhood enemy. Beyond this, the abstract category of the nation remains dormant. It is only through an activated border with a neighbouring country that the map comes alive, its inertia destabilised and its presence felt. He notes how most blind students develop a high degree of interest in international relations, where comparisons among different nations, their policies, and politics often animate discussions among their friendship groups. News media as well as theories learnt in classrooms inform these discussions where they often compare India with the rest of the world. Shrey, who was from the lush green[4] countryside of Nepal remembers having felt intimidated by the projected urbanity of New Delhi before he relocated after losing his sight. For Soma, a doctoral researcher in International Relations, borders are made porous by shared experiences of disabilities where she says the state of a blind person 'here' is the same as that of a blind person 'there', suggesting a shared experience of difficulties and affordances, sensibilities and sensations. She talks about the transcendental community that she feels is more real than borders separating them. The idea of 'Indianness' arrived at through a multitude of popular semiotic texts, but multisensory modes of experiencing them by the visually impaired communities, thus hold within them an unexplored potential for resistance against the optic discourse of nationhood.

Having lost his vision at the age of 9, Gaurav remembers having had to learn to recognise the map. This was before the age when one is typically expected to be able to reproduce the map from memory on paper in school. When asked when was the first time he remembers having encountered the idea of India as a nation, he said, 'Yes, I saw it, the map, I learnt that that was *Bhaarat Mata*', he said and both of them once again broke into laughter. This time they broke the joke for us. A student of Sanskrit, Gaurav is often unanimously taken to be right-wing sympathiser, an ideology represented by the *Akhil Bharatiya Vidyarthi Parishad* or ABVP, the student wing of the national right-wing political party. This is due to the natural conflation between the Sanskrit or Hindi languages and the political Right which champions a certain brand of *Hindutva* politics. Ajit who studies Political Sciences on the other hand was automatically welcomed by the consolidated Left. In an era of jingoistic nationalism, the figure of the *Bhaarat Mata* had resurfaced once again as a Hindu mother goddess in need of protection around the time the interview was conducted in 2019. Its invocation with a dash of humour was thus as much a reference to Gaurav's assumed political leaning based on his subject affiliation[5] as it was to the irony of icons.

The political map has become an essential and sometimes necessary tool for visualisation of the modern nation state and it is manifested, in the case of many cultures, as an embodied motherland or fatherland (Gupta, 2001; Confino and Skaria, 2002). In India, the process of visualisation of its political map as '*Bharat Mata*' (Mother India) started in the late nineteenth and early twentieth century as part of the national movement and freedom struggle against the British colonial regime. By the end of colonial rule, the pictures of *Bharat Mata* as a woman holding the Indian tricolour flag with the map in the background, was a deified presence pertaining to the Hindu religious iconography, and had its physical presence in the majoritarian discourse of the subcontinent (Ramaswamy, 2008) through calendar art (Pinney, 2004) and evocative mythologies. Among our respondents, the map and the flag emerge repeatedly as important tools for articulating the imagination of the nation and a sense of belonging to it. The mapping of visual impairment against these cultural forms or artefacts (Cheyne, 2009; Bolt, 2014), speak both of an exclusion within this symbolic discourse, as well as opening up less ocularcentric modalities of access. Sylvia and Ritu, who have congenital blindness, talk about such mythologies and the events of Independence day, Republic day, and Gandhi Jayanti (Mahatma Gandhi's birthday) as recurrent milestones in their journey of memorising their nationality. Highly dramatised and full of ritual performances, Ritu remembers her mother narrating to her the flag hoisting, 'march pasts' and other events as a part of the celebrations, that she relates to us in turn. Sylvia remembers her mother carving out the shapes of the flag and the map on malleable dirt or soil on the ground and she tracing her fingers along the lines to learn to identify India through touch. This tactile memory was later formalised with the help of tactile boards in her school, where she also learnt to remember the colours of the flag on a colour wheel.

A nation is never an inherent category, but a social reality in which one imagines oneself to be a part of it through a mediated subscription to a group of people, a piece of land and an idea of nationality (Anderson, 1983). Media such as print and electronic news, and popular culture such as movies, theatre and songs mediate the construction of this translocal and transcultural community. The flag and the map are thus remembered categories for both our respondents who are congenitally blind and who had acquired visual impairments; but for one, the memories of the sense (Seremetakis, ed., 1996) of nationalism bear a strong gendered connotation. Among these, symbolic objects such as the map and the flag bear a robust masculinity whether in its assertion or in the figure of Mother India needing protection. Their narration and recollection on the other hand, passed down by the mother's stories or narrated mythologies find a feminine preservation. It is these lived experiences that activate the liminality between the actual and virtual of these symbols and media representations. In modern processes of socialisation of an individual, the sense of belonging to a nation is generally developed in the secondary socialisation process of schooling or education attainment in India. The national flag, the map of the country, and national anthem embedded within the curriculum therefore allow the nation to be routinely learnt and memorised by the young minds of a community.

The hierarchical caste system of the subcontinent strongly informs and impacts one's sense of Indianness. This system of ascribed identity is not only an essential element for understanding the extent of socioeconomic privilege certain social groups have over others below in the caste hierarchy (Jodhka, 2017), it also regulates various life events such as marriage in an individual's life. Inter-caste marriages are a taboo and even within communities, marriages are constrained with certain rules and regulations for deciding one's life partner (Béteille, 2012). But in case of disability, caste identity is only seen to be operational against the backdrop of the disability. Disability becomes the primary marker of one's identity which carves out its own segregated social space. Soma describes her understanding of marriages among her friends and acquaintances who are visually impaired, as different from caste regulations and a bit complex. Inter-caste and inter-faith 'love marriages' are frequently approved by families and kin when both partners share an impairment. But within the social space of disability, the gender and extent of impairment plays a crucial role in formation of hierarchies in the dynamics of marriages. The desirability of a visually impaired man marrying a sighted woman, she notes, is higher than a visually impaired woman marrying a sighted man. In case of the extent of impairment, a partial impairment is deemed more desirable over complete impairment. 'It is like a caste system where a partial vision becomes the upper caste and complete blindness the lower caste', she said with a cheeky smile. Ajit echoes a similar idea when he says, 'among us, disability becomes the caste and blindness is the sub-caste'.

Chunnu dismissed caste as an overbearing presence in his life. With all our sociological knowledge, we quickly attributed that to his own dominant caste position and privilege that turns one 'caste blind'. The dominant caste in India is a complicated caste category that often does not conflate with the scriptural four-fold caste order. Instead these are regionally defined hierarchies based on occupations, land ownership, power structures, and economic capabilities of the caste groups (Jodhka, 2017). But central to each model of caste irrespective of its internal specificities is the ideas of purity and pollution that guide the actions of caste groups and make it a felt part of their everyday realities (Srinivas, 1978). Such ideas of purity and pollution amount to what Douglas (2003) would call 'matter out of place', where dirt amounts to the prefigured undesirability of substances based on religious and cultural proscriptions. What Chunnu guided us into however was a discussion about dirt as a very felt, material and tangible presence of undesirability that was closely related to his impairment. Dirt for him was a materiality encountered and contacted through proximity. He spoke about how important it was for him above everything else to ensure that the space around him was decluttered and in order, so he did not run into something unexpectedly. Surroundings for him were thus always mapped in the anticipated possibility of phantom objects, their effect and affect on his being at that moment. It is all fair and square when it is about a stray towel or a coffee mug left in disarray, but an example he cited was of walking into shit. What we understood through the rest of his narration was that faeces was often a placeholder for an entire polluting universe that he had to avoid, but straight into which his lack of sight would often lead him. He lamented how a sighted person '*dekh ke samajh jaate hai*' (can see and understand/gauge) the presence of dirt, and avoid it from a distance, whereas he is naturally disposed after his loss of vision at the age of six to try to pre-empt dirt and maintain the sanctity of one's pure self, one's caste self. Hull (2017) notes how the white cane is a mode of sensing the world and not a substitute of vision as an anticipatory sense but a new sensory orientation altogether that is felt corporeally by the bearer. The cane, Chunnu laments, must thus encounter dirt on his behalf, as an extension of his body self that can be disembodied from time to time.

Gaurav, Shrey and Ritu are all musicians. While Shrey plays the flute, Ritu is a vocalist and Gaurav is a rap artist with his own YouTube channel, and plays the piano and mouth organ. He releases his rap songs under the name of Gahari Singh[6]. 'For us, language is everything', says Gaurav, and Biju and I nod in unison, having had one of our presuppositions confirmed. In the absence of visuals, words help him interact better with the world. Sylvia cannot relate with this, saying it is only possibly a trait among those with acquired blindness. She appears uncomfortable with our question about language learning and we immediately check our optic bias. Gaurav describes his songwriting as a means to explore his understanding of new words, and thus the language itself. When asked about his idea of 'Indianness', he performed a rather evocative rap which he proudly proclaimed was his version of the national anthem. In his song, Gaurav mentions the names of all the states in India, and how none of those define him. He identifies with the land of hearts that is India, that is *Hindustan*, as a composite, and not a sum of its many parts. With sharp beats and a scintillating rhythm, we were taken on a journey with this rap. Therefore we wanted to represent his song here as it is, without ableist analysis seeping into the authenticity of his words, his Indianness:

> My name is Gahari, I say deep things,
> All the people in the village listen to me, so do the city folks
> All are my friends, No enemy
> Heartbeats come to a halt to listen to me

My music sings loudly, now is the time for Gahari Singh to shine
Days are yours, so are the nights
So let me talk things about my nation
Neither do I belong to Haryana, nor Madras, or Punjab, nor Gujarat
Not UP, not MP, not Uttarakhand, not Bihar Chhattisgarh or to Jharkhand
Not Kerala, Odisha, also not Himachal, not Sikkim, Manipur or Arunachal
Come.. let's move on together . . .
Don't think, just listen from where I belong
I live in hearts, I am from land of hearts
I am not from Goa, Karnataka or Assam, and not from Telangana
    or Mizoram
Not Jammu and Kashmir, nor Kohima, and no one says I am from
    Andhra Pradesh
Not with Meghalaya or West Bengal, don't relate me with Tripura either
Neither am I from Dilli, nor Rajasthan . . . I belong to my dear . . .
My dear, I belong to Hindustan . . . Yes, to Hindustan!!!

Concluding Discussion: The Spectre of Incompletion and Writing Multiporous Futures

What we have in place of a formal conclusion is a spectre of necessary incompleteness, a lack of finitude. The India that we trace in the above section is effectively a composite of many lives lived in conjunction where many experiences, symbolisms and affects are internalised through shared tales among peers while living together on campus. The India formed as a result is an amalgam of this 'throwntogetherness' (Massey, 2005), it shifts in form as we move from one individual to another and assumes new essence each time. We recognise the centrality of the symbols like the flag and map, but as felt presences in the real-life worlds of visually impaired persons. Be it in a father's absence or a flag etched on dirt, a caste reconfigured or a rap battle in a college fest, the many Indias that we find are scattered across a set of life events, observances and performances. It resists homogenising and opens up less explored ways of sensing its presence. It tests assumptions and makes us porous to new insights. Therefore we gladly submit to the failure of our research– to find a monolith specific to the sightless ontology that can inform an understanding of Indianness. Instead we infuse the conventional notions, signs, and symbols of the nation with much more holistic, multisensory, and engendered articulations to further complicate and diversify the very sense of nationhood in the subcontinent. Our contribution is therefore a return back to our first cultural station of blindness– a gradual dispelling of assumptions, orientations, and dispositions to appreciate making, unmaking, and 'becoming' together in diversity. Together, the two cultural stations – one of which continues to be available to us in audio recordings, as data shared with a lot of trust and patience, and the other retained through a set of impermanent scribbles in a notebook and more permanent unlearnings in our orientation – inform one another.

Notes

1   In this text, we use blindness interchangeably with the term visual impairment or its acronym VI as and how they had appeared in conversation with our respondents. For all purposes of representation and bureaucracy, the progressive term 'visually impaired' is preferred over others such as disabled or blind. Refer to Bolt (2005) for a detailed discussion on the evolution of terminologies in the disability context.

2   Most of my respondents lived in such dyads of cohabitation where students with complimentary conditions would most often be allotted rooms together. These hostels also housed persons without physical disabilities and these close living spaces with shared toilets, bathrooms, and dining halls or the dining hall were aimed to facilitate a social, corporeal, and sensory sensitivity to develop and shape attitudes around them. Despite this, Sylvia felt that the campus lacked an inherent inability to empathise, where heightened sensitivities came in the way of forming pure unadulterated friendships and alienated those with disabilities. 'They would help you, escort you, but not befriend you', she says. Healey and Michalko (2021) note how 'help' is an intrinsic part of the metanarrative of blindness.

3   The presence of a bedbug had caused a similar stir in our dispositions. I was visibly disturbed, my face giving away what I struggled to conceal in my voice. The joint interflow of the environment that was composite of ourselves, the assortment of objects and non-human actors thus coalesced into a collective affect that made us feel, do, and 'become' in the process (Deleuze and Guattari, 1987).

4   While speaking of his earliest memories of Nepal, where he was born and brought up sighted, he strongly recollects the colour green to be the predominant characteristic of the village he lived in – a colour that he naturally associates with an idea of the homeland left behind.

5   Karah (2021) in talking about the metanarratives of blindness in India calls out the disciplinary gatekeeping and positivist assumption prevalent in the social sciences that makes the pursuit of subjects such as sociology prohibitive for the visually impaired. Our situatedness within the same discipline and its predecessor, anthropology, compels us to be further reflexive of the disciplinary barriers that distance us from our respondents.

6   'Gahari' or *gehri* means deep in Hindi. As a name, it is intended to reflect the quality of a person whose spoken words have a deep meaning.

References

Anderson, B. (1983) *Imagined Communities*, London: Verso Books.

Anderson, B. (2009) Affective atmospheres. *Emotion, Space and Society* 2 (2): 77–81.

Béteille, A. (2012) The peculiar tenacity of caste. *Economic and Political Weekly* 47 (13): 41–48.

Bolt, D. (2014) *The Metanarrative of Blindness: A Re-Reading of Twentieth-Century Anglophone Writing*, Ann Arbour: University of Michigan Press.

Cheyne, R. (2009) Theorising culture and disability: Interdisciplinary dialogues. *Journal of Literary & Cultural Disability Studies* 1 (1): 101–104.

Confino, A. and Skaria, A. (2002) The local life of nationhood. *National Identities* 4 (1): 7–24.

Deleuze, G. and Guattari, F. (1987 [1980]) *A Thousand Plateaus: Capitalism and Schizophrenia*, trans. B. Massumi, London: Continuum.

Douglas, M. (2003) *Purity and Danger: An Analysis of Concepts of Pollution and Taboo*, London: Routledge.

Dufrenne, M. (2005) The phenomenology of aesthetic experience, in E. Casey and D. Howes (eds.) *Empire of the Senses: The Sensual Culture Reader*, Oxford: Berg.

Durkheim, E. (1961 [1912]) *The Elementary Forms of the Religious Life*, New York: Collier Books.

Emerson, R. M., Fretz, R. I. and Shaw, L. L. (2011) *Writing Ethnographic Fieldnotes*, Chicago: University of Chicago press.

Goffman, E. (1955) On face-work: An analysis of ritual elements in social interaction. *Psychiatry* 18 (3): 213–231.

Gupta, C. (2001) The icon of the mother: 'Bharat Mata', 'Matri Bhasha' and 'Gau Mata', in C. Gupta (ed.) *Sexuality, Obscenity, Community*, New York: Palgrave Macmillan.

Healey, D. and Michalko, R. (2021) Meaning, feeling, and feel, in D. Bolt (ed.) *Metanarratives of Disability: Culture, Assumed Authority, and the Normative Social Order*, New York: Routledge.

Hull, J. M. (2017) *Notes on Blindness: A Journey Through the Dark*, London: Profile Books.

Jodhka, S. S. (2017) *Caste in Contemporary India*, Abingdon: Routledge.

Karah, H. (2021) The metanarrative of blindness in India: Special education and assumed knowledge cultures, in *Metanarratives of Disability: Culture, Assumed Authority and the Normative Social Order*, London: Routledge.

Massey, D. B. (2005) *For Space*, London: Sage.

Mazzarella, W. (2017) *The Mana of Mass Society*, Chicago: The University of Chicago Press.

Pink, S. (2009) *Doing Sensory Ethnography*, London: Sage.

Pinney, C. (2004) *'Photos of the gods': The printed image and political struggle in India*, London: Reaktion Books.

Ramaswamy, S. (2008) Maps, mother/goddesses, and martyrdom in modern India. *The Journal of Asian Studies* 67 (3): 819–853.

Seremetakis, C. N. (Ed.). (1996) *The Senses Still*, Chicago: University of Chicago Press.

Spinoza, B. (1667) *Ethics Part III: On the Origin and Nature of the Emotions*, Indianapolis: Hackett Publishing Company.

Srinivas, M. N. (1978) *The Remembered Village*, New Delhi: Oxford University Press.

5

BLIND STUDENT AS A BYPASSED READER

Analyzing Blindness in Required Reading for Schools in Poland

Monika Dubiel

Preliminary Discussion: Unnoticed Stations

The world of disability studies, as Eyre (2014) points out, is impaired by a tendency toward explicating predominantly Anglophone cultures; for the field to develop further, its scope should embrace European cultural areas which have thus far been omitted. Since Poland is undoubtedly one such area, I was eager to contribute a proposal when I found out about this edited volume. I felt that my perspective could be a necessary and important addition to a certain process. I started to meditate on what my cultural stations of blindness were exactly, and when I reached them. I had to ask myself when I had started identifying myself as a blind person, when I had got to know other blind people's perspectives, as well as when and how I had started to reflect on representations of blindness in culture. I was very surprised to discover that although I had been experiencing serious problems with my eyesight from the age of four and had functioned as a blind person practically from the age of 12, my real connection with blindness and blind identity started in my late twenties. I interrogated myself accordingly: how was it possible that I had navigated the first quarter of my life without a single cultural station of blindness along the way? It seemed unbelievable. Around that time, a friend of mine contacted me and asked me to participate in a panel discussion about the absence of disability in Polish school textbooks. That stimulated the process of thinking back again, more profoundly, about my school days. And I discovered that blindness had not, in fact, been absent in the curriculum. It had been mentioned in various required reading texts, but I had merely disavowed them from my own story. I realized that that while passing through several cultural stations of blindness during my early childhood and adolescence, I had not recognized them as such. Moreover, it occurred to me that the nature of these cultural stations and the way they were introduced to my life made me completely disconnect myself from them and made me want to

DOI: 10.4324/9781003275060-7

isolate myself from the topic of blindness for a long time. Inspired by David Bolt's point about cultural representations of blindness – namely that while they seem to be about blindness, they focus on sight instead (Bolt, 2014b) – I understood that the required readings at school featuring blindness are actually directed at sighted children. Nevertheless, they have an impact on blind children. How is this so? This is the main question that I address in this chapter.

In the educational system, required readings play multiple roles. On the one hand, they develop students' language skills and aesthetic sensibilities; and on the other, they transmit didactic messages about desirable behaviors and attitudes. They promote commonly appreciated values and very often serve out the first portions of knowledge about unfamiliar phenomena (Gamble and Yates, 2002). They can become yet another boring requirement or a starting point for an exciting adventure with literature. For some students, however, required reading at school can become a cultural station in a journey to forming an identity. That was my experience, concerning two compulsory texts at primary school in Poland. Nevertheless, I did not understand their meaning until years later. In this chapter, I explore the significance that 'Katarynka' ('The Barrel Organ') and *Spotkanie nad morzem* (*A Meeting by the Sea*) had to my journey in search of a personal understanding of blindness, and also what it means to be blind in Poland. In subjecting these two texts to analysis, I also contemplate the role that school readings play in shaping social attitudes toward visual impairment in my country.

In compliance with the general methodological profile of this volume, I use autocritical discourse analysis in my investigation (Bolt, 2021). Since it is a hybrid method, combining autoethnography and critical discourse analysis, the analyzed material is twofold: first, two literary works are mentioned; and second, my memories and personal reflections from childhood and adulthood are presented. I compare and confront two sets of impressions: those first made about 20 years ago when I was at school; and those made most recently, triggered by the writing of this chapter. I am aware of the risk of this operation. Having in mind that memory is fallible and that my current knowledge from the field of disability studies may significantly impact my perception while reading, I have been particularly cautious while coursing between these two cultural stations.

Although the situation has recently begun to change, children's literature used to lack empowered, happy or at least positive disabled protagonists. When they appeared, they were rarely figures with whom one would like to identify. Their depiction was far from being an attractive role model (Gervay, 2004; Saunders, 2004; Adomat, 2014). Since the default recipient of the school readings is a non-disabled child, texts are selected in compliance with what such students need, or (more accurately perhaps) with what a teacher thinks such students need. Consequently, the image of disability plays a subservient role in the narrative, in relation to the main educational goal of the reading, for example, in promoting attitudes such as courage, generosity, or helping the weaker. Herein, I address a question which has apparently been overlooked in this scheme: what message about their own disability do disabled children receive from the required reading text? I argue that in both analyzed works, where disability representation is strongly formed by the charity model and the medical model, the message is that disability is negatively valued and strongly undesired social disturbance, whose only *raison d'être* is to support self-development of the non-disabled. The former paradigm interprets disability in ethical terms; that is, the existence of people with disabilities enables, encourages, and even obliges the non-disabled to do good deeds (Zames Fleischer and Zames, 2011). The latter paradigm sees disability as a deficit that should be remedied. In both cases, disability is a misfortune that requires precise actions. The active ones, however, are always the non-disabled, while people with disabilities are the passive recipients of help. It leads to the discriminatory practice of ableism that David Bolt (2019, 4) defines as the 'process by which non-disabled people are systematically rendered supreme'.

When presenting the two cultural stations, I maintain the chronological order understood as the order in which I reached them in my life, not in the order of publication. I reflect first on *Spotkanie nad morzem*, the novel that I read in the fourth grade, and then *Katarynka*, which I analyzed at school one year later.

A Meeting by the Sea: Who Is That Strange Girl?

Spotkanie nad morzem (*A Meeting by the Sea*) by Jadwiga Korczakowska is a 1962 literature classic for Polish children. The novel takes place in a Polish coastal village in the mid-twentieth century. It tells the story of the friendship between two girls: a non-disabled vacationer, Danusia, and the blind local, Elza. The former is a Pole, and a pampered only child of a middle-class family from the city of Toruń. She is spending the holiday with her mother's friend, Doctor Ada. Elza is a poor orphan who lives with her grandparents in the fishing village. They are Kashubians – an ethnic minority living on the coast of the Baltic Sea. Elza is very active and independent, moves around the village on her own, and performs several types of housework. She is also deprived of the typical attributes of the blind, namely the white cane and dark glasses, so Danusia does not realize that her new friend is blind during their first few encounters. While Danusia enjoys the privilege of living at home with a servant, Elza peels potatoes, herds goats, and picks blueberries in the forest. Initially, Elza impresses Danusia with her practical skills and knowledge about nature. However, when the vacationer discovers that her new friend is blind, her attitude starts shifting toward compassionate caring. By the end of the novel, Elza has already been presented as a completely helpless individual. The only task she can perform is to catalyze positive changes in Danusia's character (Fidowicz, 2020a). The story is told from Danusia's point of view; therefore, her perspective dominates, and the worldview represented by her (and her family) automatically becomes privileged. Elza's disability, combined with several other characteristics, all result in her alienation and social marginalization. The only way to improve her situation is by passing into Danusia's world, which takes place in the climax of the story. The girl is adopted by Doctor Ada and goes to Toruń with Danusia, where she is to undergo eye surgery. What was planned to be an optimistic and happy end, is in fact a traumatic experience for Elza. She has to abandon her roots and be subordinated to the dominating forces of able-bodiedness, Polishness, and formal education (Pamuła, 2020). The controlling regime is formed by the charity model and the medical model of disability, embodied by Danusia's mother and Doctor Ada. In compliance with the charity model, the two ladies feel obliged to help the blind girl. In line with the medical model, they arrange medical intervention. As Donoghue (2003) observes, since disability is considered an undesirable condition, persons with disabilities are expected to seek professional assistance to bring relief to their situation. The necessity of Elza's surgery is obvious to those surrounding her, to the extent that no one asks her opinion about it; no one even informs her about the true purpose of her journey to Toruń. As Oliver observes (1983, 1996) medicalization leads to the tragedy theory of disability. This mechanism is evident in the case of Elza, as her blindness is always referred to as a misfortune.

Among all of the differences between the two girls, there is one that I especially like to emphasize because, in my opinion, it strengthens the ableist dimension of the novel to the greatest extent: there is clear antagonism between the aspects of nature and culture, in which the blind character represents the former. The novel clearly promotes the culture-related achievements of the socialist state, such as living in a big city or education at school. In order to achieve that, it discredits nature, natural knowledge, and a natural lifestyle in the fishing village. Elza, as a figure in that inferior world, is deprived of access to books and school (signs of culture which are entirely obvious in Danusia's life), but she feels perfectly comfortable in the bosom of nature, of which Danusia is often afraid. As a representative of nature, the blind girl is strongly animalized. She talks to a bumblebee, a woodpecker, and a snail, calling them 'little brothers'. Nevertheless, what is perhaps given more prominence are her extraordinary senses, which as David Bolt asserts (2007) are often a sign of a blind character's animalization. Elza's haptic, aural, and olfactory sensibilities are stressed several times throughout the novel:

> 'The bumblebee is humming, can you hear?' the girl smiled
> *(Korczakowska, 1962, 57).*

> 'Can you smell the hay?' Elza interrupted. 'It smells strong.'
>   'Where is it?'

> 'In the meadow near the forest they raked such huge stacks! The scent comes all the way here'
> *(Korczakowska, 1962, 58).*

Elza's animal-like senses allow her to adapt to what is going on around her, and also orient herself temporally:

> 'It is almost six o' clock, I guess.'
>   'How do you know that? You don't have a watch.'

'What I need a watch for!' she laughed. 'I can feel it in the air, in the cold coming from the ground'

(Korczakowska, 1962, 60–61).

Even though this meta-narrative of blindness (Bolt, 2014a) is supposed to present Elza's resourcefulness, it instead emphasizes her otherness and widens the gap between the two girls. Additionally, the animalization of Elza is reinforced by the way her face is repeatedly referred to as 'pyszczek', which can be translated as 'little muzzle', or 'little snout'. This word in Polish is an affectionate term used among loved ones, especially in relation to children. It would not be surprising if it were used in reference to both girls; however, it is only used with reference to Elza. It evokes tenderness, but a kind which is tinged with indulgence and a sense of superiority that adults often feel toward children, or which humans feel toward animals, or – as in this case – the non-disabled might feel toward disabled people. This cordial yet paternalistically tinged attitude shown by the representatives of the dominating group toward Elza is also visible in Doctor Ada's remark about her that she 'unexpectedly exhibits much innate intelligence' (Korczakowska, 1962, 109). Although meant as a compliment, it is underpinned by an ableist and classist belief that one cannot expect too much from a poor, blind girl. One cannot even expect that she might be beautiful. Indeed, Elza's physical unattractiveness is stressed several times in the novel. She is a plain girl wearing a faded dress: 'What a pity that she is unattractive', Danusia assesses. 'But when she smiles, she immediately becomes very nice' (Korczakowska, 1962, 55).

The blind protagonist is constructed to convince both Danusia and the reader that physical appearance is less important than a person's inner life. Indeed, Elza's personality is very interesting and rich. She loves fantastic stories and legends. She has a very vivid imagination. The message for the reader is thus: blind and unattractive children can be very nice; it is worth playing with them, and it is not worth judging people by their appearances. However, it is a message for sighted readers. But what about the blind readers? I read this novel for the first time in fifth grade, so I was more or less Elza's age. I remember my initial impression of the situation described in the story and how I completely failed to understand it. Instead, a number of questions popped up in my head. Why doesn't Elza go to school? Why doesn't she read in braille? What is this strange language that her grandparents speak? The typical primary-school analysis of the novel did not give me any answers. It focused on the characteristics of the protagonists, on the beautiful story of their friendship, and the message about helping the weaker. Nobody explained to me why Elza's situation was so strange. When discussing the blind child, nobody concerned themselves with the cognitive dissonance of the blind student. It was the end of the 1990s, meaning that four decades had passed since the encounter between Danusia and Elza. My life and the lives of my classmates were completely different from those of Korczakowska's protagonists. Ten years had already passed since the collapse of the communist regime in Poland. In our houses, instead of memories of the Second World War, there were washing machines and vacuum cleaners, and instead of *The Arabian Nights*, we read a teen magazine called *Bravo*. I attended a private school in a big city. I had a lot of extracurricular activities, and numerous friends. Both girls in the story seemed light years away from me then, but if I had needed to identify with either of them, it would have been Danusia, for sure. Elza seemed particularly strange to me. I did not understand her, and I did not even like her. I sensed that I was supposed to identify with her to some extent, but I could not. Obviously, I did not know about the charity model and the medical model of disability at that time, though I instinctively felt that the way in which the disabled character was being presented in the novel was improper and did not work in my favor. Although I did not identify with Elza, I paradoxically felt that somehow, we belonged to the same tribe. I knew that while reading about her, many of my friends would think about me: 'so this is the way she lives'. That was why I was ashamed that she did not go to school and could not read. I did not want people to think about me through the lens of a poor, uneducated girl who owes everything to her sighted friend and her generous family.

'The Barrel Organ': Just Another Tiny Tim

'Katarynka' ('The Barrel Organ') is a short story by Bolesław Prus from 1880. The main protagonists are Pan Tomasz (Mr Thomas) and a nameless little girl who is his neighbor. Pan Tomasz is a retired, unmarried, and neatly dressed attorney who is strongly committed to high culture. Due to his good taste, Pan Tomasz hates the sound of a barrel organ. The little girl in the story is blind, due to a serious illness before the short story starts. Since that time, listening to sounds from the outdoors has become her only entertainment. After moving into the apartment across from Pan Tomasz, she is very upset because the courtyard is closed and completely silent. One day, an organ grinder arrives. Upon hearing the sounds of a barrel organ, the old attorney gets angry, but when he realizes that his little neighbor is enjoying the music, he finds himself yielding to her charm, and as a further outcome, he decides to support her medical treatment.

As in the previous example, the story is told from the perspective of a sighted protagonist. Although the author gives the appearance of narrative balance by telling the story of the girl after introducing Pan Tomasz, the narrative construction and the portrayals of the characters are greatly imbalanced, as the story of the little neighbor is reduced to that of her illness. While the older gentleman is presented through his profession, private life, hobbies, daily routine, habits, and interests, we do not know anything about the little girl except the fact that one day she had woken up blind. Where is her father? Why have she and her mother moved from the previous flat? Why does her mother's friend live with them? These questions are not addressed, because they are unimportant to the plot of the story. In consequence, the sighted protagonist is presented as a unique and multidimensional person, while the blind child is a stock character, deprived of subjectivity, and who works only as an indispensable element of the narrative (Mitchell and Snyder, 2000). Her subordinate role is additionally underscored by her anonymity. She is always referred to as 'dziewczynka' – 'little girl'. It may recall the paradigm that Georgina Kleege (2018) denominates as the Hypothetical Blind Man – a blank figure that recurs as a stock character in the Western philosophical reflection upon whom the assumptions of the sighted author are projected.

Despite these flaws, which are rather typical of formulaic, nineteenth-century depictions of disability, 'Katarynka' could be a required reading text to introduce sighted children to the subject of non-ocularcentric perception and to permit visually impaired children to share their own experiences. The blind girl's haptic and aural sensibility is stressed, but not exaggerated in stereotypical ways as in the former case:

> 'The red cherry has become smooth, round and soft cherry for her. The shiny coin has been a hard, clinking puck' (Prus, 1994, 201). The author maintains a high degree of realism when describing the sensorial functioning and epistemic dilemmas of the blind girl
>
> *(Wietecha, 2015)*

Perhaps it is related to the fact that the author himself was a visually impaired person. Throughout his life, he used very strong glasses (often utilizing two pairs of them at once), and by the end of his life, he was almost completely blind. At the same time, he had agoraphobia and acrophobia and often closed his eyes, for example during train journeys (Grabowska-Kuniczuk, 2014). Due to those circumstances, his non-ocularcentric perception was sensitized, and his description of the blind girl's functions is realistic. 'Katarynka' could be a good means for a teacher to discuss the theme of the lives of blind people in Poland earlier and now. It could be an opportunity to do exercises with blindfolding sighted children and teaching them the principles of guiding a blind person. Blind children could show their peers the braille alphabet and white canes and explain that now, a day in a blind child's life is not as sad as presented in that short story. In other words, As Mitchell et al. (2014, 295) put it 'to set the stage for disabled students to recognize their experiences as something to be cultivated as a form of alternative expertise rather than as useful only to the degree that disability can be disguised and hidden away'. Unfortunately, nothing of this sort happened when I was at school.

After reading *Katarynka*, my classmates and I were given an assignment to write a continuation of the story told by Prus. I was very happy, because I felt that it was a moment of glory for me when I would be able to shine with my unique knowledge. I wrote an epistolary story composed of various letters written by the girl from the school for the blind, in which she explained her education and newly gained skills of reading in braille and typing out on the typewriter, exactly as I used to do my homework. However, my work did not capture my teacher's interest at all; it was assessed as neither interesting nor impressive. At that time, our homework was evaluated more for rich vocabulary, an innovative plot, and correct structures than substantive value. Of course, I cannot remember what exact phrases I used to write my composition. Probably the linguistic quality of the text was not very high, and the teacher assessed it in compliance with official guidelines. However, I still remember the feeling that I had after receiving the teacher's comments. I understood that the real experience of disability is not perceived as a theme worth writing about, and the message was thus very simple: disability is nothing to be proud of, so there is no need to boast about one's knowledge about it. In other words, it is better to hide your disability as much as possible than expose it.

Last year, a post scriptum was added to this story. One day, a friend called me and said that her son was reading 'Katarynka' in class and had gotten an assignment to prepare an audio description of the school, as if the protagonist of the short story was about to become his new classmate. My friend asked me to talk with him and explain what information would be useful, and how it should be formulated. I was very happy to help her son, as that is exactly what I would like 'Katarynka' to be used for at school. A few days later, I called my friend back to ask about the assessment of the homework. She told me that the teacher had rated it very highly; however, in the end, he had added that 'fortunately', they would never need that description in real life, because a girl like that would never come to their school. In that moment, my initial enthusiasm for the creative and progressive approach by the teacher collapsed. 'Fortunately'? After 20 years, it appears that nothing has changed in Polish schooling as far as the approach to talking about disability. We have inclusive education with teaching assistants in many schools, but to the majority of the teachers, it is still 'fortunate' not to have a disabled child in the classroom. School readings impact students – not only through their literal content but also through the interpretations and contextualization given in classrooms. That is why discussion about the disability depicted in the readings is so important (Adomat, 2014). Polish language teachers are responsible for training students in critical thinking about the stereotypes present in the analyzed works. Therefore, their role as intermediators between the children and the reading, in order to understand the phenomenon of disability properly, is so important (Fidowicz, 2020b). Unfortunately, as my experiences and those of my friend's son have shown, Polish language teachers tend to strengthen the stereotypical interpretations of disability instead of questioning them. Consequently, the real educational potential of the short story by Prus has been wasted. It is still being used to reproduce discriminatory and stigmatizing social relationships.

Today, when reading 'Katarynka' through the lens of disability studies, I find considerable similarities to Charles Dickens' *A Christmas Carol*. Although Pan Tomasz is undoubtedly much nicer than Ebenezer Scrooge, the little girl and Tiny Tim seem to be very similar figures. In both cases, the disabled children are plot devices for encouraging old, lonely gentlemen to take up charitable activities: 'Poor child' Pan Tomasz whispered repeatedly looking at the sad little thing. 'If I could do something for her?' He though seeing that the child is getting more and more miserable. (Prus, 1994, 205). The barrel organ in the story by Prus performs a very similar role to the that of the crutches in *A Christmas Carol*; the instrument catalyzes a change in the adult protagonist, due to the impact of the child protagonist's disability. This narrative construction is a literary version of the poster-child strategy, in which the children depicted are innocent victims that with their bravery and charm inspire and motivate the non-disabled to support charity campaigns. In order to receive generous donations, such campaigns specialize in evoking pity. Although one could say that these initiatives are beneficial to disabled people, they do more harm than good, because in the long run, the social dimension turns out to be more important than the financial dimension. As Shapiro (1993) observes, pity oppresses and reinforces the image of people with disability as helpless beneficiaries of charity. According to Hughes (2012) pity, besides fear and disgust, is the major building block of the emotional infrastructure of ableism. Following this reflection, I argue that pity is a tool of authority which a dominating group uses to control the dominated. The promotion of a perspective on disability founded on pity in required reading in schools only contributes to strengthening an unequal social system.

Concluding Discussion: Disability and Relations of Power

Thinking back on how it felt to read these texts at school, I can hardly remember my feelings at the time. However, the message that blindness is a tragic and strongly undesired condition impacted on me so much that I disconnected from the topic for a long time. The image of a blind child as a kind of cute animal that their non-disabled peers can take care of seemed ridiculous to me, because I was anything but a cute creature at the time. For many years, I obsessively tried to prove to myself and my surroundings that I am neither a helpless victim nor a cute animal. Nowadays, trying to find out the reasons behind my reactions in the past, I have concluded that there are three levels: the first of these is the way in which disability was presented in required reading; the second concerns the interpretations in the classroom; the last but not least was found in the spontaneous reactions of classmates.

At all of these levels, the non-disabled perspective is privileged. In the above-examined works, while the non-disabled protagonists are presented in detail along with their interests and characteristics, the blind are essentially reduced to their disabilities. In both stories, disability is a narrative device rather than a real human experience, and as such, is subordinated to the main didactic purpose of the text. Disability is presented according to the narrative prosthesis model (Mitchell and Snyder, 2000) as a social deviance that should be eliminated. This impression is stressed by a strong linkage between disability and lower material and social status. In both analyzed works, the narrative scheme is very similar: a blind, poor, orphaned, or half-orphaned girl is confronted with a sighted adult from the upper social class, who when moved by her misfortune, decides to offer material help and medical treatment. This fictional construction contributes to justification and consolidation of already-existing relations of power. Although the classics in the literature for children and young adults seem to be innocent tales of friendship, love, and character development, they instead confirm the colonial order in which the weaker members of society, such as children, disabled people, ethnic minorities, or non-humans are subordinated to those stronger than them. As a consequence, power plays a crucial role between the disabled and non-disabled protagonists (Yenika-Agbaw, 2011; Pamuła, 2020). Hodkinson (2016, 61) makes a very important point about the way disability is presented and represented in school textbooks. In his opinion, 'authors may be observed as a repressive force who avoid as well as occlude the heterogeneity of society, recasting the strong and positive image of disability within an institutional homogeneity of normalisation and ableism'. I agree with him, though I argue that this observation can be extended to all school readings, including selected literary classics. As Said (1994) observes, literature reveals the relation between culture and authority, because the ability to promote some narrations and hide others is a manifestation of power. Narration is a way of forming and confirming both a dominating and a dominated identity. That is how examined in this chapter school readings become the site for formulating and sustaining a disabling social structure. The instrumental use of blindness in discussed cases reinforces ableist stereotypes and relations of power, instead of empowering disabled students and opening non-disabled students to human diversity.

References

Adomat D. S. (2014) Exploring issues of disability in children's literature discussions. *Disability Studies Quarterly* 34 (3).

Bolt, D. (2007) Saramago's blindness: Humans or animals? *The Explicator* 66 (1): 44–47.

Bolt, D. (2014a) *The Metanarrative of Blindness. A Re-Reading of Twentieth-Century Anglophone Writing*, Ann Arbor: University of Michigan Press.

Bolt, D. (2014b) The supremacy of sight: Aesthetics, representations, and attitudes, in D. Bolt (ed.) *Changing Social Attitudes Toward Disability: Perspectives from Historical, Cultural, and Educational Studies*, Abingdon and New York: Routledge.

Bolt, D. (2019) *Cultural Disability Studies in Education: Interdisciplinary Navigations of the Normative Divide*, Abingdon and New York: Routledge.

Bolt, D. (2021) The metanarrative of arthritis: Playing and betraying the endgame, in D. Bolt (ed.) *Metanarratives of Disability: Culture, Assumed Authority, and the Normative Social Order*, Abingdon and New York: Routledge.

Donoghue, C. (2003) Challenging the authority of the medical definition of disability. *Disability and Society* 18: 199–208.

Eyre, P. (2014) Impaired or empowered? Mapping disability onto European literature, in D. Bolt (ed.) *Changing Social Attitudes Toward Disability: Perspectives From Historical, Cultural, and Educational Studies*, Abingdon and New York: Routledge.

Fidowicz, A. (2020a) *Niepełnosprawność w polskiej literaturze XX i XXI wieku dla dzieci i młodzieży*, Kraków: Wydawnictwo Uniwersytetu Jagiellońskiego.

Fidowicz, A. (2020b) Recepcja tematu niepełnosprawności w literaturze dziecięcej wśród uczniów polskich szkół podstawowych. *Przegląd Pedagogiczny* 2: 271–281.

Gamble, N. and Yates, S. (2002) *Exploring Children's Literature. Teaching the Language and Reading of Fiction*, London: Paul Chapman Publishing.

Gervay, S. (2004) Butterflies: Youth literature as a powerful tool in understanding disability. *Disability Studies Quarterly* 24 (1).

Grabowska-Kuniczuk, A. (2014) "Sąd oka"? O sposobach postrzegania świata w twórczości Bolesława Prusa. *Napis* 20: 140–153.

Hodkinson, A. (2016) School textbooks and the avoidance of disability: Emptied of representation, in D. Bolt and C. Penketh (eds.) *Disability, Avoidance and the Academy: Challenging Resistance*, Abingdon and London: Routledge.

Hughes, B. (2012) Fear, pity and disgust: Emotions and the non-disabled imaginary, in N. Watson, A. Roulstone, and C. Thomas (eds.) *Routledge Handbook of Disability Studies*, Abingdon and New York: Routledge.

Kleege, G. (2018) *More Than Meets the Eye: What Blindness Brings to Art*, Oxford: Oxford University Press.

Korczakowska, J. (1962) *Spotkanie nad morzem*, Warszawa: Nasza Księgarnia.

Mitchell, D. T. and Snyder, S. L. (2000) *Narrative Prosthesis. Disability and the Dependencies of Discourse*, Ann Arbor: University of Michigan Press.

Mitchell, D. T., Snyder, S. L. and Ware, L. (2014) "Every child left behind" curricular cripistemologies and the crip/queer art of failure. *Journal of Literary & Cultural Disability Studies* 8 (3): 295–313.

Oliver, M. (1983) *Work With Disabled People*, Basingstoke: Macmillan.

Oliver, M. (1996) *Understanding Disability: From Theory to Practice*, Basingstoke: Macmillan.

Pamuła, N. (2020) Violent inclusion: Disability and the nation in Polish 1950s and 1960s young adult literature. *East European Politics and Societies and Cultures* 20 (10): 1–21.

Prus, B. (1994) Katarynka, in B. Prus (ed.) *Nowele wybrane*, Warszawa: Państwowy Instytut Wydawniczy.

Said, E. W. (1994) *Culture and Imperialism*, New York: Vintage Books.

Saunders, K. (2004) What disability studies can do for children's literature. *Disability Studies Quarterly* 24 (1).

Shapiro, J. P. (1993) *No Pity: People With Disabilities Forging a New Civil Rights Movement*, New York: Times Books.

Wietecha, A. (2015) *Sięgnąć poza wzrok. Doświadczenia percepcyjne w krótkich formach prozatorskich Bolesława Prusa*, Teksty i konteksty, Warszawa: Wydział Polonistyki Uniwersytetu Warszawskiego.

Yenika-Agbaw, V. (2011) Reading disability in children's literature. Hans Christian Andersen's Tales. *Journal of Literary & Cultural Disability Studies* 5 (1): 91–108.

Zames Fleischer, D. and Zames, F. (2011) *The Disability Rights Movement: From Charity to Confrontation*, Philadelphia: Temple University Press.

PART II

The Blind Reading the Blind

Politics and Religion

6

FROM WORLD WAR TO SOCIAL INTEGRATION AND BEYOND

Experiences of Blindness in Twentieth-Century Italy

Ugo Pavan Dalla Torre

Preliminary Discussion: War Blindness and Integration as Cultural Stations

The recent anniversary of the First World War offered the opportunity to re-examine the Italian war experience (Gibelli, 2016; Gentile, 2016); to insert it in an international framework. Above all it is important to reflect on aspects seldom covered by Italian historiography, such as the history of war medicine, the study of the medical and social assistance given to wounded soldiers, the role of the state in the provision of assistance to the soldiers (Quagliaroli, 2018), and the theme of war disability and the associative organisation of the mutilated and disabled veterans (Labanca, 2016; Pavan Dalla Torre, 2016). In numerous recently published studies, it has been reaffirmed that, among these disabilities, blindness has taken on a particular relevance in the context of war, for symbolic issues as well as physiological reasons. Starting from the study of the experience of the veterans of the Great War, this chapter considers how – thanks to that tragic experience – the concept of blindness and the identity of blind people in Italy have changed. As historiography – both Italian and international – has demonstrated, world wars constituted a significant moment for the construction of a new identity of disability, and this also applies to the figure of the '*ciechi di guerra*' (war blinded), who after the Great War emancipated themselves from their status as objects of public charity and became active subjects in Italian society. But once the wars were over, what was the fate of blind people in Italy? How have wars formed the basis of further reflection on the theme of blindness? Has there been an evolution in society's perception of blindness and in the self-perception of the blind?

The analysis conducted in this chapter focuses on two aspects. The first aspect to be addressed is the history of disabled ex-servicemen and, in particular, the war-blinded during and after the Great war, precisely because this event made a

DOI: 10.4324/9781003275060-9

decisive contribution to the redefinition of the identity of blind people, but also to the modalities of their self-representation. Starting from the fundamental experience of the First World War, the emancipation of the 'handicapped', and therefore also of blind people, continued after the conclusion of the Second World War, and this is the second aspect explored in this chapter. The Constitution of the Italian Republic emphasised the equality of citizens' rights, the institutions implemented the constitutional provision, the legislation was updated accordingly, and the practices began to move towards greater integration if not inclusiveness. This is particularly evident in the educational reforms that have taken place over the years in Italy. If world war can be considered a first cultural station for changing understandings of blindness, integration if not inclusion in education and employment constitutes the second.

World War: The Creation of a New Identity

One of the most important legacies of the Great War was certainly the birth of a new social group: the veterans. Every war has had its veterans, but the industrial dimension of the First World War and the introduction of enrolment based on compulsory conscription, rather than being voluntary, considerably increased the number of soldiers recalled to the front line, transforming this phenomenon – until that moment numerically contained – into a mass phenomenon, in all countries involved in the conflict (Gerber, 2012; Prost, 1977; Perry, 2014). The massive use of new automatic weapons, as well as the improvement and the enhancement of traditional weapons, caused an exponential increase in the wounded and an aggravation of injuries: many soldiers suffered the amputation of parts of the body, in particular legs and arms, the most exposed limbs to gunshots. The precarious hygienic conditions of the trenches and dressing places also led to the onset of pathologies related to septicemia: many soldiers in the weeks and months following their wounding had to undergo further amputations due to the onset of gangrene, which in many cases proved fatal.

The eyes were a particularly exposed organ susceptible to serious injuries, due to the violence of the explosions; to the type of ordnance, which scattered dangerous metal splinters within a radius of tens of meters; to the high temperature caused by the explosions, but above all due to the lack of adequate protection. The damage to sight, unlike that to other parts of the body for which there were numerous types of prostheses, was in fact almost irremediable. Precisely because of this irreversibility, the war-blinded, especially those who suffered bilateral loss of sight, became emblematic of mutilation and symbolic of the sacrifice of Italian soldiers (Salvante, 2015, 2016).

After being hospitalised in military hospitals, the permanently disabled soldiers were discharged and sent on leave, ending their service in the army. In Italy, however, there was no organisation capable of guaranteeing the continuity of medical care and orthopaedic assistance to these soldiers. In the cities and small villages, some citizens established several 'Comitati di Assistenza' (Assistance Committees) which, through donations received from private citizens and thanks to public contributions, organised re-education houses. In these environments, the disabled soldiers learned a new job or were instructed to work using orthopaedic prostheses. Soldiers who became blind were taught, among others, the jobs of radio operator and chair straw maker. In 1916, the Committees met in a Federation which aimed to coordinate the actions carried out at the local level and to interact with the Government (Pavan Dalla Torre, 2018a).

The idea that work constituted the privileged path to the emancipation of war invalids had its roots in the pedagogical axioms of the nineteenth century, which had been applied in many European states to blind people (Wanech, 1969; Canevaro and Gandreau, 1988). However, as Fabio Levi notes, during the nineteenth century, the construction of institutions for the blind, like many institutions created to protect other categories of so-called invalids, had in fact caused the confinement of these people in a culturally and socially restricted area. This situation was in fact perpetuated through the recruitment of blind teachers, coming from the same institutes: the blind teachers perpetuated the teaching received within the institutions, contributing to further narrow the horizons of blind people (Levi, 2017).

During the Great war some situations began to change. After almost a year of work, the Italian Parliament, recognising the need to institutionalise medical and social assistance to disabled soldiers, on 25 March 1917 promulgated the law 481 which established the Italian National Opera for the protection and assistance of invalids of war (in Italian: Opera Nazionale per la protezione e l'assistenza degli invalidi di guerra – ONIG).[1] For the first time, the Italian state took on the responsibility of assisting permanently disabled soldiers not only by guaranteeing them war pensions (Pironti, 2015; Pavan Dalla Torre, 2018b), but also by activating an institution with its own budget that was supposed to provide both medical and social assistance (Balestrazzi, 1967). But the most important novelty was the birth of associations between veterans: on 29 April 1917 the Italian National Association of Mutilated and War Invalids (in Italian: Associazione Nazionale fra Mutilati ed Invalidi di Guerra, ANMIG) was founded in Milan (Zavatti, 2009; Pavan Dalla Torre, 2012) and in November 1918, thanks to the initiative of the Central Committee of the ANMIG, the Italian National Association of Veterans (in Italian: Associazione Nazionale Combattenti – ANC) was established. The ANMIG became the most authoritative association among veterans, precisely because it represented the interests of those soldiers who had sacrificed something of their physicality.

Within the ANMIG, the war-blinded had a great importance: these veterans had in fact suffered not only serious physical injury but also a symbolically significant impairment. Several blind men became members of the Central Committee of the ANMIG, and Gino Neri and Carlo Delcroix were also presidents of the association (Vittoria, 1988). Delcroix, whose hands were both mutilated, was probably the best known of the war-disabled in the 1920s and 1930s. However, it is important to underline one aspect, perhaps apparently taken for granted: these former soldiers were not born blind, they had become blind due to participation in the war. For this reason they tried to obtain living conditions as close as possible to those experienced before their wounding, but they also tried to give a different connotation to the figure of the war-blinded, untying it from the pietistic stereotypes typical of the nineteenth and early twentieth centuries (Levi, 2017): 'We blind veterans, we want to be considered equal among equals and we do not want to be considered assisted. Many, to consider us as unfortunates, have forgotten that we are men and with this they make us feel more the weight of our infirmity. Too much have stopped in our misfortune and have forgotten that strong souls know how to light an unquenchable fire even in the shadows' (ANMIG, 1919).[2]

The initiatives for the protection of the war-blinded continued in those same years with the establishment of the Italian Blind Union (UIC), founded in 1920 by Aurelio Nicolodi (Salvante, 2013). The latter, wounded in the eyes and discharged from the army in 1916, already at the beginning of 1917 had given life to a specific association for the war blind, which later merged with the ANMIG. The birth of the UIC aimed to give greater representation to the blind from war, but also – starting from the experience of war blindness and from the welfare and pension gains deriving from that experience – to better protect blind civilians, favouring their progressive integration into Italian society.

There are two other relevant aspects. The first is the issue of work, to which two different provisions refer. The first is the promulgation of the law of 21 August 1921, called the 'Labriola Law', from the name of its rapporteur in the Chamber of Deputies. This law provided for the compulsory hiring of war maimed, as a percentage of the number of people employed in private companies and public offices (Fumi, 2002). Although the private sector struggled to transpose and apply this new legislation, numerous war invalids were hired in the public sector. The law on compulsory employment was a provision much awaited by war invalids, who – as we have seen – understood how work was key to integration into the social fabric of the country. Starting from the second half of the 1900s, the provisions included in this law would also have been extended to disabled civilians. Still on the subject of work, in 1934 a new national agency was founded, called the National Labor Body for the Blind (in Italian: Ente Nazionale di lavoro per i ciechi) This new body provided work to blind people, employing them mainly in weaving and metalworking, and had the Italian state as its main client.

The second aspect is the reform of the war pension system, carried out by the first Mussolini government in 1923. Since Italy's entry into the war, the legislator had tried to harmonise the pension system and adapt it to the needs of a war of mass and industrial warfare.[3] However, up to the early 1920s, legislative interventions had only constituted a corrective to a system that had kept the same structure. When, after the march on Rome, Mussolini was charged with forming a government, he understood that he also needed the support of the veterans and undertook to study a new structure of war pensions, which also contained an update of the impairment tables. Both the Central Committee of ANMIG and Alfredo Rocco, one of the most successful jurists of the time (Simone, 2012; Pavan Dalla Torre, 2020), were involved in the preparatory study work. The new system of war pensions, while not making the war-maimed completely satisfied, nevertheless gave widespread recognition – especially in economic terms – to eye injuries, in particular bilateral blindness.

Between the two world wars, the social and working situation of blind people stabilised around the points analysed. However, with the promulgation of the new civil code, in 1942, a fairly significant novelty was introduced. In the new text the blind – as well as the deaf, another category of disabled people that was numerous but very often not well represented – were not considered incapacitated a priori, but could be declared as such if they had not received an adequate education. This aspect may seem obvious, in fact he centralised the education of the blind – and, consequently, that of all the so-called invalids – also marking an important expansion of social benefits in favour of a substantially higher number of disabled people.

Integration If Not Inclusion: School and Employment for the Blind

The conclusion of the Second World War was a moment of caesura in Italian history. In 1946, an institutional referendum sanctioned the birth of the Italian Republic and a Constituent Assembly was elected to draft a new Constitution, which entered into force on 1 January 1948. Unlike what happened during the Kingdom of Italy and especially during the Fascist regime, the new Constitution aimed to guarantee the equality of citizens before the law, underlining that it is 'a task of the Republic to remove the obstacles of an economic and social nature, which, by limiting the freedom and equality of citizens, prevent the full development of the human person and the effective participation of all workers in the political, economic, and social organisation of the country'[4](art. 2). From this point of view, disability – both congenital and acquired, due to war or work related – should no longer have been an obstacle to the fulfilment of individuals or even a brake on their participation in the social and economic life of the Republic. Thanks to the experience of the Great War, to the work carried out by associations between veterans and to the welfare benefits obtained in the first post-war period; thanks above all to a close confrontation with the Italian governments, a radically different vision of the 'handicapped' had emerged from that of a few decades earlier. An evident sign of this change was the birth of two associations which, even in their name, referred to the experience of the mutilated in wars: the National Association between the mutilated and disabled of work (in Italian: Associazione Nazionale fra Mutilati e Invalidi del Lavoro, ANMIL), founded in 1943 (Salvini, 2018) and the National Association of the Civilian Disabled (Associazione Nazionale Mutilati e Invalidi Civili, ANMIC), founded in 1956. These two associations aimed to give representation to situations of illness and disability that had always existed in Italy, but which had never obtained proper recognition. The exaltation of war invalidity conveyed a more general reflection on more common events than wars, but was no less relevant.

The experience of the Second World War also made a contribution in another area. The Second World War was really a total war, in which even civilians were involved, suffering the consequences of war actions, in particular those of bombing in Italian cities. The National Association of Civil War Victims (in Italian: Associazione Nazionale Vittime Civili di Guerra) was born in this period (De Ninno, 2020a, 2020b): even civilians who had suffered a disability as a result of the war were granted the status of war invalids. The nefarious effect of the war and bombings continued to cause victims even in the decades following the end of hostilities, in particular among children who were mutilated by the explosion of unexploded war devices: precisely because of these events there were cases of bilateral blindness and of mutilated limbs, especially hands.

But what are the useful stages to describe the path of emancipation travelled by blind people since the end of the Second World War? The first aspect is certainly the integrated employment of blind workers. After the Second World War, the Italian 'National Employment Agency' (Ente Nazionale di Lavoro) had in fact taken the road of decline and blind people, without their preferential placement in state factories, during the 1950s were directed to other professions and, more importantly, to workplaces that were also shared with sighted people: those with a massage therapist's diploma had the opportunity to be hired in hospitals; those who had completed their university education were able to access competitions for school teaching of subjects such as history and music; finally there was the recruitment of blind people to fill the posts of switchboard operators.

Another important aspect is education. School surely had a great role in this integration of blind people. Two laws (n. 517/1977 and the 'legge-quadro' n. 104/1992) established that disabled people, and therefore also blind people, may have the opportunity to attend 'normal' schools, thus closing the experience of 'scuole differenziali', special schools such as those created within institutions for the blind (Schianchi, 2021). This was a passage that indicated in the school one of the areas of inclusion of blind young people in Italian society. Scholastic integration also resulted in the progressive decay of institutions for the blind which, deprived of internal schools and vocational training, were lacking in their most important function, the education of blind young people. As Fabio Levi correctly points out, the progressive closure of Institutes for the blind was the reflection of a broader paradigm shift in the management of disability in Italy. Another relevant measure, such as the reform of mental hospitals proposed by Franco Basaglia, also dates back to the end of the 1970s (Foot, 2014). Beyond the single measures, it was a change of cultural paradigm that had an immediately perceptible form in the lexicon: in Italy words such as 'invalido' (invalid person), 'handicappato' (handicapped people), or 'minorato' were replaced by 'disabile' (disabled person) with the intent to emphasise the different abilities of people rather than their impairment.

Of course, after the end of the Second World War, blind people continued to receive public assistance, but there was an important cultural development, as they became active subjects of this assistance. The path of emancipation also continued from the associative point of view: in 1979 a group of war blind established the Associazione Nazionale Ciechi di Guerra (Italian National Association of the War Blind – ANCG) aimed at obtaining greater recognition of the disability deriving from the loss of sight: 'Why did we associate independently, despite the fact that the Association of the blind (UIC), the Association of Disabled Ex Servicemen (ANMIG), the Association of the civilian victims of war (ANVCG), the Association of the disabled for service (UNMS) already existed? Because the war-blind, great invalids almost always multi-mutilated, constitute a minority of which the larger associations, sensitive to the needs of the most numerous members rather than those most affected, are not very concerned. We first formed as a grassroots movement in existing organizations and then, from 23 May 1979, as the Italian Association of the Blind of War (AICG)'.[5] This Association is currently affiliated with IKK (International Congress of War-Blinded).

In the last years the improvement of living and health conditions in Italy led to a significant increase in the average age and, at the same time, an increase in geriatric diseases, including those related to vision: pathologies such as maculopathy and progressive decrease in vision, closely linked to the progress of age, have increased their incidence among the Italian population, in the face of a progressive decrease in blindness due to birth. To better protect these subjects and to highlight how the concept of blindness has expanded over the years to include experiences that are also very different from the traditional one, that described the blind man as blind from birth or as a soldier who had suffered an impairment in war, in 2007, the Italian Union for the Blind changed its name to the Italian Union for the Blind and Visually Impaired precisely to underline the transformation of blindness during the twentieth century. In this way, over the years, blind people became more and more a part of society, even if no longer only and exclusively as the blind, but as elderly people with visual pathologies, as adolescents with visual difficulties and so on.

Concluding Discussion: Which Path for Inclusion?

The experience of the Great War and the founding of associations between veterans gave blind people a new identity, disconnected from the stereotype of persons unable to look after their needs and devoted to begging. Furthermore, the initiatives set up to protect war invalids contributed to giving medical and social assistance a different character from the charitable character typical of the nineteenth century. At the end of the First World War, blind people obtained unprecedented social recognition, based on the rhetoric of sacrifice for the homeland and the sufferings as a result of the war. However, after the end of the First World War, the path of emancipation for the war-blinded was still in its infancy.

The conclusion of the Second World War marked an acceleration in this area, leading – through a gradual process – to the exit of blind people from the Institutions, initially only from the point of view of work and, subsequently, also from the point of view of education. If the identity of blind people and their role in society now seems to have reached an almost complete maturity, a level of integration at least, with all the paradigmatic changes mentioned in this chapter, the process of building an inclusive society for blind people – and people with disabilities – is, on the other hand, still underway.

Notes

1 In December of the same year, Italian Parliament also created the National Agency for Veterans (in Italian: Opera Nazionale Combattenti, ONC) for the labour assistance of veterans.
2 'Noi ciechi – Delcroix said, talking during the second National Congress of the ANMIG held in Palermo in 1919 – vogliamo essere considerati uguali fra gli uguali e non vogliamo essere considerati degli assistiti. Molti per considerare noi come dei disgraziati, si sono dimenticati che siamo degli uomini e con questo ci fanno sentire maggiormente il peso della nostra infermità. Troppo si sono fermati nella nostra disgrazia ed hanno dimenticato che le anime forti sanno accendere anche nell'ombra un incendio inestinguibile' It should be borne in mind that, at that time, the blind and the deaf were considered – under the civil code (art. 340, *Codice Civile del Regno d'Italia,* 1865) – incapacitated unless the court ruled that they were unable to provide for their livelihood.
3 The Italian pension system was linked to the Napoleonic provisions of the nineteenth century and had as a premise the existence of an army of professionals. The amounts of pensions were adjusted and the categories of invalidity increased.
4 'È compito della Repubblica rimuovere gli ostacoli di ordine economico e sociale, che, limitando di fatto la libertà e l'eguaglianza dei cittadini, impediscono il pieno sviluppo della persona umana e l'effettiva partecipazione di tutti i lavoratori all'organizzazione politica, economica e sociale del Paese'
5 www.aiciechiguerra.it/chisiamo/chisiamo.html, consultated 05/05/2022: 'Perché ci siamo associati autonomamente, nonostante esistessero già le associazioni dei ciechi (UIC), dei mutilati e invalidi di guerra (ANMIG), delle vittime civili di guerra (ANVCG), dei mutilati per servizio (UNMS)? Perché i ciechi di guerra, grandi invalidi quasi sempre plurimutilati, costituiscono una minoranza di cui le grandi associazioni, sensibili alle esigenze degli iscritti più numerosi piuttosto che a quelle dei più colpiti, non si sono molto preoccupate. Ci siamo costituiti dapprima come movimento di base nelle organizzazioni esistenti e poi, dal 23 maggio 1979, come Associazione italiana ciechi di guerra (AICG)'.

References

ANMIG. (1919) Il Congresso di Palermo, in 'Il Bollettino', anno II, n. 1, maggio 1919.
Balestrazzi, G. (1967) *L'opera nazionale per gli invalidi di guerra in mezzo secolo di storia: 5/3/1917–25/3/1967,* Roma: Apollon.
Canevaro, A. and Gandreau, G. (1988) *L'educazione degli handicappati. Dai primi tentativi alla pedagogia moderna,* Roma: La Nuova Italia Scientifica.
De Ninno, F. (2020a) *Civili mutilati e ciechi di guerra, 1940–1945. Cause, conseguenze ed esperienze,* Milano: Unicopli.
De Ninno, F. (2020b) *Civili nella guerra totale 1940–1945. Una storia complessa,* Milano: Unicopli.
Foot, J. (2014) *La repubblica dei matti. Franco Basaglia e la psichiatria radicale in Italia, 1961–1978,* Milano: Feltrinelli.
Fumi, G. (2002) Politiche del lavoro e portatori di handicap: il collocamento obbligatorio (1917–1968), in S. Zaninelli and M. Taccolini (a cura di) *Il lavoro come fattore produttivo e come risorsa nella storia economica,* Milano: Vita e Pensiero.
Gentile, E. (2016) *Due colpi di pistola, dieci milioni di morti, la fine di un mondo. Storia illustrata della grande guerra,* Roma-Bari: Laterza.
Gerber, D. (Ed.). (2012) *Disabled Veterans in History,* Ann Arbor: University of Michigan Press.
Gibelli, A. (2016) *La guerra grande. Storie di gente comune,* Roma-Bari: Laterza.

Labanca, N. (2016) Studiare la disabilità di guerra, in N. Labanca (ed.) *Guerra e disabilità*, Milano: Unicopli, pp. 11–38.

Levi, F. (2017) *Un mondo a parte. Cecità e conoscenza in un istituto di educazione (1940–1975)*, Torino: Zamorano [ed. originale Bologna: il Mulino, 1990].

Pavan Dalla Torre, U. (2012) Le origini dell'ANMIG in V. Del Lucchese (ed.) *Passato, presente e future. Compendio di storia dell'ANMIG*, Roma: Associazione Nazionale fra Mutilati e Invalidi di Guerra, pp. 19–117.

Pavan Dalla Torre, U. (2016) L'ANMIG fra la sua fondazione e il suo primo manifesto, in N. Labanca (ed.) *Guerra e disabilità*, Milano: Unicopli, pp. 95–117.

Pavan Dalla Torre, U. (2018a) Tra assistenza e propaganda: medici e notabili cittadini e l'azione dei Comitati di Assistenza, in S. Magni (a cura di) *Gli italiani e la Grande Guerra. Dalla guerra delle idee alla guerra degli uomini*, Roma: Aracne, pp. 359–371.

Pavan Dalla Torre, U. (2018b) Reforming the war pensions system for disabled ex-servicemen. Notes and research perspectives on the Italian case, in D. Deroussin (ed.) *La Grande Guerre et son droit*, Issy-les-Moulineaux: Cedex, pp. 395–406.

Pavan Dalla Torre, U. (2020) Alfredo Rocco e la riforma delle pensioni di guerra in Italia (1923), in M. De Prospo and S. Mura (a cura di) *Il governo dei migliori. Intellettuali e tecnici al servizio dello Stato*, Verona: QuiEdit, pp. 255–276.

Perry, H. R. (2014) *Recycling the Disabled: Army, Medicine and Modernity in WWI Germany*, Manchester: Manchester University Press.

Pironti, P. (2015) Grande guerra e stato sociale in Italia: assistenza a invalidi e superstiti e sviluppo della legislazione sulle pensioni di Guerra. *Italia contemporanea* 277: 63–89.

Prost, A. (1977) *Les anciens combattants et la societe francaise. 1914–1939*, 3 vol., Paris: Presses de la Fondation nationale des sciences politiques.

Quagliaroli, F. (2018) *Risarcire la nazione in armi. Il Ministero per l'assistenza militare e le pensioni di guerra*, Milano: Unicopli.

Salvante, M. (2013) Italian disabled veterans between experience and representation, in S. McVeigh and N. Cooper (ed.) *Men After War*, London and New York: Routledge.

Salvante, M. (2015) Mutilati e Invalidi in Trentino-Alto Adige: il caso dei ciechi della Grande Guerra, in *Annali del Museo Storico Italiano della Guerra, 23*, Rovereto: Museo Storico della Guerra.

Salvante, M. (2016) I ciechi di guerra nella Firenze del primo conflitto mondiale, in N. Labanca (a cura di) *Guerra e disabilità Mutilati e invalidi italiani e primo conflitto mondiale*, Edizioni Unicopli, Milano: Unicopli, p. 68.

Salvini, P. (2018) *Storia. Anmil – Associazione Nazionale fra lavoratori mutilati ed invalidi del lavoro*, Firenze: Arsal.

Schianchi, M. (2021) *Disabilità e relazioni sociali. Temi e sfide per l'azione educativa*, Roma: Carocci.

Simone, G. (2012) *Il guardasigilli del regime. L'itinerario politico e culturale di Alfredo Rocco*, Milano: FrancoAngeli.

Vittoria, A. (1988) *Delcroix, Carlo*, in Dizionario Biografico degli Italiani.

Wanech, O. (1969) *Geschichte der Blinden-padagogik*, Berlin: Marhold.

Zavatti, F. (2009) *Mutilati ed invalidi di guerra: una storia politica. Il caso modenese*, Milano: Unicopli.

7

A STATE OF SPIRITUAL DERANGEMENT

Blindness in Seventh-Day Adventist Theology, 1860s–1950s

Talea Anderson

Preliminary Discussion: A Personal History of Healing

Writing in 1891, Mrs Woelfe of Spring Arbor, Michigan, begged an elder at the General Conference of the Seventh-day Adventist church for help. She wrote that her daughter had taken ill with 'brain fever', and while the child ultimately recovered, she lost all vision. Mrs Woelfe asked Elder Olsen to come and lay healing hands on the child because, as she wrote, 'I cannot but believe [my daughter] was left in this condition to try our faith and I believe that God is able to restore her eyes' (Woelfe, 1891).

Mrs Woelfe's letter betrays some of the contradictions evident in Adventist interpretations of blindness. The distraught mother clearly viewed her child's disability in negative terms, as an affliction at odds with God's intentions for humanity. On the other hand, she implied that God chose for the girl to be blind in order to 'try' the family's faith. In both of these interpretations, the blind child is seen as an object lesson for able-bodied people – whether as an example illustrating the impacts of sin or as a faith-strengthening exercise for onlookers. The focus placed on the blind child has the contradictory effect of reducing her to an object of able-bodied scrutiny while also elevating her story within the community. To be blind was both to be figuratively cut off from God while also having the singular opportunity to experience God's healing first-hand. For a church founded on the desire to commune directly with God, the experience of disability would seem at once terrifying and awe-inspiring.

These contradictory understandings of disability were still evident nearly one hundred years later when I was born blind into an Adventist home in the 1980s. Like Mrs Woelfe, my mother also asked church elders to intervene on my behalf with prayer and anointing. When I regained partial vision after undergoing eye surgeries, my church and family understood my recovery as divine intervention. An

DOI: 10.4324/9781003275060-10

Adventist children's book author underlined this point when he wrote a devotional about my story using pseudonymous names for me and my parents (Mills, 1993). In his story, God healed my eyes thanks to my mother's prayers on my behalf. Much like Mrs Woelfe, the author ultimately presented my blindness as a faith-building exercise for church members' eager spiritual insights. In the final scenes of the story, my pseudonymous mother assured readers that I had emerged from these trying circumstances as a 'normal' child – happy and healthy albeit with very thick glasses. The author of the devotional thus invited readers to understand my blindness as a fearful experience to be covered over with the tropes of inspirational storytelling.

Growing up in the Adventist faith tradition, I often struggled to understand my disability amidst an array of contradictory messages provided by the church. I understood that blindness should never happen to truly 'good', truly faithful people. I understood that blindness made me more righteous than most because it was God's way of testing me like a pot in a kiln. I understood that my story was an inspiration to others but only if couched in proper terms. I understood that my blindness drew others' attention without necessarily giving me my own voice. I understood that I was not even blind at all because how could a person who had received God's healing still bear the lingering signs of disability? As June Eric-Udorie (2016) writes in her essay, 'When You Are Waiting to Be Healed', I understood that 'God does not make mistakes; everything God created was perfect; God corrected the things that were imperfect', and yet my vision loss remained.

Some of my confusion as a child no doubt emerged from the Adventist church's own grappling with disability as an experience within the community. In this chapter, I examine the writings of two church members to explore evolving perceptions of blindness in the nineteenth and twentieth centuries. By examining these works, I consider how founding religious narratives influenced my early conceptions of disability and, in particular, blindness.

Ellen G. White: A Disabled Prophet

The Seventh-day Adventist church emerged from the religious revivals that swept the United States in the early nineteenth century. Itinerant preachers made impassioned calls for ordinary people to study the Bible for themselves and form their own understanding of God based on personal experience. Simple farmers and young women – people who usually had little authority in society – became influential as religious leaders who had learned through visions and close Bible study to understand the true will of God (Cott, 1975).

The Adventist church began to coalesce in 1844, after church members were devastated at finding that the world had not ended as predicted by William Miller, an enthusiastic student of biblical prophecy. Seeking answers, church members found leadership in Ellen G. White, a woman they soon identified as a prophet due to her particular spiritual insight. White reported receiving visions from God since she was a teenager, and she drew on these revelations when making calls for theological reform (White, 1985).

Under White's leadership, the early Adventist church assumed as a core belief the understanding that the body is the 'temple of the Holy Spirit' and should, therefore, manifest health and purity (1 Cor. 6:19). The church ascribed many physical and mental limitations now regarded as disabilities to the consequences of sin and maintained a strong belief in the individual's ability to achieve strength, health, and mental vigour through rigorous attention to spiritual principles such as chastity outside of wedlock, abstention from alcohol and drugs, and vegetarianism (Skrzypaszek, 2014).

As her work evolved, White identified linkages between spiritual 'derangement' and conditions that we would today regard as disabilities (1887). Writing in 1864, she instructed church members to carefully avoid vices like masturbation and meat-eating because succumbing to these sinful practices had produced what she regarded as physical and mental aberration. In one instance, she described the gradual decline of the 'kind husband and father' who begins by eating meat and then succumbs to 'a feverish state of the system' characterised by 'impure' blood, 'not equalized' circulation, chills, and fever. Ultimately, men like this were necessarily 'degraded . . . to beasts' (White, 1864b, 125.2).

Like others in the nineteenth century, White included blindness on the list of disabilities that she regarded as the consequence of spiritual failing. In one account, she explained that God had shown her the clear connection between disability and sin (especially masturbation):

> Everywhere I looked, I saw imbecility, dwarfed forms, crippled limbs, misshapen heads, and deformity of every description. Sins and crimes, and the violation of nature's laws, were shown to me as the causes of this accumulation of human woe and suffering.
>
> *(White, 1864a, 16)*

This visionary account suggested that disability, or deviation from perceived physical and mental norms, was a consequence of lust, greed, and generally poor behaviour. White was particularly concerned with the vices of masturbation, alcoholism, and meat-eating, and she used accounts of twisted bodies to direct readers away from these behaviours. By this token, health and wholeness came implicitly to represent spiritual purity, community belonging, and a high degree of scrupulosity in adhering to recommended lifestyle choices.

It merits noting that Ellen White was hardly alone in identifying blindness and disability with moral failing. Victorians frequently associated alcoholism and masturbation with a variety of maladies including impotence, epilepsy, hysteria, and vision loss. Dr William Mackenzie, Surgeon-Oculist to Queen Victoria, noted in 1843 that masturbation produced everything from sleeplessness to headaches and insanity. Still more influential for White were the teachings of Sylvester Graham and John Harvey Kellogg, who both suggested that all sorts of physical and mental illnesses afflicted those who eschewed a bland whole-grain diet in favor of rich foods that excited sexual passions (Engs, 2001).

Although White indicated that an individual's spiritual failing might well result in blindness, she offered a different interpretation of disabilities acquired by happenstance or from birth. Writing about one of the blind men healed by Jesus in the New Testament, she indicated that it was 'an error to suppose that everyone who was a great sufferer was also a great sinner' (White, 1863, par 2). She suggested that God allowed or even preordained that these men would be blind because they served a purpose as object lesson for the devout. In the case of the blind men, Jesus healed them 'that the works of God should be made manifest' (White, 1863, par 1). Their blindness – and subsequent healing – demonstrated Jesus's divinity and drew people to Christianity. Therefore, blindness could be useful as a lesson to others, a talking point, the focus of a devotional account.

It is perhaps revealing to note that childhood disability was central to Ellen White's own experience as a visionary and church leader. While still in elementary school, she was assaulted by a girl who broke her nose and caused her to fall into a coma for three weeks. Upon waking up, White found her strength depleted and her face changed beyond recognition. Friendships dried up as it became clear that 'looks make a difference in the feelings of many' (White, 1860, 10.1). Wishing for death, White took comfort in religion and thereafter began having the visions that she recounted throughout her life.

White's near-death experience is often cited in Adventist literature, including children's books designed to instruct young people about the power of God's intervention. These stories suggest that those who fall short of physical health due to no error of their own will find spiritual recompense for their suffering. Their physical imperfection will be made up for by deep religious insight in the present and later by rewards in heaven.

Indeed, these accounts often dwelled on White's disability and its manifestation in her body. Authors like Everett Dick pointed out how White's hands trembled after her accident, making her continued education impossible. To church members like Dick, it was significant that White received a limited education due to physical disabilities because she later proved to be a prolific writer. Dick indicated that the 'simplicity, purity, and directness of [White's] style' belied her meagre three or four years of education, implying divine intervention in her work (Dick, 1938, 203.1). Other church members agreed – White's writing career was a sign of her close connection to God and part of the blessing she received in compensation for her disability.

Dick further commented on White's physical mannerisms while in vision. On one occasion, she:

> Held a large family Bible in one hand, open above her head, and turned the leaves with the other hand, repeating correctly certain texts and pointing to them, although her eyes were turned upward.
>
> *(Dick, 1938, 210.1)*

White's ability to lift heavy objects, remember lengthy texts, and see without use of her eyes were presented as impossibilities for any woman but particularly one racked with physical impairments. White's ultimate emergence as a prophet and church founder thus parallels the story of the healed blind men. Through careful scrutiny of her broken yet healed body, church members were taught to find renewed belief in God and his divine intervention.

White's writings and example suggest two somewhat conflicting views of blindness. On the one hand, she pointed to blindness as a sign of individual spiritual failing to be corrected through rigorous adherence to proper behaviour. On the other hand, she also spoke of it as an almost preordained condition, a kind of divine mandate designed to inspire the able-bodied to greater heights of devotion. The former interpretation implies little intersection between the church and disability because how could any true believer remain unhealed? In contrast, the latter view suggests disability as a high calling – cause for elevating the disabled and healed body so that it might be gazed upon and in some sense admired by ordinary church members. For White, her disability story certainly helped secure tremendous authority, though her example suggests no particular role in the church for a blind or disabled individual who does not display preternatural spiritual gifts as a result of their condition.

Jungle Thorn: An Object Lesson in Spiritual Hierarchies

Moving forward to the middle of the twentieth century, we find another set of writings that deal with blindness in the context of the Adventist church's evangelical work. Adventists at this time were focused on the expansion of the church. Drawing on Ellen White's teachings about health reform, they came to practice 'health evangelism' – a form of missionizing that combined medical care with theological instruction. Missionaries provided care via clinics scattered around the world. While doing so, they had the opportunity effectively, or at least partially, to recreate Jesus's miracle of curing the sick and blind. Through these living examples of modern-day miracles, they could 'introduce the Bible as a valuable resource for total health' (Adams, 2012).

In this context, the Adventist church cast disability firmly within a medical model. By this, I mean that disability was largely perceived as an individual problem to be cured through the use of modern medicine. As a positive side effect of medical interventions, the disabled person could then take their place as a productive member of Protestant-capitalist society (Bunbury, 2019). Early church members like John Harvey Kellogg had devoted themselves to restoring health through lifestyle changes that they regarded as harmonious with God's original intentions for humanity. These lifestyle choices included vegetarianism, outdoor exercise, and hydrotherapy – practices that remained in favour into the twentieth century. In fact, health remained a key focus for mid-century evangelists. As W.H. Branson wrote in 1944, the church had a responsibility to carry the 'rules and laws of health' around the world in order to assure the 'buoyant health that we ought to have in order to serve the Lord most acceptably' (Branson, 1944). Much as Ellen White had suggested when denouncing the deforming effects of sinful behaviours, this sentiment implied that people who had not attained health – people with disabilities – needed to be recouped by church members equipped with the teachings of modern medicine paired with the teachings of God. Left unclear was the status of anyone who did not achieve health by following the church's approved medical regimen, though their moral shortcomings might well be assumed by other community members.

In the twentieth century, Adventist missionaries began publishing books about their evangelical work in South America, Asia, Africa, and Soviet/eastern Europe. These books often bore a certain resemblance to the devotional written about me and my blindness. They tended to present non-Christians living around the world as sickly, superstitious, and impoverished folk to be transformed into healthy and productive members of society through conversion by hard-working Adventist missionaries. I grew up surrounded by these stories as my own grandparents were missionaries in Indonesia. Our bookshelves at home were filled with books by authors like Eric B. Hare, Josephine Cunnington Edwards, and Norma Youngberg – authors who wrote stories for children based on their time in Myanmar, Borneo, Malawi, or other parts of the world.

One of these books presented an understanding of blindness that reiterated themes from Ellen White's writings. *Jungle Thorn* was published by Norma Youngberg in 1951. It was one of a series that remained popular into the 1980s, when I first read it as a young child. Each book purportedly drew from the author's experience 'among headhunters . . . of Sarawak' with the intention of 'revealing the power of the gospel among primitive jungle peoples' (Adventist Book Center, no date). As this quote suggests, the books often betrayed racist assumptions, showing white Protestant missionaries as the saviours of backward peoples living far from Western technologies and medicines. Specifically, in *Jungle Thorn*, Youngberg told the story of Kondima, a young Bornean girl who encounters missionaries after losing an eye in an accident with thorny jungle creepers.

Kondima's story begins in a remote jungle village. Before her accident, she is described as 'pretty and lively' but, afterwards, as her vision fails, she becomes timid and self-conscious, knowing that she is 'no longer pretty'. Her own mother admits that she can hardly look at her daughter, who will grow up to be 'blind and useless' if no man wants her as a wife (Youngberg, 1951, 16, 30, 58).

Kondima's fortunes turn when white missionaries arrive and take her away to a hospital in Singapore. Along the way, the missionaries replace her faded, tattered clothes with an array of bright dresses. They wash and cut her hair in imitation of their own children's hairstyles, and at last they replace her ruined eye with a glass one so convincing that she shocks her neighbours upon returning home.

Kondima's transformation is the centrepiece of Youngberg's story, and her blindness greatly impacts the villagers who welcome her home. Seeing how Kondima has changed, the village residents come to accept Ellen White's teaching about the parity between physical and spiritual health. For them, Kondima's story suggests that blindness and disability can be kept at bay by effecting their own religious and cultural transformations to imitate the missionaries who – like Christ – have acted as their saviours. Gradually, they convert to Adventism, a change typified by the removal of the pigs that live in the spaces under their houses. As Kondima says, 'The pigs and devils are being driven out' (Youngberg, 1951, 158).

Although Kondima's blindness was not cured in the course of *Jungle Thorn*, her disability offered an object lesson to the mostly white children who read Youngberg's book. Readers were taught to be thankful for their own able-bodied privileges as they watched the impoverished, disabled child receive the missionaries' gifts with gratitude.

Jungle Thorn also acted to assuage any sense of guilt over the inequities between brown and white, disabled and able-bodied characters because, as Kondima insists, everyone in the Adventist community is loved 'regardless of race or color' (Youngberg, 1951, 86). When Kondima receives a crudely carved doll from a village friend and a white baby doll from the missionaries, she explains that she loves both the same even though 'one [is] beautiful and one [is] ugly' (Youngberg, 1951, 115–116). These statements reveal how Kondima denies all sense of racial and corporeal difference within the spiritual space of the church even though she never loses her sense of real-world hierarchies. To be dark-skinned or disabled was to be inferior – only loved through an act of condescension. Putting on a veneer of normality as Kondima does might help matters along but the hierarchies remain the same.

Present at the fringes of *Jungle Thorn* are hints of physical and socioeconomic differences left largely unacknowledged by the author: Indonesian and Chinese people act as porters, drivers, and laundresses for white missionaries; Kondima, despite her warm welcome into the missionaries' home, is sent to sleep with local converts; and the villagers who give up their pigs in the interest of Christian cleanliness no doubt suffer financial losses as a result. These racial and economic divisions are left unexplored in the book, tacitly accepted by all of the characters in the story as the mere facts of life. Similarly, Youngberg did little to explore Kondima's lived experience as a person with a single eye, instead presenting her blindness as an experience distant from white readers – merely the centrepiece in a story about sin and the curative power of religion. The glass eye not only hides Kondima's unsightly disability, it soothes readers who have learned to see Western culture, medicine, and religion as powerful cure-alls that can hide disparities from view under cover of equal love for all.

Concluding Discussion: Constructing a New Vision of Blindness

Certainly, texts by Ellen White and Norma Youngberg cannot speak for every Adventist's understanding of disability over the last two hundred years. However, for generations of church members, White's and Youngberg's writings created powerful founding narratives about disability. As such, it is no wonder that two mothers at the turn of the twentieth and twenty-first centuries regarded their children's blindness with sadness and disbelief. Church members had imagined blindness as a distant experience – a problem of sinners and poor peoples in far-off lands. Believers could not be blamed for supposing that a righteous life would keep the disabled 'other' at bay. Spiritual transcendence coupled with God-given medical knowledge would always bring the body back to health. Thus, no child of the church could remain unhealed.

Unsurprisingly, texts by White and Youngberg betray themes common in representations of disability. As Rosemarie Garland-Thomson (2002, 58) outlined in her essay 'The Politics of Staring', disability representations often follow tropes including the wondrous, the exotic, the sentimental, and the realistic. Adventist accounts of healing, including the devotional about me, contain hints of the sentimental and exotic. My story – and Kondima's and Ellen White's stories – held meaning for the church because our bodies played out spiritual narratives regarded as sensational and inspiring. As Garland-Thomson wrote (2002, 74), these stories confirmed a 'culturally fabricated narrative of the body' by showing disabled people as object lessons for able-bodied viewers. These stories effectively assured able-bodied people that they were beautiful, healthy, capable, and intelligent by comparison to the unfortunate other.

Adventist understandings of blindness and disability contained contradictions that I found confusing to navigate as a child. I read stories suggesting that my blindness was both pitiable and 'other' but also extraordinary and potentially empowering if White's example was any indication. Ultimately, these texts and teachings gave me no inkling of a more complex story – one without the soothing veneer of 'normality' or healing. All these years later, I find myself wondering what Kondima actually saw with her one eye and wishing that her story had helped me imagine a more complicated, more expansive, future for myself.

References

Adams, E. (2012) 'What is health evangelism?' [online]. *Ministry Magazine*. Available from: https://ted.adventist.org/sites/default/files/Pages%20from%20Ministry-12-11-final2.pdf [accessed 1 December 2021].

Adventist Book Center. (No date) *Norma Youngberg*. Available from: https://adventistbookcenter.com/authors/norma-youngberg/ [accessed 23 November 2021].

Branson, W. H. (1944) Health evangelism and the gospel ministry. *The Ministry* 17 (12): 28–30.

Bunbury, S. (2019) Unconscious bias and the medical model: How the social model may hold the key to transformative thinking about disability discrimination. *International Journal of Discrimination and the Law* 19 (1): 26–47.

Cott, N. F. (1975) Young women in the second great awakening in New England. *Feminist Studies* 3 (1/2): 15–29.

Dick, E. N. (1938) *Founds of the Message*, Washington: Review and Herald Publishing Association.

Engs, R. (2001) *Clean Living Movements: American Cycles of Health Reform*, Westport: Praeger.

Eric-Udorie, J. (2016) *When You Are Waiting to Be Healed*, Catapult [Magazine].

Garland-Thomson, R. (2002) The politics of staring, in S. L. Snyder, B. J. Brueggemann, and R. Garland-Thomson (eds.) *Disability Studies: Enabling the Humanities*, New York: Modern Language Association.

MacKenzie, W. (1843) On asthenopia, or weak-sightedness. *The Edinburgh Medical and Surgical Journal* 60 (156): 73–103.

Mills, C. (1993) *The Master's Touch: Adventists Share Stories of God's Leading*, Hagerstown: Review and Herald Publishing Association.

Skrzypaszek, J. (2014) The heart of the Seventh-Day Adventist health message. *Ministry: International Journal for Pastors* 86 (12): 6–8.

White, A. L. (1985) *Ellen G. White: The Early Years, 1827–1862*, Washington: Review and Herald Publishing Association.

White, E. (1860) *Spiritual Gifts*, Nampa: Seventh-day Adventist Publishing Association.

White, E. (1863) The signs of the times [online]. *Ellen White Estate*. Available from: https://m.egwwritings.org/en/book/820.11847 [accessed 23 November 2021].

White, E. (1864a) *An Appeal to Mothers*, Nampa: Seventh-day Adventist Publishing Association.

White, E. (1864b) *Spiritual Gifts*, New York: James White.

White, E. (1887) Correspondence to brother covert. Ellen G. White Writings, Volume 5, Lt. 26d. *Ellen White Estate*. Available from: https://m.egwwritings.org/en/book/14055.4087001 [accessed 20 November 2021].

Woelfe, Mrs H. C. (1891) *Correspondence to Elder Ole Andres Olsen. Presidential Incoming Letters, 1891-W. MS 11, Box 5*, Washington: General Conference Archives.

Youngberg, N. (1951) *Jungle Thorn*, Nashville: Southern Publishing Association.

8

FAITH HEALING AND BLINDNESS ACROSS CULTURES

Disability, Religion, and the Scientific Milieu

Aravinda Bhat

Preliminary Discussion: The Social Model of Disability, Social Constructionism, and Autoethnography

One day in December 2021, a friend and I sit in his office discussing my inability to walk independently – using the white cane – across the road and down uneven paved steps in front of the campus to drink a cup of tea. In a slow, thoughtful voice, he says that current ways of doing ordinary things – day-to-day functioning – have been determined by non-disabled people. It is they who have, this non-disabled friend explains[1] to a blind person, defined what are the acceptable ways of walking, negotiating crowded streets, finding tables in restaurants, locating commodities in shops, and so on (Siebers, 2006, 174; Elder-Vass, 2012, 4). If people like me – those with visual and other disabilities – were, he continues, to be present in significant numbers in various institutions and social settings, we would have a say in making pertinent decisions.

Thus he outlined to me – unaware that it was the kernel of an influential concept in disability studies – a social model understanding of disability. Mike Oliver and Colin Barnes explain it thus:

> Unlike previous traditional individual, medical approaches, the social model breaks the causal link between impairment and disability. The 'reality' of impairment is not denied but is not the cause of disabled people's economic and social disadvantage. Instead, the emphasis shifts to how far, and in what ways, society restricts their opportunities to participate in mainstream economic and social activities rendering them more or less dependent.
>
> *(2010, 548; Tremain, 2005, 9, 10)*

According to this liberatory analysis emerging out of sociology, the responsibility for the discrimination faced by disabled people lies squarely with society, and is

DOI: 10.4324/9781003275060-11

not located in the impaired body of the individual. It is instructive to note that the definition of weak social constructionism given by Tobin Siebers exposes the similarity between the two conceptions: '[I]t posits that the dominant ideas, attitudes, and customs of a society influence the perception of bodies' (2006, 174). Three noteworthy points flow from these considerations. First, 'the reality of impairment is not denied' in either case: the altered sensory, locomotor, and/or intellectual functioning of persons with disabilities receives recognition (Linton, 1998, 25; see Crilley, 2016, 306, for a different view). Both understandings make it clear that such psycho-somatic features can no longer be cited as reasons for the oppression of said people. Second, the social model has given rise to the academic field of disability studies which, along with disability rights movements around the world, understands 'disability as a social, political, and cultural phenomenon' (Linton, 1998, 21). Third, this conceptual innovation has enabled individuals with different impairments to forge a collective identity (Linton, 1998, 25) by laying bare the common complex of problems facing them, viz. negative attitudes of people whose thinking is shaped by ableist norms, institutional stumbling blocks, and infrastructural barriers in the built environment erected by insensitive authorities. As is clear from these remarks, this conception of disability fashions disabled people into political actors.

However, over the last two decades, disability scholars have moved away from the social model and formulated a theory based on what Siebers calls 'strong social constructionism' (2006, 174). This development has been shaped by the poststructuralist thought, among others, of Michel Foucault. Philosopher Shelley Tremain's explanation of impairment and disability is illustrative. She criticises the social model for succumbing to bio-power, 'inadvertently extending' 'contemporary social and political arrangements', and legitimising 'modern governmental practices' which form, define, and reproduce impaired subjects (Tremain, 2005, 10). She claims, contra the social model, that 'there is indeed a causal relation between impairment and disability, and it is precisely this: the category of impairment emerged and, in many respects, persists in order to legitimise the governmental practices that generated it in the first place' (Tremain, 2005, 11, 2006, 186, 192). Whereas the social model and the weak version of social constructionism shift the responsibility for the oppression of disabled people from the medicalised individual body to society, the social constructionist theory that Tremain develops voids the body of substance and the power to experience and speak out. This it does by side-stepping experience altogether, and reducing impairment to 'an historically specific effect of knowledge/power' (Tremain, 2006, 185; Swan, 2002, 284–285; Siebers, 2006, 174–175; Bhat, forthcoming, 23–26). The present volume's subtitle, 'International Constructions and Deconstructions', indicates an interest in constructionism. Therefore, this discussion pertinently acts as a conceptual frame that underpins my analysis.

Truth to tell, until my friend personalised the social model/constructivist notion – while reading David T. Mitchell and Sharon L. Snider (2000) for a collaborative paper – I regarded the idea that disability was socially constructed with intense suspicion. But when my friend laid out the concepts involved with brilliant lucidity, my resistance to the view relaxed a little, if not dissipating. I conceptualise my new position in opposition to how disability theorists governed by Foucauldian thought explain it. The sensory and corporeal experience of persons with disabilities should, I hold, actually occupy a central place when the social construction of disability is theorised. If non-disabled, normative discourse mandates how people in general, and persons with disabilities in particular should behave, how might I understand blindness and my long-term adaptation to it? I inquire into this problem by carrying out a comparative autocritical discourse analysis of two cultural stations.

The following sections exemplify a number of values central to autoethnography: 'a respect for contingency and chance; . . . an interest in subjectivity, emotionality, spirituality, and performativity; a commitment to vulnerable observation and writing; and a regard for relational ethics' (Bochner and Ellis, 2016, 214). They emerge, first, in a personal narrative of my family's multi-generational negotiations with blindness; and second, in the textual analysis of John M. Hull's diary entries and letters which reject faith healing for the blind, and stake a claim for the respectful treatment of disabled people. If anything, my critical writing exposes the difficult situations that the various persons involved in the two stories navigate, and their adherence to conflicting value systems with respect to blindness. It is for this reason that Critical Discourse Analysis (CDA) becomes useful. It 'enables ethical explorations of disability via multiple levels and forms of textual representation' (Bolt, 2021). While my autoethnographic narrative emerges in the first-person voice, it even-handedly treats the ethical commitments represented therein in concert with a comparative analysis of Hull's writing.

Multi-generational Negotiations: The Affirmation of Blind Selfhood

In 1940 or 1941, a nine- or ten-year-old boy reads to his mother regularly while she takes rest. She encourages him, her second son, to read aloud. This is because, due to a visual impairment, print is inaccessible to her. That lady is my great-grandmother, Venkatalakshmi, and the boy, my late maternal grandfather, Munglimane Subramanya Bhat (known to everybody as M. S. Bhat). He reads news reports on the ongoing Second World War appearing in the Kannada newspaper entitled Samyuktha Karnataka. The reports are written by a journalist under the nom de plume of Sanjaya.[2]

Speaking about his mother[3] some years ago, my grandfather tells me that two of her siblings also had vision problems. The former, C. S. Narayana, was a leading lawyer in his town, Madikeri (the British colonial administration of India rechristened it Mercara). During an interview conducted on 28 May 2017, Umagowri Shivaprasad told me that her father acquired a thorough legal education, most likely at Madras Law College, and practiced the law with the help of people who read to him. Venkatalakshmi's sister, Padmavati, was married but did not have children.[4] The latter had learned Hindi and held a degree called Hindi Visharad, awarded by Dakshin Bharath Hindi Prachar Sabha. During an interview conducted on 27

May 2017, S. S. Bhat and L. M. Bhat recall how Padmavati would unfailingly serve coffee and snacks or laddus to all her guests. Due to these circumstances, reading aloud has never been alien to my family.[5]

My mother started reading aloud to me and my non-disabled sister[6] soon after we turned one. My parents (Gupta and Singhal, 2004) not only raised me to love books, but also as a person in my own right. I grew up in the 1980s and 1990s in Manipal, a university town on the south-Western coast of India. My father was a professor of dental surgery at the Manipal College of Dental Sciences. Although my family's social standing and economic situation were good and I attended the local school, every now and then we had to negotiate with relatives, neighbours, university, and government authorities to enable me to have a happy childhood. But as I have remarked to my parents before, growing up visually impaired in the last two decades of the twentieth century in a small town was most fortunate for my development as a person with a disability. Although the word *normal* did crop up in relation to me in public discourse, it did not prevent my mainstream schooling and play with other non-disabled children. An old friend brought to my notice some years ago that my educational and economic privileges – cultural and financial capital – had protected me from experiencing discrimination.

Thus, my parents, sister, friends, and teachers treated me as a 'normal' child. The appearance of this adjective hardly suggests that any of these people expected me to conform to ableist norms.[7] They encouraged me to be myself and grow to my full potential. But I realise now that my maternal grandparents and paternal grand-father[8] grieved because their beloved grandson was blind. While they showered me with abundant love and made sure that I had confidence to deal with other peo-ple and face the world, they expected that the quality of my life would always be poorer than that of my non-disabled peers. They feared that I might face bullying at school or on the streets. Although the three of them were aware of how blind children could be brought up to participate fully in society thanks to the blind law-yer of Madikeri and his sisters, they never stopped hoping that my eyes would be cured when science had advanced sufficiently.[9] While they did not go to the extent of dragging me to traditional healers as L. Subramani's mother did (2014), they did succumb to the idea of faith healing for my retinitis pigmentosa (RP).

One day around 18 years ago, my maternal grandparents, uncle, and I drive to my native village in the South Indian state of Kerala to visit a relative and his wife, both of whom are old friends of my grandparents'. We stay for lunch. At table, our host offers to cure my blindness through Pranik healing.[10] Immediately, my grandfather says forcefully[11] 'Say yes!' I am taken aback by their words. Sensing my discomfort, my psychiatrist uncle asks his father to let me make my own decision. Although I find the idea of faith healing dubious, I catch myself acquiescing. The reason for this submission is simple enough. I do not wish to say no to the kindly old man just after my grandfather has exhorted me to accept his offer. While in India youngsters hesitate to fly in the face of their elders' words, I find that Hull too reports his initial inability to refuse point-blank a faith healer's offer (1997, 63). This professed faith healer, whom Hull calls Mr Cresswell, as well as the elderly

Pranik healer and my grandfather are figures of authority in their respective societies, the first religious and the latter two familial.

After lunch, when I go to the long living room in the front of the old house, our host explains how Pranik healing works, and what my responsibility is: every Tuesday evening he will send healing energy to cure my vision. I must sit quietly with my palms open and have full faith in the procedure. My grandmother is present, and hears his words. She says with emotion that this sort of healing will give me courage. I ask her angrily, 'Courage for what? I do not fear anything'. She replies uncertainly, 'Courage to face life'. In the face of my grandparents' bewilderment about blindness, I am at a loss for words. Luckily the others are not present to witness this exchange. But the Pranik healer tells me gently that if I do not want this therapy, he will not insist. Not wishing to disappoint him, I capitulate once again. The amount of emotional pressure that relatives can apply staggers me.

Then the healer relates the following success story – to be repeated a couple of times over the next few years – to give me hope (Hull, 1997, 75, 2001, 47). A lawyer from a nearby town who started losing his sight came to him one day seeking urgent help. The man feared greatly that he would have to give up his profession if he became blind. Then our elderly gentleman gave him Pranik healing. He even instructed the recipient to continue the medication prescribed by his ophthalmologist. After a few months had passed, the lawyer reported improvement in his vision and showed a graph that plotted the positive change (Davis, 2002, 101, 104, 106). Our host relates these details to underscore not only the compatibility of his alternative therapy with modern scientific medicine, but also their equal footing. The chart depicting a graph of the patient's vision attests to the efficacy of both systems of cure. This narrative shows how the discourse of medical science lends authority to the alternative healing method.

To satisfy my relative, I make a half-hearted effort on a few Tuesdays to sit in meditation. I even donate money every month to charities because it is part of the healing process. But I really cannot sustain the practice much longer because first, I was forced to submit to faith healing, and second, I do not desire to have 'normal' eyesight. I feel this way because I have grown into blindness and have created a world comparable in richness to that of sighted people by using my other sensory, intellectual, and spiritual resources (Hull, 1997, xii–xiii).

A dozen years later, in early October 2016, I meet the Pranik healer at my maternal grandparents' home. The final rites for my grandfather have been performed; he passed away on the intervening night of the eighteenth and nineteenth of September. Towards the end of the religious programme, my mother and I weave our way among the chairs placed for guests and greet the faith healer. He asks me why I do not walk independently among the crowd of people and chairs. 'Son, can you not see well now? I have been giving you Pranik healing for many years'. (See Hull, 1997, 76–77, for a very different attitude displayed by Mr Cresswell.) I tell the elderly gentleman that I cannot see well, that my vision is as it was earlier. He then offers to continue the therapy, but this time I tell him honestly that I do not wish it. While he believes that his alternative healing method has been proved efficacious by modern science, I regard faith healing with scepticism, and myself as a whole person.

John Hull: Faith Healing and Blind Epistolary Self-Declaration

In late 1997, Hull receives 'a letter' from a 'would-be faith healer' named J. P. Morris urging him, a blind man, to accept 'divine healing': 'There is a man by the name of Peter Scothern who has been mightily used of God in divine healing. He conducts divine healing services in various areas of Britain. He goes to various areas, if invited to do so, to lay his hands on needy and afflicted persons' (Hull, 2001, 46).[12] Hull is 'distressed' (2001, 48) by the patronising contents of the letter. It paints a detailed picture of the ill and disabled as 'needy and afflicted persons' who require to be cured. So the blind man posts a reply rebutting the discriminatory attitude of both Mr Morris and Mr Scothern, thereby claiming full disabled personhood[13]:

> I do not interpret my blindness as an affliction, but as a strange, dark and mysterious gift from God . . . . I have learnt that since I have passed beyond light and darkness, the image of God rests upon my blindness . . . . we are told in Psalm 139, v. 12 that God is beyond light and darkness . . . . I am a Christian like yourself . . . . This loss has helped me to think through many of my values in living, and in a way I have learnt a greater degree of intimacy with God.
>
> *(Hull, 2001, 48)*

Hull's conviction about the value of blindness to his life, personhood, and faith – achieved painfully over many years – invites the conclusion that he lives in the world by relying on resources of the self that are not constrained by light and darkness. In this sense, he has achieved nearness to God. But the situation was vastly different when he started maintaining a cassette diary on 1 June 1983 (Hull, 1997, 10). Concluding the introduction to his diary (1997), Hull states that when he finally came to recognise his total blindness in 1983, he 'began to sink into the deep ocean', meaning 'despair' (1997, 9). Of direct significance to my purpose here is his diary entry headed 'To Accept or not to Accept 8 January 1984' (Hull, 1997, 45–47). There he admits reluctantly, to quote his own words, that 'blindness is, for me, a kind of religious crisis' (Hull, 1997, 45). The everyday reality of not being able to see after living as a sighted man more or less for 45 years, having to adapt to the 'fact' of disability, and being forced to learn new ways of performing his activities drives him to this conclusion. At this delicate juncture in his psychological life, he is approached by two would-be faith healers, Mr Cresswell and Mr Benito Luigi, who claim that they can heal his blindness; he is also encouraged by a friend to accept the latter's offer (Hull, 1997, 63–65, 74–77, 2001, 46–48).

Mr Cresswell ascribes Hull's blindness to sin. This theme runs through the two diary entries in which he appears. He refers first to 'a fall' (Hull, 1997, 63) – the reference is to the Fall of humanity from the Garden of Eden – as the cause of blindness. He then tells Hull and his wife, Marilyn, that they are missing their home, which according to him is heaven. Next, Mr Cresswell accuses the blind man of having 'ceased to read the Bible', and warns that 'the moment we stop reading the Bible these things come upon us'. He even implies that Hull's 'parents or grandparents' may have sinned, which God has visited upon him (1997, 64, 2013, 22–23). But when Hull demonstrates conclusively that he knows his scripture, the faith healer proceeds to exorcise the 'evil influences' (1997, 65) from his body. Finally, when the blind man declines to carry 'a small Bible' in his pocket as advised by the faith healer, the latter rebukes him for being a wilful sinner[14] who refuses 'to obey the word of God'; warns him that he is 'treading a very dangerous path', and that he 'would not find healing that way' (Hull, 1997, 77). Tracking these instances where the faith healer applies cumulative pressure on the blind man to accept healing, we uncover the discourse of guilt informing the evangelist's creed.

Although Hull desires to recover his eyesight at the time he is accosted by the faith healers (1997, 75–76, 2001, 45–46), he considers faith healing to be deceitful, manipulatory (2001, 37–38), and superstitious (1997, 76). So he rejects it. This act bespeaks his belief in modern science and his sceptical bent of mind (Hull, 2013, 25). However, Mr Cresswell too concedes the efficacy of modern medicine when he grants that doctors may have correctly diagnosed Hull's eye condition (1997, 63). By contrast, the faith-healing Mr Morris displays a disparaging attitude towards doctors. In spite of his scepticism, he describes persons who need 'divine healing' by providing a detailed list of anatomical anomalies, physical and intellectual impairments, and illnesses (Hull, 2001, 46). Thus, it is clear that in the case of the faith healers, the religious discourse of sin combines with the scientific discourse of normalcy to produce a toxic religious milieu for disabled people.

Many years after writing his letter in reply to the one sent by Mr Morris, Hull composes his 'Open Letter from a Blind Disciple to a Sighted Saviour: Text and Discussion' (2013, 13–41). I comment briefly on the discourse of faith healing as it appears in this work from a modern perspective. This caveat is necessary because Hull analyses the Gospels. The New Testament is an ancient document, and tracing the discourse of faith healing in the society depicted therein lies outside the scope of this chapter. Deborah Beth Creamer cautions the modern reader about stories of disabled people being healed in the New Testament: 'We do not know if physical healing actually happened. We must not look at the healing stories as historical accounts but, regardless of their factuality, remember that what has survived for us today is a message that was crafted for a specific audience with a specific purpose' (2009, 45). So, this 'message' has come down to our day carrying, despite the passage of two millennia, a potent power to move the modern evangelist. We must remember that 'these inherited images and notions still function in church and society today, and thus we must always keep an eye on the contemporary significance, contributions, or dangers of the images that we explore' (Creamer, 2009, 39). Thus, Hull addresses his open letter to Jesus Christ, and challenges the link between sin and disability that the Gospels communicate (2013, 22–23). This sanctioned connection encourages faith healers to draw inspiration from the ministry of Jesus, and set out to heal blind and other disabled people.

Concluding Discussion: Critical Autoethnographic Integration of Blindness

In presenting and analysing the autoethnographic narratives of two blind men, one Indian and the other English, this chapter concentrates

> On the functions of stories and storytelling in creating and managing identity; the expressive forms for making sense of lived experience and communicating it to others; the entanglements that permeate how interpersonal life is lived and how it is told to others; the reflexive dimensions of the relationship between storytellers and story listeners; and the canonical narratives that circulate through society, offering scripted ways of acting.
>
> *(Bochner and Ellis, 2016, 210)*

My analysis of the two cultural stations articulates a conception of blindness as a valid sensory experience to be integrated with life, and the two men's respective struggles against 'canonical narratives' about ability, faith, normalcy, self, and world.

Notes

1 I wish to thank Dr Arjuna SR, Assistant Professor at the Department of Liberal Arts, Humanities and Social Sciences, Manipal Academy of Higher Education, Bengaluru, India, for his acute insight into the social determinants of disability. His fresh statement of the social model approach to disability led me to perceive the link between that conception and social constructionism. This new inkling gave me the impetus to write this chapter.
2 This name carries immense significance in South Asia because, in *The Mahabharata*, Sanjaya is the name of the minister who sat by the blind king Dhrtarashtra and narrated to him the fratricidal war being waged by the rival cousins, the Pandavas and the Kauravas. The minister's name bears significance for me because my grandfather became a Sanjaya to his visually impaired mother.
3 She died in 1943 when he was just 12 years old.
4 In the early twentieth century, the two sisters could not have practised any profession outside the home because girls had few prospects of education then. They were simply raised to be wives and mothers. However, this condition changed somewhat when the next generation of girls came of age in the mid-twentieth century. M. S. Bhat's elder sister, Dr Saraswati S. Rao, was a professor of political science in Bombay University, India. This doughty lady once remarked that her grandfather had given his daughter in marriage to an impoverished schoolteacher (her father) because she was visually impaired.
5 This narrative opens an article I wrote nearly a decade ago for a now defunct online magazine called *The Alternative*. I have modified the original paragraph in order to improve the writing.
6 Sometimes I wonder whether my sister, who is just over two years younger than I, felt neglected as a child because our parents had to give me more attention on account of my visual impairment and the resultant negotiations with social institutions. But she has assured me at least a few times that she never felt that way. When my mother asked her

whether she had felt less loved as a child, my sister replied that such a thought had never crossed her mind.

7 This is not to say that I have not encountered bad apples. In mid-2015, I met a man in his sixties at a religious gathering in Hyderabad, India. He said that he was a journalist and advised me that if I woke up at five o'clock every morning and read the *Bhagavad-Gita,* my sight would be restored. With barely contained rage at his presumptuous interference, I told him in a tight voice that I did not appreciate such advice.

8 His wife died even before my parents got married.

9 This wish was repeated by my grandmother as a refrain until one day my mother got fed up and explained to her that I really did not want to get back my vision; in fact I had never had good eyesight; and that I regarded myself as a full person with capabilities. At this, my grandmother retorted that such a thing was a lie; it could never be possible that someone didn't wish to see. But eventually my mother was able to convince her that this was really the case. To her credit, my grandmother remarked to me some years later that it took her a while to recognise that I had my own personhood.

10 It is an alternative therapy which involves energising *cakras* or certain points in the human body which are considered to be vital.

11 is his voice charged with enthusiasm or some other emotion? I think I understand now what it is. My uncle said to me the year before his father died that the latter blamed himself for passing on to me the gene causing blindness.

12 Comparing the letter written by Mr Morris (Hull, 2001, 46–47) and the passages critiquing the social model by Tremain (2005, 10–11), we may discern a common stylistic feature. It consists in the repetitive employment of certain word-forms and imperative sentences which build into a hectoring rhetoric. Far from persuading the reader, such passages end up alienating him or her.

13 The material discussed in this cultural station appears elsewhere in other forms of expression (Bhat, 2021, forthcoming).

14 Similarly, Mr Luigi, the Sicilian hypnotherapist, alleges that Hull does not have willpower (1997, 75) to actively recover his eyesight, and Hull's 'loyal and affectionate friend' thinks that 'it must be a combination of pride and complacency' (1997, 76) which are the reasons for his rejecting hypnotherapy.

References

Bhat, A. (2021) Being on the brink of a blind abyss: Stepping back from a religion defined by the opposing archetypes of light and darkness, in J. M. George (ed.) *De Natura Fidei: Rethinking Religion Across Disciplinary Boundaries vol. 3*, New Delhi: Authorspress.

Bhat, A. (forthcoming) *Blind Narrations and Artistic Subjectivities: Corporeal Refractions*, Abingdon: Routledge.

Bhat, S. S. and Bhat, L. M. (2017) Interview with Aravinda Bhat, Manipal.

Bochner, A. P. and Ellis, C. (2016) The ICQI and the rise of autoethnography: Solidarity through community. *International Review of Qualitative Research* 9 (2): 208–217.

Bolt, D. (2021) The metanarrative of arthritis: Playing and betraying the endgame, in D. Bolt (ed.) *Metanarratives of Disability: Culture, Assumed Authority, and the Normative Social Order*, Abingdon: Routledge.

Creamer, D. B. (2009) *Disability and Christian Theology: Embodied Limits and Constructive Possibilities*, Oxford: Oxford University Press.

Crilley, M. (2016) Material disability: Creating new paths for disability studies. *CEA Critic* 78 (3): 306–311.

Davis, L. J. (2002) Bodies of difference: Politics, disability, and representation, in S. L. Snyder, B. J. Brueggemann, and R. Garland-Thomson (eds.) *Disability Studies: Enabling the Humanities*, New York: The Modern Language Association of America.

Elder-Vass, D. (2012) *The Reality of Social Construction*, New York: Cambridge University Press.

Gupta, A. and Singhal, N. (2004) Positive perceptions in parents of children with disabilities. *Asia Pacific Disability Rehabilitation Journal* 15 (1): 22–35.

Hull, J. M. (1997) *On Sight and Insight: A Journey Into the World of Blindness*, Oxford: Oneworld Publications.

Hull, J. M. (2001) *In the Beginning There Was Darkness: A Blind Person's Conversations with the Bible*, Harrisburg: Trinity Press International.

Hull, J. M. (2013) *The Tactile Heart: Blindness and Faith*, London: SCM Press.

Linton, S. (1998) *Claiming Disability: Knowledge and Identity*, New York: New York University Press.

Mitchell, D. T. and Snyder, S. L. (2000) *Narrative Prosthesis: Disability and the Dependencies of Discourse*, Ann Arbor: The University of Michigan Press.

Oliver, M. and Barnes, C. (2010) Disability studies, disabled people and the struggle for inclusion. *British Journal of Sociology of Education* 31 (5): 547–560.

Shivaprasad, U. (2017) Interview with Aravinda Bhat, Madikeri.

Siebers, T. (2006) Disability in theory: From social constructionism to the new realism of the body, in L. J. Davis (ed.) *The Disability Studies Reader 2nd Ed*, New York: Routledge.

Subramani, L. (2014) *Lights Out: A True Story of a Man's Descent Into Blindness*, Noida: Random House India.

Swan, J. (2002) Disabilities, bodies, voices, in S. L. Snyder, B. J. Brueggemann, and R. Garland-Thomson (eds.) *Disability Studies: Enabling the Humanities*, New York: The Modern Language Association of America.

Tremain, S. (2005) *Foucault and the Government of Disability*, Ann Arbor: The University of Michigan Press.

Tremain, S. (2006) On the government of disability: Foucault, power, and the subject of impairment, in L. J. Davis (ed.) *The Disability Studies Reader 2nd Ed*, New York: Routledge.

9

THE ACCEPTANCE AND TRANSCENDENCE OF BLINDNESS

A Collaborative Autoethnography

Neng Priyanti and Taufiq Effendi

Preliminary Discussion: Politicization of Blindness

Indonesia has ratified a number of legislations (i.e. ILO discrimination convention, the UN convention on the Rights of People with Disabilities) and made Disability law No. 8/2016 for state and non-state companies to adopt the 1–2% quota for the employment of persons with disabilities. However, even though blindness as an impairment does not affect cognitive or adaptive ability, recent data suggests that employment of people with blindness is typically confined to manual labour and, hence, informal sectors. This is due to the inadequate knowledge of family, society, and government about blind people's potential for education and professions, as well as the lack of employer commitment to the provision of necessary accommodations for prospective employees (Gunawan and Halim, 2020). In this chapter, we add that the establishment of a metanarrative, coupled with collectivist cultural values that view inequality as part of the existing social system (rather than a subtle form of oppression), affects how blindness and the acceptance and/or resistance to it is perceived, responded to, and represented. The chapter describes the journey of two people in their understanding of blindness within a collectivist society – one without blindness and the other with blindness (the first author and second author respectively). We offer different angles in our exploration of how the two cultural stations that we visited as we grew up shaped and re-shaped our understandings of blindness.

The study adopts a mixed method approach of collaborative autoethnography and critical disability theory. Underpinned by the social model of disability, critical disability theory views disability as social, cultural, and political practices, and in so doing challenges the taken-for-granted beliefs and traditional norms about disability; it explores the embodiment and normalization of disability and, by extension, the politicization of marked bodies within contemporary societies. In particular, it

DOI: 10.4324/9781003275060-12

examines the social and institutionalized mechanisms and practices of disablement occurring in a variety of forms and degrees within certain cultural groups, as a means to produce knowledge to fight for the justice of marginalized people with biologically and mentally marked bodies. In our attempt to gather data and/or to revisit our past shared experiences, we rely on autoethnography as it allows us to explore and examine our personal experiences, and empirically tie them to wider sociocultural and political issues (O'reilly, 2012). These connections to wider issues are further used to make our theoretical assumptions (Fetterman, 2010), which therefore can be taken as a credible account of culture. The selection of a collaborative approach for this chapter is driven by the fact that it provides room for collective interrogation and discussion, which makes use of our dual lenses (unsighted and sighted angles) to guide our examination of our possibly biased and culturally rooted ableist perspectives. In other words, our revisiting of the collective shared experiences which start from opposite directions – the second author's personal experience from being sighted to being unsighted and the first author's interactional experience as an able-bodied social worker – makes it possible for us to gain an enriched understanding of the embedded cultural and social practices of blindness in Indonesia. We limit our experiential exploration to two cultural stations that have constructed public imagery of blindness and have subsequently shaped and re-shaped our understanding of it – particularly the rehabilitation programs for the blind and massage parlours. We utilized two ways of memory recollection for our data collection: the first involved revisiting and reflecting on past interactional experiences that usually generated wordless images; these wordless images were then transcribed into words, which were critically examined through collaborative discussion to produce contextualized narratives.

Rehabilitation: The 'Realistic' Narrative and Learned Acceptance

In Indonesia and around the world, vision has been placed as the favoured mode of information transfer due to its so-called practicality (Putzar Goerendt et al., 2007, cited in Cattaneo and Vecchi, 2011); when compared to other sensory modalities, it seems to offer an enormous amount of information in one go. This preference has been culturally engrained in contemporary societies. Through osmosis it has been passed down from generation to generation and, as a result, has been received and accepted as an unquestionable, natural tendency of human bodies.

With regard to this state of affairs, Bolt (2015) argues that ocularcentrism leads to ocularnormativism, as the huge emphasis has made visuality the normative example against which other modes of sensory information are judged. He further argues that placing sightedness as the only legitimate source of knowledge leads to biased epistemology. To provide an illustration, we analyse vision-related metaphors that reflect and thus guide day-to-day normative conceptual systems existing in particular communities (Lakoff and Johnsen, 2003). These visual metaphors function to 'alert us to the metaphorical entailments and in modelling metaphors as creative explanation of abstract notion' (McKnight and Whitburn, 2017, 1). In other words, visual metaphors colloquially used in a certain cultural group carry linguistic elements, which can help to explain traditional ableist notions circulating in that community. For example, the common metaphors *seeing is believing* or *a picture is worth a thousand words* can be found across nations and in different cultural contexts. They discursively represent visual perception as the dominant way to achieve knowledge, or as synonymous with knowledge, leaving people with a lack or absence of vision epistemologically 'othered'.

Similar ableist presuppositions can be found in many Indonesian everyday discourses, such as the symbolic phrase '*yang buta menuntun yang buta*'.[1] Even though the metaphor in question is not exclusively related to people with blindness, the double utilization of the lexicon of blindness and the connotations of incompetence carries a semantical presupposition that in order to perform in, say, managerial/leading positions, eyesight is necessary. Not only does such an idiom, when used in context, project agential scepticism towards a group of people that are marked with the loss of eyesight in a given situation, it also positions atypical ability as inferior in achieving knowledge and performing agentive positions, which further leads to institutionalization.

This ocularnormativism has contributed to the reductive program definition, design, and development of Indonesian rehabilitation institutions, especially the occupational choice offered to people with blindness. These rehabilitation institutions generally aim to empower people with blindness through predetermined trainings and employment opportunities, and in so doing enable future independent living. The career choices, however, are mostly limited to professions assumed to be advanced through touch and hearing, such as massage, Shiatsu, and Spa training, as well as Music and making coffee[2] (BRSPDSN Wyata Guna Bandung, 2022). Such occupational boundaries seem to have stemmed not only from ocularnormativism but also from the sensory compensation phenomenon that presents the improvement of tactile and hearing acuities on people with the absence of eyesight as empirical facts. Such a phenomenon suggests that the remaining senses available improve significantly to compensate the sensorial deficits. In other words, the absence of vision (or the partial lack thereof) makes people with congenital and acquired blindness depend on their skills in identifying different objects by touch in order to function, which leads to enhanced tactile and hearing acuities (Cattaneo and Vecchi, 2011; Collignon et al., 2006, 2009; Collignon and Volder, 2009).

The established metanarrative about what people with blindness can and cannot do speaks volumes about assumptions of authority over the non-normative bodies cloaked under a variety of discourses specific to collectivism. We explicitly relate these blindness issues to collectivism; to the cultural upbringing, the context in which we were both raised and, specifically, to the cultural values that shape our views and beliefs about what is considered desirable. In a collectivist society, the degree of interdependence is relatively high as people exist in relationship with others, and self-image is defined within a social framework. Each person is communally nurtured and taken care of, particularly the weak and the less fortunate (which includes people with disabilities and blindness), and the sighted counterparts presume and assume that people with blindness, for instance, have more tactile memory and thus should be trained to do certain occupations. In other words, the assumed authority performed through the reductive choices of employment, that we know reduces the agency of people with blindness (Bolt, 2016), becomes translated as care.

The current political situation has further presented the rehabilitation program which provides training within a six-month timeframe as *a realistic option*. The issues encountered by people with visual impairments have been well documented and thus acknowledged within Indonesian legislation and policies. For example, a number of international conventions such as the UN convention on Rights of People with disabilities and the ILO Discrimination convention have been ratified. At the national level, there are Law Number 70/2009 (i.e. providing inclusive education for students with disabilities), Law No. 25/2009 (i.e. enforcing accessibility and inclusivity of public services), Law No. 28/2002 (i.e. enforcing inclusive built environment), and Law Number 8/2016 (i.e. ensuring that each company allocates 1–2% quota for the employment of persons with disabilities into the workforce); all of which have been developed to ensure the welfare of people with disabilities in general, including people with blindness.

However, the political acknowledgement and support do not seem to translate on grassroot levels; classic issues such as unequal access to education, in particular access to curriculum and classroom instruction, as well as inadequate facilities have been widely recognized in Indonesia and also in other countries such as India (Palan, 2021). The second author – who became legally blind when he was 15 years old[3] and as a result experienced first-hand studying and living as both a sighted and non-sighted person[4] – noticed that some basic requirements for the establishment of integrated schools were not provided. The curriculum and instructions at the integrated school were, despite the political endorsement, mostly inaccessible for students with blindness, as learning materials were not made available in braille nor audio format.[5] Teachers' pedagogical approaches, decisions, and skills had also been found not to be inclusion-friendly.[6] The second author also mentioned how the narrative of what was 'realistic' circulated within the institutions and, coupled with wider economic pressure, pushed people with blindness to take very particular career options.

The second author, nevertheless, stated that social supports from a handful of volunteering individuals and certain communities had been overflowing and managed to keep him and his other three schoolmates with blindness from being marginalized. He especially recalled the kind assistance offered by a number of sighted volunteers and paid readers 'lending' their eyes,[7] organised by a non-government organization.[8] The second author's social interaction with volunteers and this foundation (which was founded by, and an employer of, people with visual impairments) helped him view blindness in a relatively positive manner. Such educational support and interactional exposure[9] gave hope and motivated the second author to continue his studies into Higher Education and then his position on a university faculty.

However, such 'inspiring' stories (Muharam, 2020)[10] are those of exceptionality and might be unrepresentative of the majority. Although research on blindness is relatively rare in the Indonesian context, the stories above suggest one similar issue: access to quality education and instruction remained poor when compared to sighted counterparts, leading to the low participation rate of people with visual impairment in Higher Education (ILO, 2022).[11] Although the number of people with blindness might be relatively high[12] when compared with people with other disabilities, the participation rate and representation of people with disabilities in the formal workforce is still low (Hidayatullah and Noer, 2021). And despite the fact that blindness does not affect cognition and adaptive skills, people with blindness, to a certain degree, have experienced inequality in terms of accessing quality education and employment opportunities evident in those inspiring stories (including the second author's) which further confirms research findings (Kustini and Dianti, 2020; Gunawan and Halim, 2020; Hidayatullah and Noer, 2021). The unequal distribution of education and employment opportunities, as suggested in different success stories, seem to indicate a lack of countrywide enforcement of constitutionally established laws and policies within the Indonesian political system. This places, for instance, the decisions to grant access to quality education (as bases for future employment) and employment opportunities in the hands of leaders of schools, government offices, and companies, instead of being nationally enforced. Such 'flexible' arrangements and the choices made on grassroot levels, as reflected by the rate of participation and institutional challenges faced by people with blindness on a daily basis, unfortunately reflect the culturally entrenched negative stigma and scepticism.

We have also observed similarities between career options of the rehabilitation institutions with that of empowerment programs offered by non-governmental organizations that have inadvertently contributed to the social construction of disability, in particular the agential ability of people with blindness, and henceforth neutralized the bio-medical divide. Through the lens of a then social worker,[13] the first author learned that the empowerment programs designed, developed, and delivered by non-governmental organizations, including a variety of faith-based organizations, as a response to blindness, despite their good intentions, were practicing ableism. For example, when the first author worked for a non-government organization in Nusa Tenggara Timur, a province in the eastern part of Indonesia, she observed that empowerment programs which were subtly displacing the agency of people with the absence of vision were considered culturally noble and religiously appropriate. The first author had also mentioned that her decision to become a frequent patron of *Panti Pijat Tunanetra* and *Salon Tunanetra*[14] was driven by her social and religious obligations. It was not until she was intellectually engaged with disability studies, where her cultural beliefs and biased social and cultural practices were challenged and contested in the academic arena, that she experienced a paradigm shift, and thus viewed the reductive career options as ableist instead of noble. We argue that such a dilemma is also experienced by members of a collectivist society, with and without blindness.

The empowerment program – which is similar in approach and nature to the practice of giving social care conducted by government and non-government agencies, including individuals in Indonesia – is therefore 'entangled in generosity but also in domination and power over bodies (Erlina, 2020, 200). The predetermined career pathways, political policies, and practices that have been enacted towards people with blindness seem to be paradoxical as government and non-government agencies, including individuals in general when carrying out their social and spiritual responsibilities, can inadvertently maintain the status quo and/or practice ableism. Enclosed within the institutional mechanism, such ableist practices may carry the bio-medical power that can further marginalize people marked with biological differences (Das and Addlakha, 2007), placing them at the bottom of the social hierarchy within the collectivist society. Through osmosis advanced by circulating discourses, the inexorably politicized dichotomy is presented as a natural consequence of an impairment, and influenced by cultural norms and value systems specific to collectivism, which tends to be accepted by both worlds – the sighted and unsighted – as, therefore, culturally appropriate and desirable.

Massage Parlours: Finding Happiness

In the previous section, we discuss how ocularcentrism leads to ocularnormativism reflected in the establishment of (and the reductive choice of) career paths for people with blindness in Indonesia, and how this seems to be accepted as part of the social system. We now draw on recollections of selected dialectic conversations we had with people with blindness who, due to wider socioeconomic forces, have taken the career path politically designated for them. We also explore practices and ways that people with blindness have taken as sociocultural and political responses to the public construction of blindness, in a spiritual move towards happiness. This transcendence of blindness means going beyond limitations levied by emotional reactions and societal expectations. In their book *Psychology of Disability*, Vash (1978 in Vash and Crewe, 2004) condensed five acknowledgements of disability into three levels: recognition of the facts, acceptance of implications, and embracing the experience. Although a bit outdated, this model remains relevant here.

The second author, whose blindness developed gradually, almost took the Shiatsu when he went through the shock and denial stage and went on to take several curative options before he was able to accept and embrace his blindness for its non-normative positivisms (Bolt, 2015). He vividly described how, when asked by family members to learn braille, he was offended and furious. This was because his understanding and social interactional experience of blindness prior to becoming legally blind was filled with stigma influenced by the 'negative' public images of 'tunanetra'[15] (Effendi et al., 2021). Similar emotional and political struggles were shared by other people whose blindness occurred at a later stage, such as his cohort at the Tanmiyat residential school,[16] who were not age-appropriate for formal education, and most, as the second author recalled, needed to be financially independent and/or were expected to provide financial support for their families. This economical and societal pressure, to an extent, seems to affect the speed of self-acceptance. In other words, the 'realistic' narrative re-surfaced, forcing each individual with blindness to understand the limitations and assess the available options.

On the other hand, the first author, through years of frequenting different *Tunanetra* massage parlours, learned that the message projected by therapists with blindness was one of contentment. She is especially reminded of the conversation she had with a married couple who established and ran a three-room massage parlour; how they both narrated with pride their achievement of sending their children to college and thus to live a life socioeconomically better than theirs. They, taking turn, reminisced about their journey, where they met, and how they started their small business. During our dialectic conversation, they did not mention or suggest any resistance or bitterness. Both of them kept mentioning the word 'bersyukur',[17] and seemed to have accepted the 'norm' that, once eyesight is lost, employment options would *realistically* be limited. When asked why they did not take other options such as continuing to a higher degree, they explained they did not know anything back then, but were *grateful* they could be like they were today.

Vash and Crewe (2004) argue that one's spiritual and/or religious beliefs affect how people come to terms with their loss of eyesight. People who view blindness as Karma for past mistakes, for instance, are likely to interpret their own visual impairments differently from those who view it as a blessing. In fact, there have been several research studies suggesting how spiritual beliefs affect one's acceptance of disability and spiritual orientation (Claassens et al., 2018; Hasnain et al., 2019; Johnstone et al., 2007; Otieno, 2009; Selway and Ashman, 1998). In a country with the largest Muslim population in the world, Islamic beliefs about disability affect how disability is perceived and received by the affected person and by the public. Erlina (2020, 191) found that in Islam, disability is understood spiritually as God's blessing, that one therefore needs to practice 'nrimo' (acceptance with passion) and keep practicing gratefulness before being able to 'transcend' their loss of eyesight. In other words, such spiritual beliefs have assisted the process of transcending blindness. The practice of 'bersyukur' (gratefulness), repeatedly mentioned by the married couple, seems to have been drawn from their Islamic belief to aid the paradigmatic shift to a view of blindness as part of their 'fate', where they needed to walk on with compassion, which aided their journey in accepting and transcending constructs of blindness.

This form of internal spiritual submission seems to be the first stepping stone towards happiness. Several researchers (Brebahama and Listyandini, 2016; Harimukthi and Dewi, 2014), who explored the psycho-social well-being of Indonesian people with acquired blindness, have found that the loss of eyesight is viewed as a catalyst for spiritual growth – the loss of eyesight makes life more purposeful and meaningful (Harimukthi and Dewi, 2014, 74). Doing similar research, Fikriyyah and Fitria (2015) revealed that university students with blindness have higher adversity quotient compared to their sighted counterparts, which further indicates how blindness is navigated spiritually and therefore has aided mental and spiritual growth. Habsyiyah et al. (2015) argue that 'the Indonesian culture and beliefs' affect the quality of life of persons with visual impairments and blindness, which is also put forward by researchers (Brebahama and Listyandini, 2016; Harimukthi and Dewi, 2014). As members of a collectivist society, we agree that our upbringing affects how blindness is viewed, received, and responded to. Borrowing the cultural dimension framework provided by Hofstede (Hofstede et al., 2010), we unpack and explain the culturally rooted barriers towards inclusion.

The therapist couple's acceptance and contentment, which can also be interpreted as their agentive submission to the government power, is arguably influenced by the collectivist preference for *uncertainty avoidance* and *harmony*. For example, the different inclusion 'alternatives' in terms of inclusive education as a basis of future employment and occupational choice offered to people with blindness are ineffective, if access to them is still troublesome compared to access to segregated and predetermined career options which are fully facilitated. The politically limited occupational pathway from the Indonesian Ministry of Social Affairs therefore provides *certainty of future employment* compared to the inclusive education and/or employment from the Indonesian Ministry of Education, and in a collectivist society geographically situated in a developing country with its preference for avoiding uncertainty, such employment uncertainty itself is an institutional barrier. However, this does not mean that there is no resistance; to say so would only undermine agency. The resistance is often expressed in subtlety through the cultural adoption of a non-confrontational conflict management style (Lim, 2009), which is assumed to maintain harmony.

In our interactions with massage therapists with blindness, none has explicitly expressed resistance to the political and cultural establishment, and the same is true in some success stories such as those in Muharam's YouTube videos and DPP Pertuni.[18] In fact, despite their 'rocky' journey in achieving their current state, none expressed explicit resistance. What was mentioned repeatedly is the problem of inaccessibility and prejudicial hiring practices,[19] and often the blame was directed to the *self* rather than the *wider political mechanism*. In one of Muharam's YouTube videos, for instance, a woman recollected the challenging journey she had to endure before successfully being employed as a civil servant. She experienced first-hand the prejudicial hiring practices; in particular the test and its delivery formats that were not blind user-friendly. She struggled but found her way by contacting necessary connections to get herself familiarized with the device and application used specifically for the screening test and other follow-up tests. The second author also had expressed his lived experiences being rejected by various institutions on the basis of his impairments. His persistence and perseverance are factors that enable him to be in his current academic and leadership role.

The personality aspects found in success stories seem similar in principle and pattern with supercrip stories[20] (Silva and Howe, 2012; Schmiesing, 2014) which, due to the advancement of information technology, are raising in number.[21] These supercrip stories discursively project a similar message and pattern – that working hard and a fighting spirit can defeat disablement. Such an implicit narrative seems to project biased expectations in which people need to overcome their blindness in order to fit the collective standard and in so doing need to have certain attitudes, mindsets, and personalities. It is true that personality, argued by Vash and Crewe (2004), influences one's reaction to disablement. However, when disablement is represented as a personal struggle or mentality problem (rather than a societal issue), 'motivational' representation, despite good intentions, may carry ableist effects. In other words, although such representation creates positive images, placing disablement and blindness as a personal struggle opposes the social model of disability, and hence the inclusion for which Indonesia is aiming.

As members of a collectivist society, we know this phenomenon and its complexities, especially when it is tied down to the issues of inclusion. In a collectivist society, a well-defined social framework is seen and thus accepted as a standard ideal which governs each member of the in-group, leading to the notion of the 'We-Image' rather than the 'I' image. Each member is therefore dependent on the others to create a harmonious society and maintain harmony. Under such a cultural establishment, social hierarchy is unavoidable or, to say it another way, is the by-product of the cultural establishment in question. Within such a cultural framework, people with disabilities are taken as the 'weak' members that need to be taken care of and protected. Growing up with such public images, where *disablement is understood as care*, people with blindness accept the limited occupational choices as *a form of care*, and with the help of other members of the society seek solace and solution. This inclination to live in harmony with the 'disabling'[22] environment, rather than moulding the established environment to fit personal needs and agenda, is specific to collectivism.

Even so, we have seen that people that we had met and interacted with, at least within our social circles, seemed to have reached the adjustment stage and found ways to meet their needs and despite the lack of eyesight accept themselves as an adequate person. We have observed that the 'marginalizing constructs are subverted and reconceived in terms of identity, pride and new epistemology' (Bolt, 2015, 141). Blindness, in their journey, was initially regarded as an unpleasant reality that should be recognized, accepted, and therefore adjusted to, like other realities. The adjustment journey, in particular for those massage therapists with blindness, was aided and thus sustained by the spiritual strength which comes from the Islamic practice of 'bersyukur' as well as the new spiritual take on and/or perspectives on disability. Such spiritual strength functions as a new form of personal power which helps massage therapists with blindness psychologically and spiritually transcend their loss of eyesight and enable them to embrace blindness as part of their identity and thus navigate the God-given 'period' for spiritual growth (Erlina, 2020; Idler and Kasl, 1997). The first author visited the married couple again in 2022, when she noticed changes inside the parlour; the waiting room now had more displayed certificates (which showed that they have upgraded their massage skills) and a variety of offers and pamphlets with a different price range. They have also started, with the help of their children, advertising their services through online platforms. They, aided by the helpful perspective and spirituality, have acknowledged, accepted, and transcended their blindness, and thus proved that people with blindness are not 'powerless in the matrix of power and control that regularly targets and disempowers them' (Erlina, 2020, 200).

Concluding Discussion: The Paradox

In this chapter, autoethnographic insights shed light on the paradoxicality of barriers to employment within the Indonesian political landscape. The politicization of occupational opportunities reflects the enactment of assumed authority towards people with blindness and how such 'tradition' is culturally understood as part of the social system within the Indonesian collectivist society as a social hierarchy, where the agential ability of those at the bottom can be controlled by those at the top as a form of care. As members of a collectivist society who have studied and thus been exposed to disability studies, we have seen that such a 'tradition', though perceived as socially desirable, can function as an oppressive power, pushing people marked with a biological difference further into the margins. At the same time, we have also found that throughout their journey, people with blindness rely on their spiritual beliefs and practices which, as this chapter suggests, serve as internal powers that enable each individual with blindness to adapt to changed circumstances, accept their loss, embrace blindness as part of their identity, and live a happy life. In the end, these autoethnographic insights suggest that blindness, in the Indonesian context, is not always associated with unhappiness, which contradicts research findings in other cultural contexts, where, as projected in a variety of literary works (Leduc, 2020; Sunderland et al., 2009), disability is synonymous with unhappiness.

Notes

1 The blind is guiding the blind.
2 The last two were new additions and were not available when the second author studied at the institution in question.
3 In 1997 due to gradual retinal detachment developed caused by the accident in 1988.
4 The second author enrolled and lived in rehabilitation institution and studied at a nearby integrated school.
5 In 1999, textbooks in Braille format and computer-assisted technologies were rare, if not almost non-existent in integrated schools. Those were only available in special schools and rehabilitation institutions.
6 Teachers were kind and helpful; however, their lack of knowledge and inclusive pedagogy training prevented them to practice inclusive pedagogy.
7 The volunteers served as 'paid' voluntarily assistive readers, reading non-Braille textbooks for students with blindness.
8 Yayasan Mitra Netra provides training and advocacy for the rights of people with blindness.
9 This is one of many interactions that the second author experienced.
10 Muharam is blind and owns a YouTube video channel that shares inspiring stories of people with visual impairments and blindness.
11 Based on the ILO, only 5% of people with disabilities classified as high skilled and/or having university degrees.
12 There has not been any data about this, but this study suggests that employment of people with blindness in government sector in the capital city of Indonesia, Jakarta, is approximately 1%.

13 The first author was a social worker for an NGO before deciding to become a disability researcher and an academic.
14 Massage parlours and beauty and Spa parlours managed and operationalized by people with blindness.
15 Tunanetra is an Indonesian term for people with blindness, the gloss translation is without eyesight.
16 The second author stayed and spent 3.5 years at this residential school.
17 Gratitude, gratefulness.
18 DPP Pertuni is an association developed to support and advocate for the rights of people with blindness.
19 Indonesian's preference for harmony contributes to the extensive use of euphemism.
20 Supercrip stories are those where characters with disabilities are portrayed as a hero and thus against the odds overcome his/her disabilities.
21 With the advacement of technology, Indonesian disability activists and scholars have tried to put blindness as in a different spotlight through different YouTube Channels.
22 We use this word 'disabling' as we are not sure people experiencing this see this as disabling.

References

Bolt, D. (2015) Not forgetting happiness: The tripartite model of disability and its application in literary criticism. *Disability and Society* 30 (7): 1103–1117.

Bolt, D. (2016) *The Metanarrative of Blindness*, Ann Arbor, MI: University of Michigan.

Brebahama, A. and Listyandini, R. A. (2016) Gambaran Tingkat Kesejahteraan Psikologis Penyandang Tunanetra Dewasa Muda. *Jurmal Mediapsi*, 1–10.

*BRSPDSN Wyata Guna Bandung. (2022) *Sejarah*, Bandung: s.n.

Cattaneo, Z. and Vecchi, T. (2011) *Blind Vision: The Neuroscience of Visual Impairment*, London: The MIT Press.

Claassens, L. J., Shaikh, S. and Swartz, L. (2018) Engaging disability and religion in the global South, in B. Watermeyer and L. Swartz (eds.) *The Palgrave Handbook of Disability and Citizenship in the Global South*, Charn: Palgrave Macmillan.

Collignon, O. and Volder, A. G. D. (2009) Further evidence that congenitally blind participants reacts faster to auditory tactile spatial targets. *Canadian Journal of Experimental Psychology* 63 (4): 287–293.

Collignon, O., Voss, P., Lassonde, M. L. and Lepore, F. (2009) Cross modal plasticity for the spatial processing of sounds in visually deprived subjects. *Experimental Brain Research*, 192 (3): 342–358.

Collignon, O. et al. (2006) Improved selective and divided spatial attention in early blind subjects. *Brain Research* 1075 (1): 175–182.

Das, V. and Addlakha, R. (2007) Disability and domestic citizenship: Voice, gender, and the making of the subject, in B. Ingstad and S. R. Whyte (eds.) *Disability in Local and Global Worlds*, Berkeley: University of California Press.

Effendi, T., Suyudi, I. and Ali, A. (2021) EFL vision impaired teacher's classroom management in the eyes of his teenaged, sighted students. *TESOL International Journal* 16 (1): 73–101.

Erlina, E. (2020) *Open research ANU Library* [online]. Available from: https://openresearch-repository.anu.edu.au/handle/1885/212365 [accessed 28 June 2022].

Fetterman, D. (2010) *Ethnography: Step-by-Step 3rd Ed*, London: Sage.

Fikriyyah, W. R. and Fitria, M. (2015) Adversity Quotient Mahasiswa Tunanetra. *Jurnal Psikologi Tabularasa* 10 (1): 115–128.

Gunawan, T. and Halim, G. M. (2020) *Rapid Assessment on Employment for Persons With Disabilities in Indonesia*, Jakarta: International Labour Organization.

Habsyiyah, H., Lestari, Y. D., Ariawan, I. and Gondhowiardjo, T. D. (2015) Relationship of Socio-economic factors with vision-related quality of life on severe low vision and blind population in Indonesia. *Medical Journal of Indonesia* 24 (4): 245–251.

Harimukthi, M. T. and Dewi, K. S. (2014) Eksplorasi Kesejahteraan Psikologis Individu Dewasa Awal Penyandang Tunanetra. *Jurnal Psikologi Undip* 13 (1): 64–77.

Hasnain, R., Queijo, J., Laher, S. and Sandahl, C. (2019) Islam, leprosy and disability: How religion, history, art, and storytelling can yield new insights and acceptance. *Societies* 10 (6): 1–17.

Hidayatullah, F. and Noer, K. U. (2021) Implementasi kebijakan rekrutmen tenaga kerja disabilitas tunanetra di BUMD DKI Jakarta. *Delega Lata Jurnal Ilmu Hukum* 6 (2): 406–422.

Hofstede, G., Hofstede, G. J. and Minkov, M. (2010) *Cultures and Organization, Software of the Mind: Intercultural Cooperation and Its Importance for Survival*, New York: McGraw Hill.

Idler, E. L. and Kasl, S. V. (1997) Religion among disabled and non-disabled persons II: Attendance at religious services as a predictor of the course of disability. *The Journal of Gerontology* 52B (6): 306–316.

International Labor Organization (ILO). (2022) *International Labour Organization* [online]. Available from: www.ilo.org/wcmsp5/groups/public/–asia/–ro-bangkok/–ilo-jakarta/documents/publication/wcms_233426.pdf [accessed 15 March 2022].

Johnstone, B., Glass, B. A. and Oliver, R. E. (2007) Religion and disability: Clinical, research and training considerations for rehabilitation professionals. *Disability and Rehabilitation* 29 (15): 1153–1163.

Kustini, E. and Dianti, R. (2020) Pemenuhan Hak Aparatur Sipil Negara (ASN) Penyandang Disabilitas di Pemerintah Provinsi DKI Jakarta. *Jurnal Ilmiah Manajemen Forkamma* 4 (1): 24–36.

Lakoff, G. and Johnsen, M. (2003) *Metaphors We Live by*, London: The University of Chicago Press.

Leduc, A. (2020) *Disfigured: On Fairy Tales, Disability, and Making Space*, Toronto: Couch House Books.

Lim, L. L. (2009) The influences of harmony motives and implicit beliefs on conflict styles of the collectivist. *International Journal of Psychology* 44 (6): 401–409.

McKnight, L. and Whitburn, B. (2017) The fetish of the lens: Persistent sexist and ableist metaphor in education research. *International Journal of Qualitative Studies in Education* 30 (9): 1–9.

*Muharam, D. P. (2020) *Tiga tahun dicuekin Guru Matematika, Pemuda Tunanetra ini dapat lulus dari Unair dengan Bangga*, Surabaya: YouTube.

O'reilly, K. (2012) *Ethnographic Methods 2 Ed*, New York: Routledge.

Otieno, P. A. (2009) Biblical and theological perspectives on disability: Implications on the Rights of persons with disability in Kenya. *Disability Studies Quarterly* 29 (4).

Palan, R. (2021) "I seriously wanted to opt for science, but they said no": Visual impairment and higher education in India. *Disability and Society* 36 (2): 1–24.

Schmiesing, A. (2014) *Disability, Deformity, and Disease in the Grimms' Fairy Tales*, Detroit: Wayne State University Press.

Selway, D. and Ashman, A. F. (1998) Disability, religion and health: A literature review in search of the spiritual dimension of disability. *Disability and Society* 13 (3): 429–439.

Silva, C. F. and Howe, P. D. (2012) The (in)validity of supercrip representation of Paralympian Athletes. *Journal of Sport and Social Science*, 174–179.

Sunderland, N., Catalano, T. and Kendall, E. (2009) Missing discourses: Concepts of joy and happiness in disability. *Disability and Society* 24 (6): 703–714.

Vash, C. L. and Crewe, N. M. (2004) *Psychology of Disability 2nd Ed*, New York: Springer Publishing Company.

10

ENCOUNTERING THE MYTH, TRANSFORMING UTOPIAN REALITIES OF BLINDNESS

Counter Narrative Notes on Intersectional Interdependence and Critical Hermeneutics

Alexis Padilla

Preliminary Discussion: The Futurity and Mythology of Intersectional Disability Journeys

I write this chapter as a blind, diasporic global south Latinx critical race, critical ableism and intersectional decoloniality scholar. My purpose is to reflect axiologically and ontologically on the epistemological processes which made possible my transit through two stations of blindness, both of which connect to the same blind figure. I have opted to call this male figure Ricardo Torralba (R.T.). Like me, R.T. was a Venezuelan lawyer; the first blind lawyer to graduate from my alma mater in the early 1970s. He was one of the first blind lawyers to graduate from a public Venezuelan university which made him into a sort of mythical, almost messianic role model within the first identitarian station I describe in the chapter.

Thematically speaking, the chapter as a whole is about forging a critical hermeneutics analysis (Roberge, 2011) of futurity and mythology in the making and re-making of intersectional disability identitarian spaces of becoming. I engage in the myth/mythology (Barthes, 1972) and the evolving identitarian reality of my personal encounter with R.T. in the mid-1980s in Caracas, Venezuela, during a research engagement.

At another level, the chapter is about what I am opting to call moral decoloniality. This nomenclature emerges in dialogue with thinkers who, like Maldonado-Torres (2007; see also, Mignolo and Tlostanova, 2006) talk of three enactments of coloniality in action: power, knowledge, and being. For me, there needs to be a fourth dimension. This fourth dimension consists of existential features which expose the coloniality of morals or broader axiological modes of coloniality (e.g. Fanon, 1965, 1967, 2004; Memmi, 1991; Memmi and Roditi, 1992, notwithstanding the fact that both Fanon and Memmi frame these existential features

DOI: 10.4324/9781003275060-13

within psychoanalytical theoretical clothing which often hides their underlying moral relationality connotations).

I Rely on the critical hermeneutics and decolonial ethos of what I call elsewhere LatDisCrit's radical exteriority which centres on the identitarian dimensions intrinsic to extreme forms of alterity (Padilla, 2021a; see also Vallega, 2014). I thus use this chapter as a critical space to interrogate embodied modes of independence and interdependence. I regard these spaces as intersectional cross–coalitional constructs which get built through the transimmanence (Nancy, 1992, 1993, 2000, 2008). Here otherness works as the source for identitarian and justice seeking collective action. It awakens vocations and opens emancipatory relationality avenues of anti-ableist struggle across global north and global south contexts.

Before articulating the counterstories which constitute the two cultural stations of blindness at the heart of the chapter, I dive into the relational theory and epistemology of what Jean-Luc Nancy calls transimmanence as a horizontal open space of axiological and ontological futurity in the making. I use this examination as an existential interrogation of the dichotomy of dependence versus interdependence in justice-seeking anti-ableist movement building. While I emphasise in my foregoing discussion global south contextual features due to the counter-narrative specificity of the present chapter, my aim is to plant a seed for critical reflexive engagements applicable to global north disability justice contexts of relational, grassroots movement building as well (Obourn, 2020; Piepzna-Samarasinha, 2018). I thus conclude the chapter with reflections which emphasise decolonising moral/axiological spaces of intersectional agency in anti-ableist justice dreaming and enacting.

The time sequence of my identitarian examination of transimmanent futurity is worth elevating. In this chapter, I am traveling to the past to unearth the epistemological contours of disability justice dreams in their complex moral and identitarian relationality. As such, I pursue an important intersectional disability agency quest, whose decolonial intersectionality critical hermeneutics reaches into anti-oppressive resistance spheres of race, masculine configurations, and class. I privilege in this chapter representational memories which most likely derive from a sense of congruency with the horizontality of the present in its current nonlinear sense of identitarian becoming. Hence, this quest's potential for revolutionary significance in the theorising of anti-ableist resistance is not entirely disconnected from existentially informed psychoanalytical musings (and although Marcuse, 1948 rejects in his early writings Sartre's existential philosophy as essentially ideological in its distortion of Hegel, some of Marcuse's own psychoanalytical reflections are perhaps in order here; see, e.g. Marcuse et al., 2017).

Part of the issue which I am convinced gets exacerbated by the normalising pressures experienced by folks with disabilities, especially in global south contexts, is the uncertainty of any kind of futurity. This is so whether one analyses it individually or at the level of collective action.

For thinkers like Derrida, the future is absolute uncertainty. This is congruent with Derrida's view of transcendence, a view which Stoker and Van der Merwe

(2012) describe in terms of immanent transcendence, that is, as an approximation to the unknown, to otherness, which we attempt individually and collectively only through our own inherent and ineluctable sense of immanence. Derrida (1992, 78) indicates that transcendence encompasses 'every other (in the sense of each other) is every bit other (absolutely other)'. This is a philosophical position which impacts not only his perspective on the future but also his view of relationality as fundamentally othered and othering on the basis of our immanent experiencing of radical uncertainty. 'The future as the unknown (l'avenir) is described by Derrida in such a way that the transcendent nature of it cannot be escaped – this future is 'impossible to figure' . . . it is the arrival of the unexpected, it is absolute. L'avenir is hyper-transcendence – totally beyond our grasp' (Verhoef, 2016, 6; see also Derrida, 2005; Martinon, 2007).

In contrast to Derrida, there are post-metaphysical philosophers like Gilles Deleuze who prefer to do away with transcendence altogether. Deleuze dwells on radical or pure immanence. For him, 'only when immanence is immanent to nothing except itself, can we speak of a plane of immanence . . . it is exactly this 'pure immanence which allows one to be creatively ethical' (Verhoef, 2016, 4, 2013). Ironically, pure immanence operates in Deleuze's philosophy as transcendence. It is essentially foundational. There is 'only a plane of immanence . . . which can be understood as a type of transcendence. . . . The point here is that the ethical creates a question with regard to transcendence, and vice versa, so that as long as we ask ethical questions, transcendence cannot be ignored in our post-metaphysical era' (Verhoef, 2016, 4–5). Since the quest for disability justice is fundamentally ethical, we are back to a terrain of transcendence.

Regarding futurity, however, philosophers like Catharine Malabou complicate the matter further by stressing that the future is malleable, transformable, and already figured and refigured. A key concept in Malabou's non-messianic understanding of futurity is plasticity which has a double meaning. 'Plasticity has the double meaning of what is susceptible to receive form, like clay or marble, and also to be able to bestow form, to give form, as we can hear in the expressions of plastic arts or plastic surgery. Plasticity also characterises what is about to explode' (Malabou, 2014, 211; see also, Crockett, 2010). Transcendence is thus totally rejected by Malabou. Time gets radically circumscribed within the biological. It has 'no outside, no transcendence, breaches, or holes' (Verhoef, 2016, 9).

Nancy's concept of Transimmanence provides the only way to bridge these radical positions on the ethics of futurity. This is especially so in the horizontal relationality of collective action such as the one would expect to observe in the movement building dynamicity of anti-ableist struggles. For Nancy, immanence and transcendence are both inadequate to help us understand existence and our being in this world. Existence expresses multiple textures, movements and relations in this world as an 'absolute immanence' – 'a world joins, plays, speaks and shares: this is its sense' (Nancy, 1997, 78). This 'absolute immanence' is not a simple dichotomy immanence against transcendence. It is the core existential expression of transimmanence. Transimmanence is not about a tension or balance between the world (immanence) and its 'outside' (transcendence), but it is 'absolutely imma-nent'. It unfolds within and through the tensions and relations among modes of being and existing in the world. It constitutes what Verhoef (2016, 10) calls an open-immanence:

> Nancy recognises an 'outside of the world' (that there is something more than the world and that it might get its sense from it), but in transimmanence he locates this in 'the inside' of human experiences. Our experiences of the world, where otherness prompts a will to posit a transcendent outside, are for Nancy really nothing more than 'the extension of the world, with no possi-ble appeal to another world'. . . . Our experience that 'the sense of the world must lie outside the world' . . . should be understood as an 'outside within' . . . the experience that the world might have or be something more, that its meaning can be found from outside it, or this 'outsideness of the world', should be understood as the inside of this world. The outside is found within the world because the world 'is lacking exteriority' and only has sense which 'circulates in the exposure of singular beings' . . . Nancy suggests that the world has really 'no present entities, only spacing of presences, always plural, always co-appearing, in co-existence'.
>
> *(Verhoef, 2016, 10)*

This radical horizontal relationality of an existential 'outside within' is similar to and explainable through Nancy's understanding of human bodies. Bodies have for Nancy their 'outside in . . . ways of opening out toward a sharing with other mov-ing and weighing bodies' Taylor, 2015, 116). Nancy speaks therefore not of bodies, but of corpuses. Corpuses relate within an 'ontological materiality' (Nancy, 1993, 103). Our sense of 'outside this world' is thus not denied. Rather, it is understood as part of how this world is 'within', that is, continually taking place, joining, shar-ing, playing, circulating between one another's corpuses, cutting across in being-with in an intrinsic ethical relationality. This 'outside' is not something to which we cross over . . . but rather is something to which we are unceasingly exposed in our existence with others 'in this world' (immanence) where meaning circulates (cuts across, trans-). Transimmanence captures this . . . 'outside within' (Verhoef, 2016, 10).

Transimmanence, on the other hand, recreates the tension between its 'outside within'. This operates via the unceasing opening of existence to itself and its con-gealing into presences that are 'immanent and enclosed, self-constituted' (Nancy, 2000, 72). In this tension, 'closed immanence', consisting of the interior of being gets determined in relation to an exteriority, a transcendent source of meaning, and 'open immanence', which consists of a 'totality of infinite relationships without exteriority' (Hutchens, 2005, 167).

The latter point is of vital importance for the purposes of this chapter. It gives to Nancy's relational ethics of transimmanent futurity and horizontality a sense in which both dependence and interdependence get transimmanently fused, intrinsically tied to our relational sense of dynamic becoming. In other words, it morphs into continuous identitarian making and re-making, regardless of purely sociocultural, socio-political, or contextual factors.

Encountering and Internalising the Myth: Experiencing Blindness as Transimmanent Relationality

The experience of blindness can best be defined poetically, that is, in the manner rendered by Kuusisto (2000):

> No Name for It
> Start with a hyphenated word, something Swedish –
> Rus-blind; 'blind drunk'; blinda-fläcken; 'blind spot';
> Blind-pipa; 'nonentity', 'a type of ghost'.

On this front, contextual dimensions, although tangible, are certainly of lesser significance (Healey and Michalko, 2021). This is the kind of inexpressible aspect I want to capture and underscore when I talk of existential becoming in the configuration of identitarian selfhood.

This configuration of selfhood is never ending, always dynamic. Therefore, one could not assert that the existential nature of blindness is universal. Quite on the contrary, its textured uniqueness is the most important part, especially as a relational expression of the processing of one's contextuality as a blind subject who continuously becomes.

In my case, this context was primarily rural. The rural texture in global south contexts is multifaceted. It is definitely hard to compare it to rural organising spaces and ways of being in global north contexts, apart from superficial similarities in scarce populations and the like.

I grew up with my grandparents, despite having spent a good deal of my childhood trapped in the cold institutional governmentality (Joseph, 2018; Lemke, 2019; Walters, 2018) of a boarding school for the blind. Guided by what Coles et al. (2021) call fugitivity, I am convinced that the existential experiencing of these institutional spaces tends to be much more of a 'going through the motions' kind of affairs. 'Not restricted to literal flight from slavery, fugitivity belongs to what philosopher and poet Fred Moten . . . describes as a capacious category of the irregular in which freedom and unfreedom perpetually coexist in persons who refuse to be objectified or reduced' (Feldman, 2021). Hence, fugitivity operates as a protective shield for some sanity in the ultimate configuration of one's sense of selfhood.

To be sure, institutionalised spaces of confinement indeed have identitarian implications. However, these implications are suspended, so-to-speak, until the ultimate configurations start taking shape in their internal existential synergy of things like decolonial intersectional agency, radical solidarity, and so on (Padilla, 2021a, chs. 1 and 6, Forthcoming, 2022).

This half narrative, half conceptual interjection underscores a crucial fact. My grandfather was, for me, the only masculine role model relationally significant to be considered as such during those childhood days. José Amador Zambrano Méndez, the son of José Maria Zambrano (hereafter, el Nono, the way we called our grandfather in the region of the country where I grew up), was born in Guaraque, Mérida state, Venezuela during the second decade of the twentieth century.

El Nono was a rustic character who had never gone to school. He was illiterate, despite being very proficient with numbers and business transactions. At some point, he had owned a covey producing little 'finca' (the meaning of this word has no precise equivalent in English, being an intermediate category in the spectrum from Coffey 'haciendas' [large estates with numerous paid and often unpaid workers] and 'conucos' survival level pieces of land, often not even owned but held in a sharecrop arrangement). Nevertheless, by the time I was growing up, el Nono's main occupation was 'sobandero' (the name given in Colombia and Venezuela to a sort of rural version of physical therapist who fixes bone fractures when folks are kicked by horses and the like).

As a matter of fact, during those days, el Nono tried initiating me in the art of becoming sobandero. Likewise, he tried teaching me complex rosary prayer structures to earn a living in 'velorios' (funeral rituals where the dead body was accompanied by folks from adjacent areas and family members) and 'novenarios' (nine night prayer rituals which followed immediately after somebody's death as well as their six month and anniversary commemorations). El Nono was convinced that, as a blind man, those were the only kinds of niches open for me to earn a living without spending my life begging, the destiny of most blind folks in those rural areas.

Even as a child, I felt intuitively that those were not things I aspired to, but, understandably, with adolescence and exposure to what I thought at the time were political maturation dynamics (Padilla, 2021a, ch. 7), that intuitional feeling turned into a strong moral aversion which in turn meant a significant relational disruption, a crossroads turning point in the directionality of my becoming. This was not so much operational at the affective level. It was an existential rupture or transgressiveness towards the traditional ways of el Nono. Yet, it was charged with normalising, morally inflamed overtones in the relational way that Valdivia (2017, n.p.) attributes to utopia. Identitarian modes of utopia can fluctuate between being either no place or a good place. Its relativity is relationally determined and always unfolding, perpetually dynamic.

It was under this existential search for directionality that I came in contact with the myth of R.T. This happened in the absence of other relationally relevant blind role models. I entered the boarding school for the blind in 1969. By the time I was a teenager, it had not produced blind college graduates.

R.T.'s story first came up during the Saturdays I served as a volunteer tutor for a middle-class girl in high school. Her mother kept telling me about this extraordinary blind man in her hometown who did this or that (mostly anecdotal incidents which corroborated their generalised belief that blind folks compensate their lack of sight with unique giftedness talents; see, Padilla, 2021b). A few years later, during my relational journey within an evangelical church in the same town, R.T.'s mythical figure came up again. This time there were details on how American missionaries had acquainted R.T. with braille through bible reading and the like, infusing a profoundly moral ethos of a 'holy man' into this blind figure who started acquiring utopian contours, very much in the omniscient way blindness gets represented in Silvio Rodríguez's song:

> And you go by touching
> The coldness with a soft silence.
> Blind man, I sentence you
> To name everything I don't know now!
> (Rodríguez, 2016, my translation)

Moral Demystifying or Anti-Ableist Decolonial Transimmanence?: On the Subaltern Intersectionality Contours of Disability Identity Journeys

R.T.'s myth contrasted with the sort of blind folks I had met throughout childhood. None of those folks I interacted with first hand ever went to college. Their moral lives were either unknown to me or covered with gossip, in the manner that proximity in relationality often disqualifies potential role models embedded in our own context.

El Nono himself was one of these extraordinary moral figures, although I was blocked from grasping those relational epiphanies at the time. Reflecting on his axiology, I now remember how he was always proud that in his private space, nothing would get lost. This is something he loved to convey to the many folks who kept coming and going through their place. Furthermore, there was at el Nono's environment an aura of absolute openness and hospitality towards folks who in many other contexts would be regarded as undesirable: the drunk, the poor, the disabled.

Therefore, in the 1980s, when I arrived at Caracas for my National Congress Archives undergraduate research, I did not imagine I would run into R.T. in his fleshly habitus (Bourdieu, 1977; Ferreira, 2008), demystified from his artificial moral coat as portrayed by sighted folks from his hometown. I stayed at the Venezuelan Blind Society. Although the organisational contours of the society were rather mysterious, their run-down building from the 1950s seemed to be well-known. It was under the control of an older blind man who seemed to run everything singlehandedly. I cannot even remember the name of this individual who was at the time so crucial to our livelihood.

Rooms were dusty. The atmosphere surrounding the area was frightening. I remember one day when a taxi driver refused to take me to the building. It was after 6:00 PM and it would soon get dark. It was simply too risky. Thus, finding R.T. under such circumstances was more than unexpected.

R.T. was a regular blind fellow. He was aging at the time and had his legal office right there, next to his bedroom in a space that faced the street. In the months I spent there, it did not seem that many clients used his legal services. At night and on weekends, heavy drinking was a common event. Joy did not abound. Nevertheless, this somehow had become a demystified home for R.T.

Concluding Discussion: The Transimmanent Tackling of Normalcy Ideologies and Radical Solidarity Quests

The relational journey of interdependence which mediates the two identitarian stations described in this chapter was nonlinear. However, I feel that the horizontal existential becoming it involved can best be captured through the idea of transformational transimmanence. Both el Nono and R.T. were morally heroic in their own yet tremendously differentiated ways. Both were impacting my identitarian sense of becoming. Even if R.T. never articulated political or religious statements of the sort attributed to him by the sighted people of his hometown, he was a survivor, a blind guy in the making, a disabled combat agent against the plight of material precarity, normalcy impositions, and much more. El Nono did enact radically and clearly these moral imperatives. Some of them, although charged with ableist contours, were profoundly caring and ethically transformational. They were part of his moral legacy which, unknowingly, was preparing me for the sort of material precarity and anti-ableist struggles R.T. had to endure in Caracas and wherever he ended up going afterwords.

My identitarian experience of blindness was certainly altered by encountering the myth. It was an enfleshment epiphany of sorts.

It is ironic that I have to assert emphatically the obvious: there was nothing wrong with R.T.'s moral standing. Without fully understanding it, I was then able to touch it, to feel it in its real disabling contours, replete with misery as well as possibilitarian cries for disability justice.

I thus started to realise that normalcy ideologies are pervasive. They colonise our own sense of morality. They create mythically idealised embodiments of disability, even for those of us who live under the existential reality of pan-disability.

In the case of blindness, their pervasive constructs get filtered through the ableist lens of ocularnormativism (Bolt, 2014). In other words, sighted people tell us what blindness 'success' should be like, setting up an alienating identitarian sense of verticality. This, in turn, places ocularnormative representations on top of everything.

For disabled people of colour, the intersectional contours of this moral coloniality process get even more complex. Through supremacist ideologies, one's own roots are experienced as foreign. True, there are important manifestations of ableism in that utopian process of becoming. This is what forms our own dialectical intersectionality. Hence, percolating its poisoning elements of dialectical oppression needs to be part of our world within.

As Nancy would probably say, this is our transimmanent testing and tasting of existential limits. Yet, only this world within will help us reach out towards possibilitarian modes of relational solidarity and interdependence. This is what helps us as intersectional beings to go beyond the confines of our circumscribed conflation of roots and wings. From there, a more authentic sense of collective action and movement building is likely to emerge, critically informing our own emancipatory learning as well as that of other partnering decolonial sojourners.

References

Barthes, R. (1972) Myth as a semiological system, in R. Barthes (ed.) *Mythologies*, A. Layers, New York: Hill and Wang.

Bolt, D. (2014) *The Metanarrative of Blindness: A Re-Reading of Twentieth-Century Anglophone Writing*, Ann Arbor: University of Michigan Press.

Bourdieu, P. (1977) *Outline of Theory and Practice*, Cambridge: Cambridge University Press.

Coles, J. A., Ohito, E. O., Green, K. L. and Lyiscott, J. (2021) Fugitivity and abolition in educational research and practice: An offering. *Equity & Excellence in Education* 54 (2): 103–111.

Crockett, C. (2010) Foreword, in C. Malabou (ed.) *Plasticity at the Dusk of Writing: Dialectic, Destruction, Deconstruction*, New York: Columbia University Press.

Derrida, J. (1992) The force of law: 'The mystical foundation of authority', in D. Cornell, M. Rosenfeld, and D. G. Carlson (eds.) *Deconstruction and the Possibility of Justice*, London: Routledge.

Derrida, J. (2005) Screenplay, in K. Dick and A. Z. Kofman (eds.) *Derrida: Screenplay and Essays on the Film*, New York: Routledge.

Fanon, F. (1965) *Studies in Dying Colonialism*, trans. H. Chevalier, New York: Grove.

Fanon, F. (1967) *Black Skin, White Masks*, trans. C. L. Markmann, New York: Grove.

Fanon, F. (2004) *The Wretched of the Earth*, trans. R. Philcox, New York: Grove.

Feldman, M. (2021) Fugitive voice. *Representations* 154 (1): 10–22.

Ferreira, M. A. (2008) La Construcción Social de la Discapacidad: Habitus, Estereotipos y Exclusión Social. *Nómadas: Critical Journal of Social and Juridical Sciences* 17 (1): 1–33.

Healey, D. and Michalko, R. (2021) Meaning, feeling, and feel, in D. Bolt (ed.) *Metanarratives of Disability: Culture, Assumed Authority, and the Normative Social Order*, New York: Routledge.

Hutchens, B. C. (2005) *Jean-Luc Nancy and the Future of Philosophy*, Montreal: McGill-Queen's University Press.

Joseph, J. (2018) *Varieties of Resilience: Studies in Governmentality*, New York: Cambridge University Press.

Kuusisto, S. (2000) *Blind Days in Early Youth, in Only Bread, Only Light*, Port Townsend: Copper Canyon Press.

Lemke, T. (2019) *Foucault's Analysis of Modern Governmentality: A Critique of Political Reason*, London: Verso.

Malabou, C. (2014) The future of Derrida. Time between epigenesis and epigenetics, in C. Crockett, B. K. Putt, and J. W. Robbins (eds.) *The Future of Continental Philosophy of Religion*, Bloomington: Indiana University Press.

Maldonado-Torres, N. (2007) On the coloniality of being: Contributions to the development of a concept. *Cultural Studies* 21 (2–3): 240–270.

Marcuse, H. (1948) Existentialism: Remarks on Jean-Paul Sartre's L'Etre et le Neant. *Philosophy and Phenomenological Research* 8 (3): 309–336.

Marcuse, H., Kellner, D. and Pierce, C. (2017) *Philosophy, Psychoanalysis and Emancipation: Collected Papers of Herbert Marcuse Volume 5*, New York: Routledge.

Martinon, J. P. (2007) *On Futurity: Malabou, Nancy and Derrida*, New York: Palgrave Macmillan.

Memmi, A. (1991) *The Colonizer and the Colonized*, trans. H. Greenfeld, Boston: Beacon Press.

Memmi, A. and Roditi, E. (1992) *The Pillar of Salt*, Boston: Beacon Press.

Mignolo, W. D. and Tlostanova, M. (2006) Theorizing from the borders. Shifting to geo- and body-politics of knowledge. *European Journal of Social Theory* 9 (2): 205–221.

Nancy, J.-L. (1992) *Corpus*, trans. R. A. Rand, New York: Fordham University Press.

Nancy, J.-L. (1993) *The Experience of Freedom*, trans. B. McDonald, Stanford: Stanford University Press.

Nancy, J.-L. (1997) *The Sense of the World*, trans. J. S. Librett, Minneapolis: University of Minnesota Press.

Nancy, J.-L. (2000) *Being Singular Plural*, trans. A. E. O'Byrne and R. D. Richardson, Stanford: Stanford University Press.

Nancy, J.-L. (2008) *Noli Me Tangere: On the Raising of the Body*, trans. S. Cliff, P.-A. Brault, and M. Naas, New York: Fordham University Press.

Obourn, M. W. (2020) *Disabled Futures: A Framework for Radical Inclusion*, Philadelphia: Temple University Press.

Padilla, A. (2021a) *Disability, Intersectional Agency and Latinx Identity: Theorizing LatDisCrit Counterstories*, Abingdon: Routledge.

Padilla, A. (2021b) The metanarrative of blindness in the global South: A LatDisCrit Counterstory on the bittersweet mythology of blindness as giftedness, in D. Bolt (ed.) *Metanarratives of Disability: Culture, Assumed Authority, and the Normative Social Order*, New York: Routledge.

Padilla, A. (Forthcoming, 2022) LatDisCrit: Exploring Latinx Global South DisCrit reverberations as spaces toward emancipatory learning and radical solidarity, in S. A. Annamma, B. A. Ferri, and D. J. Connor (eds.) *DisCrit Expanded: Inquiries, Reverberations and Ruptures*, New York: Teachers College Press.

Piepzna-Samarasinha, L. L. (2018) *Care Work: Dreaming Disability Justice*, Vancouver: Arsenal Pulp Press.

Roberge, J. (2011) What is critical hermeneutics? *Thesis Eleven* 106 (1): 5–22.

Rodríguez, S. (composer, musical performer) (2016) *Como Esperando Abril*. Available from: www.youtube.com/watch?v=-P2gyG2b7Go [accessed 4 July 2022].

Stoker, W. and Van der Merwe, W. L. (Eds.). (2012) *Culture and Transcendence – A Typology of Transcendence*, Leuven: Peeters.

Taylor, M. L. (2015) Immanence, in P. Gratton and M.-E. Morin (eds.) *The Nancy Dictionary*, Edinburgh: Edinburgh University Press.

Valdivia, A. (2017) Implicit utopias and ambiguous Ethnics Latinidad and the representational promised land, in M. E. Cepeda (ed.) *The Routledge Companion to Latina/o Media*, New York: Routledge.

Vallega, A. A. (2014) *Latin American Philosophy: From Identity to Radical Exteriority*, Bloomington: Indiana University Press.

Verhoef, A. H. (2013) Embodied religion's radicalisation of immanence. *Acta Academica* 45: 173–194.

Verhoef, A. H. (2016) Transimmanence and the Im/possible relationship between eschatology and transcendence. *Religions* 7 (135): 1–15.

Walters, W. (2018) *Governmentality: Critical Encounters*, New York: Routledge.

11

CRIP GAZES

Eye Mutilations and the 'Biopolitics of Debilitation' in Lina Meruane and Nicole Kramm

Carlos Ayram and Marta Pascua Canelo

Preliminary Discussion: Chile Woke Up But Lost Its Eyes

The social revolt that began in Santiago de Chile on 18 October 2019 and extended during the period of confinement due to the global pandemic of COVID-19 is a historic milestone in the country since the end of the civil-military dictatorship's and return to democracy. Curiously, one of the slogans that circulated through the different marches called at Plaza Italia (renamed Plaza Dignidad/Dignity Square) and in the peripheral populations of Santiago was: *Chile woke up*. This awakening turned into a weapon of agency and denunciation, driven by a collective weariness of the neoliberal policies that have privatised life and concentrated economic privilege in an obscene 3% of the population.[1]

However, during this Chilean awakening, the Carabineros police force brutally repressed the social protest. For instance, 468 people suffered permanent eye damage caused by rubber bullets fired selectively. Among the eye victims of this extreme police action were Gustavo Gatica, Fabiola Campillay (current senator), Nelson Iturriaga, Carlos Vivanco, and Nicole Kramm. As Valverde Gefaell (2015, 16) observes, this fact can be considered reliable evidence of liberal necropolitics in which 'the excluded live dead in life or are left to die because they are not profitable'.[2] The slogan *Chile woke up* and metaphors about vision and wounded eyes gained relevance in a panorama of dissent vis-à-vis political agenda. The eyes of the citizenry were opened but were extinguished by police brutality sponsored by the neoliberal state. The bodies of the mutilated protesters were sentenced to disappear as witnesses of a scene of collective demand. These were not accidents; they were crimes against humanity.[3]

While there was an impact on institutional politics and democratic life, the revolt 'in addition to its political charge, has expressive, creative and deeply subjective dimensions' (Pleyers, 2022, 21). Political coalitions and performative actions

DOI: 10.4324/9781003275060-14

that expanded 'the repertoires of protest in public space' (Cortés, 2020) became present as bodies and gestures. In this political and activist scenario, we ask ourselves: how to reflect theoretically on these disabilities assigned by the police brutality of a neoliberal state? What answers does disability studies offer us to think about these excesses of state violence? What solutions do artists, intellectuals, and activists provide? How do artistic languages process these traumatic events instead of speaking for the victims to converse with them? What politically embodied answers emanate from those subjects who have been deprived of their right to look, submerged in the opacity of blindness?

This chapter analyses two cultural manifestations of this period of repression during the Chilean social revolt. Specifically, we are interested in pointing out how, because of the eye mutilations, the Chilean State engaged in a particular activity that has been called by Jasbir Puar 'biopolitics of debilitation'. Consequently, we turn to two different media – essay and photography – twinned by a central concern: how to portray the victims of eye mutilations in Chile in order, on the one hand, to make visible the different ethical, aesthetic, and political short-circuits generated by their representations and, on the other hand, to rehearse a crip gaze (for what it represents and who represents it). *Blind Zone* (2021) by Chilean writer Lina Meruane and the series *Victims of Ocular Trauma* (2019–2020) by Chilean photographer Nicole Kramm arise from two embodied experiences of visual disability, authorising the artists to reflect. First, the aim is to think about the insurrectionary possibilities of the crip gaze; second, in the responses to the political processes involved in the 'biopolitics of debilitation' (Puar, 2017); and third, in an ethical obligation that pursues 'disabling the hegemonic gaze' (Marín, 2020).[4]

We locate our critical and theoretical analysis in the field of disability studies and blind studies, epistemologies that have mainly been produced in the Anglo-Saxon context (Garland-Thomson, 2009; Michalko, 1998; Siebers, 2010; Bolt, 2014; McRuer, 2006, 2018; Kafer, 2013; Hammer, 2019; Healey, 2021). We consider, of course, a geopolitical variant for the provenance of the two Latin American cultural materials with which we work, invoking some interdisciplinary studies from critical biopolitics and racial studies (Puar, 2017) and decolonial thought (Meekosha, 2011). Specifically, we subscribe to Meekosha's approaches in considering that the problems of inequity, environmental justice, and recognition of civil rights are not the same in the global North as in the global South. This allows us to consider the different intersections of class, gender, or race that operate in the administration of disability in contexts traversed by war, imperialism, colonialism, civil-military dictatorships, and the crises of neoliberal capitalism in the global South.

While we are interested in sustaining a notion of disability as a culturally generative and radically political model, as Robert McRuer (2006) reminded us, we are also aware of the need to question the assignment of different types of disabilities amid police repression or a military occupation in countries of the global South, as it happens in Chile during the social revolt. This violent way of injuring certain bodies, of ocular mutilation, confronts us with a challenging paradigm of representation and agency contested by the embodied and subaltern experiences of those subjects who constantly live in these dangerous scenarios of extreme violence.

According to David T. Mitchell and Sharon L. Snyder (2015), disability, as a concept and paradigm, is inseparable in modernity from a planned political activity on bodies: biopolitics. From the approaches made by Michel Foucault when he warned that 'the old right to make die or to let live was replaced by the power to make live or to refuse to die' (1984, 167), biopolitics is understood as a form of power that originates a set of practices, decisions, and technologies that intervene in a specific way both in bodies and their biological functions and in collective life. To replace 'letting die' with 'making life', we will also have to ask ourselves who are, in the end, the lives that are worth preserving or that have a future. If we think of disabled lives, there is a complexity because disabled bodies are not invested in futurity. Some bodies must be standardised, segregated, or sterilised so that they do not disturb the course of normative life.

With the rise of neoliberalism, the relationship to disabled bodies changes in the name of inclusion and patriotism, what Mitchell and Snyder call 'Ablenatiolism' (i.e. select disabled bodies that can be included in nationalist agendas because they are more able than others). This model that continues to celebrate *ableism* as a particular way of making bodies productive entities – despite their limitations – offers a new way of accumulating knowledge about disability: 'Biopolitical identifications of dysfunctional bodies productively assist nations in improved understanding of all the bodies concerning the further embedding of universal norms of functionality, appearance, and capacity' (2015, 10).[5] Now, what happens with these designs in contexts of the global South where neoliberalism is a promise for better living but generates all kinds of damages and inequities that lead its citizens to live at permanent risk? What happens when biopolitics implies the attrition of some bodies so that others can live better?

We allow ourselves to work with two concepts deployed in this chapter. Each complicates the paradigm of disability: the biopolitics of debilitation (Puar, 2017) and what we refer to as the *crip gaze*. First, we invoke the suggestive concept developed by Jasbir Puar as an inflection to Eurocentric biopolitical theorisations. This illuminates how certain bodies are available to be injured under neoliberalism and military occupation so that others can live better lives. However, Puar complicates the disability rights paradigm as she critiques that it is a specific white collective that produces rights movements at the expense of the inequities suffered by racialised bodies in the global South and even endogamically in the global North. In her approach, the notions of debility and capacity become practical terms. On the one hand, there are disabled bodies more capable than others that are co-opted by national discourses, what Robert McRuer (2010) has termed 'crip nationalisms' or what Mitchell and Snyder call 'Ablenationalism'. On the other hand, there are bodies upon which a constant debilitation operates, leading them to submit to the ordinary work of living. Second, we are interested in asking ourselves about the particularities of a type of blindness provoked by the excessive police actions during the Chilean revolt, which undoubtedly and substantially modifies the coordinates of analysis and interpretation of both cultural stations in the light of theories of disability and blindness studies. Both *Blind Zone* by Lina Meruane and *Victims of Ocular Trauma* by Nicole Kramm offer possibilities of representation and, at the same time, critically and politically portray the victims of ocular trauma. It should also be noted that this portrait they offer somehow has its point of origin in the authors' visual impairment. While the writer Lina Meruane suffered an episode of temporary blindness due to her diabetes, the photographer Nicole Kramm was a victim of ocular trauma during the Chilean uprising. Hence, these embodied positions from which their work emerges make us think about the double insurrectionary condition of their gaze.

If Crip Theory emerges, as Robert McRuer points out, 'from cultural studies traditions that question the order of things' (2006, 2), we think that a crip gaze offers a way of subverting the normative and normalising frameworks that guide our way of looking at pain and violence. In dialogue with Karina Marin, in a certain way, the crip gaze 'disables the hegemonic gaze' to suspend its effect and power. On the other hand, it is a tactic that responds to the biopolitical undermining that operates on the body of the protesters. Echoing what McRuer and Kafer taught us about the negative charges associated with the word *crip*, we seek to recover both that painful sensation hidden in the insult and, at the same time, a political potency that allows us to register the world away from ocularcentric and ableist mandates. In our case, 'crip gaze' refers directly to the aesthetic response conjured up by the arts to contest the ocular mutilations resulting from the police repression to which we have referred. At the same time, this term, in turn, allows us to explore the embodied character manifested by the works produced by two authors who are themselves visually impaired and who bear, then, the stigma of crip corporealities subjected to the regulatory biopower of non-normative bodies.

In this case, we also notice that these disabled subjects' creative and artistic positioning presents a gender-variant that further complicates the construction conditions of this crip gaze. It is worth seeing that these are two artists who think and reject the procedures derived from a 'biopolitics of debilitation', as a policy executed by a neoliberal state in collaboration with the state's military forces. This gender marker is indispensable to think that those who question us are two women crossed by dictatorial and military violence: their writings and works account for these trajectories.

These 'crip gazes' are inscribed in the field of autocritical disability studies (Bolt, 2021). This critical stance is corroborated by the author Lina Meruane's own words when she acknowledges in an interview during the publication of her book: 'I have always been interested in that crossing between the visceral experience, that of the body, and the perhaps more distanced reflection' (Meruane in Sanz, 2022). Therefore, both authors' works develop a metanarrative of disability (Bolt, 2021) that emanates from their connection with disability and the 'biopolitics of debilitation' exercised by the Chilean state.

Blind Zone: 'Killing the Eye' by Lina Meruane or the Political Chronicle of an Ojicide

Blind zone [*Zona ciega*] (2021), by Chilean writer Lina Meruane, is a tripartite essay that summons a choral narrative of blindness. This particular interest in blindness is not trivial. It derives from the episode of temporary blindness the author experienced because of diabetic retinopathy, as she acknowledges in the book's second essay (2021, 60–61). Likewise, this event is also the basis of her autofictional novel *Sangre en el ojo* (2012), which managed to win the prestigious Sor Juana Inés de la Cruz prize for Latin American literature. Therefore, visual impairment is a subject that occupies the author due to her embodied eye disease experience. *Zona ciega* is a new entry in this autoethnographic journey.

The work, composed of the essays 'Matar el ojo', 'Ojos prestados', and 'Las casi ciegas', compiles a variety of notes and reflections derived from her personal link with blindness, as she acknowledges in the second text: 'That blood was an issue that I had been dragging for years. Years of procrastination. Years wanting to put in writing. A material that I was depositing in notebooks and loose papers' (2021, 61). The social revolt in Chile and the hundreds of ocular mutilations that took place served for Meruane to find a way to culminate this broad project of cultural and critical exploration of blindness because, as she states, 'there are forms of horror that summon the gaze' (2021, 47). Thus, writing a final text halfway between essay and political chronicle allowed her to bring closure to her personal and collective history of damaged eyes, whether for medical reasons or the war attacks mentioned earlier.

'Matar el ojo' begins, then, the journey of what we could call, using the author's term, an 'auto-eye-graphy' (2021, 90). This first essay connects with the chronicle of an ojicide directly related to the biopolitical practices that administer our societies and that turned their power against the thousands of demonstrators protesting in the streets of Chile since October 2019. This is how Meruane relates it: 'they began the chilling onslaught against the eyes. It was at the eyes where they were shooting with perfidious precision. . . . They were killing our eyes. Our eyes that were our power' (2021, 27).

As Foucault warned, states declare their right to control and govern life in modern societies. Today, in a West defined by the visual turn (Rodríguez de la Flor, 2009), being the culture of the image and the society of a thousand screens (Brea, 2007), the government of life is mainly equivalent to the control of the eyes. If the gazes of citizens rebel against the organs of power, states attack the eyes in an attempt at political domestication of lives and bodies. So, Meruane warns that 'a new repressive tactic was underway: the eye was not being made an occasional target, a serial ojicide was being executed' (2021, 34).

Hence, in a society governed by an ocularcentric sensory model (Jay, 2007), attacking the eyes and weakening or annulling the sense of sight becomes the most effective way to manage the social body of the citizenry. Having the power to decide who can and cannot see becomes an exercise to determine which subjects should participate in society and which are deprived of this capacity for agency. Moreover, according to Meruane, in the face of the brutal murders of the dictatorship, in democracy, 'piercing the eyesight could be declared as mere collateral damage and the act of leaving the victim alive could be said to be benevolent, even if it was a weakened and battered life' (2021, 36–37). According to Jasbir Puar, 'the purportedly humanitarian practice of sparing death by shooting to maim has its biopolitical stakes, not through the right to life, or even letting live, but rather through the logic of 'will not let die'. Both are part of the deliberate debilitation of a population . . . both are mobilized to make power visible on the body' (2017, 10).

Nevertheless, it is also interesting to highlight the situated and embodied character of the enunciation. Although the author usually resides in the United States and therefore writes the text from a place far from the social revolt, she insists on positioning herself as a subject qualified to narrate the horror of the ocular mutilations due to her condition as a victim of visual disability: 'I kept looking at everything from afar and doubting everything, even my eyes that did not see well since the ocular stroke that years before had almost left me blind. They were not mutilated eyes, mine, just damaged eyes. Remote eyes I could not trust; but who could trust his eyes' (2021, 25). In turn, she refers to the mediated condition of our society by the image culture and the screens through which we look at the world when she then adds: 'Our gazes were mediated either by touch screens or by smoke screens' (2021, 25).

Consequently, there are two aspects that we consider of vital importance for the narrative of blindness and crip gaze that Lina Meruane makes in 'Matar el ojo'. The author articulates her reflection both from her condition as a victim of ocular disease and, therefore, from her full awareness of the limitations and suffering that blindness entails, and from the biopolitical entity that ocular mutilation acquires. On the one hand, only the visually impaired subject can assume the competence to narrate ocular mutilations from her, his, or their embodied subjectivity. On the other hand, the biopolitics of debilitation – through provoked blindness – acquires imponderable credibility only in a society that bows to the omnipotence of sight. Hence, these two related conditions come together in the following highly enlightening sentence, where Meruane manifests both the projection of biopower over the mutilated bodies and eyes of the citizenry and the political transcendence of this event in an ocularcentric society presided over by the visual order and administered by that hegemony of sight:

> There are few things people value more than their eyes. . . . In the inventory of the most feared losses, citizens declare that losing their sight is just below death . . . given the choice of what to save, people choose the eye. Because in these times that celebrate the omnipotence of sight, that certify reality in the order of the visual, that privilege relations mediated by the image, that prioritize the organizing functions of the gaze, to blind an eye or two is much more than to kill it, it is to increase physical inequality, it is to make participation in society impossible.
>
> *(2021, 39–40)*

Victims of Ocular Trauma: Returning the Eyes Despite Everything

On 31 December 2019, the Chilean photographer and audiovisual filmmaker Nicole Kramm was injured in her left eye by a pellet fired by a Carabineros officer while marching with some colleagues to record the new year during the social revolt in Chile. Nicole joins a chorus of voices who also lost their eyes in the country and that demand justice and reparations for being victims of crimes against humanity sponsored by a neoliberal state. Karina Marin, referring to what has been happening in Chile, Colombia, and Ecuador since 2019, states that, in these scenarios, disability functions 'as a strategy to consolidate an ideology of normality' (2020, 141), which means that the bodies injured during these revolts are banished with impunity to the imaginary of the deformed and the *weird*.

Between 2019 and 2020, while it was difficult for Nicole to return to work, she undertook a photographic project entitled *Victims of Ocular Trauma [Víctimas de Trauma Ocular (VTO)]*, composed of 38 photographs, in which she recorded documents and observed – with a rebellious and a blinded eye – the routines, gestures, and repertoires of some of the people who suffered ocular mutilation during the revolt. Nicole returns to the shutter and insists on constructing testimonial scenes that can cover what the eyes of the nation refuse to see and recognise as part of its failure.

The photographs are potent documents, attentive records that do not skimp on discomfort. The victims appear as bodies that refuse to disappear. They exhibit their scars, the prostheses they wear, the ointments and gauze with which they clean their wounds, the X-rays of their eye traumas; sometimes, they point to the places where their eyes were taken away and remove the patches so that Nicole can capture with her camera the dignity that survives barbarism. In this case, Nicole Kramm deactivates the morbidity that guides the normative gaze on the one-eyed, the blind, and those who wear glass eyes. She confronts them with unusual eyes and a camera as a material representation device. Photography communicates individual pain, but it is unquestionable evidence of collective and historical trauma.

George Didi-Huberman evokes the work developed by Philip Bazine during his internship in a hospital, where he portrayed the dirty zone of the human aspect of the patients. From an 'artistic will' (Didi-Huberman, 2014, 32), Bazine recovers a parcel of humanity for those who, amid oppression, do not have the right to be figured: 'hence the need *to spend time to look better* and consider for oneself, to recognize the face of the other' (2014, 34). This act of recognition and resistance, this looking at the other as other, motivates Nicole Kramm aesthetically to pronounce herself against the violence exercised on the bodies of the demonstrators: it is not only organic damage that they received but an anguished bodily allocation for which no one takes responsibility. Nicole's camera takes time to look and continues to shutter despite the violence inscribed on her own body.

Under the monstrous look of neoliberalism, eyes that watch and punish, Nicole uses her crip gaze to develop a survival tactic. According to Susan Sontag, 'in a system based on the maximal reproduction and diffusion of images, witnessing requires the creation of star witnesses. Renowned for their bravery and zeal in procuring important, disturbing photographs' (2003, 27). But this exceptional witness, the war photographer, then has a glamour that Kramm rejects because her testimony does not account for the heroism of the eye but for her survival in a regime of terror. Her wounded body creatively and politically drives portraits that reveal the human aspect of the victims taken away by ocular injuries. Nicole's crip gaze, stemming from her exhaustion and pain, displaces photography's technical knowledge to manage an intimate space of reparation and visibility that is not contaminated by media anaesthesia.

Nicole refuses to disappear as an observer and witness from an embodied and situated character and activates an ethical dimension of photography that discourages the objectification of the bodies portrayed. Instead of statistics, histories, and diagnoses, in 'VTO', Nicole chooses to make these bodies, their pains, and shared histories, speak. For example, in photograph No. 13, on a white wall, someone draws an eye; to the left, the ocular silhouette is empty and, at the top of it, the silhouette loses contour and blurs: a suggestive and powerful metaphor about the process of decomposition of the gaze, which fades with the horror of violence. In image No. 31, a young man raises his face to the camera. His left eye is no longer there, but its material absence becomes a powerful interrogation device: the face stands up, challenges us, and accounts for this biopolitically assigned condition. This face never stops looking at us.

Nicole Kramm's photographs are nonconformist images that move away from what Robert McRuer has called 'Cripinspiration' (2018, 59; Kramm, 2019). 'VTO' is not offered as a representation of the triumph of bodies in the face of adversity. On the contrary, they are sharp, politically engaged images of other lives that matter. The photographs reveal a particular *ethos* that restores that condition denied by neoliberalism to lives that are not invested with a future. Although the photographs exhibit the marks of bodily debilitation, they insist on being defiant to the public gaze. There is a right exercised and enabled by Nicole Kramm so that those who do not have the right to an image, as Didi-Huberman mentions, have it despite everything.

Concluding Discussion: An Insubordinate Crip Gaze

In this chapter, we account for the ethical, aesthetic, and political deployments that Lina Meruane and Nicole Kramm rehearse with their crip gazes as responses to the biopolitics of debilitation deployed during the social revolt in Chile. Although the analysed works have different materialities and different geopolitical coordinates, both artists fabricate emergency devices to recognise bodies crumbled by state violence and, mainly, to produce a gesture of survival, 'a light for all thought' (Didi Huberman, 2012, 51). *Zona ciega* y 'Víctimas de trauma ocular (VTO)' have offered a critical and embodied response that constructs a crip gaze, understood in this work as that insurrectionary, defiant, and anti-normative gaze situated in a context of violence and danger, refuses to disappear. However, it is also a feminist and disabled gaze, a gaze that alters the scopic regime of our 'phalogocularcentric' era (Jay, 2007) and that registers, despite real ocular damage, necropolitical actions within a social movement where eyes also exploded.

Two aspects that stand out in the conjuncture of Chile's social revolt seem to be particularly noteworthy. In the first place, it is not at all trivial that it is the eyes that are being shot at: attacking and precisely weakening the eyes in a markedly ocularcentric society, whose 'current scopic regime has screened as its central figure' (Castillo, 2020, 11), acquires strong connotations. To mutilate and blind a common citizenry, forced to see images in mass media continuously, implies controlling the direction of their gaze. In a twenty-first century dominated by screens, the right to exercise the gaze in scenarios of social discontent is doubly dangerous. For this reason, the 'biopolitics of debilitation' identified by Jasbir Puar becomes relevant to think, in this case, about who has the right to look at the future with their eyes under the threatening shadow of neoliberalism.

In the second place, the genre marker of the *crip gazes* stands out. Meruane and Kramm cultivate a way of witnessing the horror of violence without reproducing unnecessary victimisation or shameful spectacularising. Their eyes are openly rebellious because they are born of indignation and nonconformism. They are traversed by colonialism, patriarchy, ableism, and a biopolitical regime that mainly targets women's bodies. Still, they also promise gazes because they continue to envision the future, even if it has been denied. Both authors, crossed by ocular damages and chronic diseases, seek in a hopeful way to develop incarnated and localised artistic-political actions that can serve as unusual testimonies of denunciation and that make visible and confront the drama of ocular mutilations. It is not only a matter of contingency: it is an urgency in the time now. A crip gaze located, disabled, anti-ableist, and feminist.

Notes

1 This discontent comes empowered by other mobilizations that since 2010 have reacted against the current pension model, the privatization of education and austerity policies (Pleyers, 2022; McRuer, 2018). The 2019 revolt exhibited weariness in the face of an economic model that disregards life and produced a substantial change for Chilean society: the conformation of the constituent assembly that oversees writing a new constitution.
2 We translated all Spanish quotes into English.
3 The eye mutilations produced a reaction of condemnation of the police forces. Although the government created the 'Comprehensive Eye Repair Program' to provide rehabilitation to the victims, the debate over state responsibility for these assigned disabilities is still pending.
4 In addition to Meruane and Kramm's works, many other artistic manifestations have portrayed from this shared critical perspective the ocular mutilations in Chile. Activist collectives such as 'Lxs hijxs ciegxs del Estado Terrorista de Piñera' (2019) or 'LasTesis',

performances such as Cecilia Vicuña's 'El Veroir comenzó' and numerous practices from visual art have also pursued the symbolic reparation of these bodies with works that remind us how much it costs to lose an eye for dignity and justice.

5   This strategic incorporation of disabled bodies into patriotic regimes toward the global North can be seen, as Mitchell, Snyder, and McRuer have documented, as a biopolitics of disability that is not eugenic, but ableist and dangerously nationalistic.

References

Bolt, D. (2014) *The Metanarrative of Blindness: A Re-Reading of Twentieth-Century Anglophone Writing*, Ann Arbor: University of Michigan Press.

Bolt, D. (2021) *Metanarratives of Disability: Culture, Assumed Authority, and the Normative Social Order*, New York: Routledge.

Brea, J. L. (2007) *Cultura_Ram. Mutaciones de la cultura en la era de su distribución electrónica*, Barcelona: Gedisa.

Castillo, A. (2020) *Adicta Imagen*, Buenos Aires: La Cebra.

Cortés, I. (2020) Usos políticos de las sonoridades y performances andinas en Santiago de Chile post 18 de octubre de 2019. *Boletín Música: Revista de música latinoamericana y caribeña* 54: 53–70.

Didi-Huberman, G. (2012) *Supervivencia de las luciérnagas*, Madrid: Abada Editores.

Didi-Huberman, G. (2014) *Pueblos Expuestos, Pueblos Figurantes*, Buenos Aires: Ediciones Manantial.

Foucault, M. (1984) *Historia de la sexualidad. La voluntad de saber*, Buenos Aires: Siglo XXI.

Garland-Thomson, R. (2009) *Staring How We Look*, New York: Oxford University Press.

Hammer, G. (2019) *Blindness Through the Looking Glass: The Performance of Blindness, Gender, and the Sensory Body*, Ann Arbor: University of Michigan Press.

Healey, D. (2021) *Dramatizing Blindness: Disability Studies as Critical Creative Narrative*, London: Palgrave Macmillan.

Jay, M. (2007) *Ojos abatidos. La denigración de la visión en el pensamiento francés del siglo XX*, Madrid: Akal.

Kafer, A. (2013) *Feminist, Queer, Crip*, Bloomington, IN: Indiana University Press.

Kramm, N. (2019) *Víctimas Trauma Ocular* [online]. Available from: www.nicolekramm. com/vto [accessed 29 March 2022].

Marín, K. (2020) *Sostener la mirada. Apuntes para una ética de la discapacidad*, Quito: Editorial Festina Lente.

McRuer, R. (2006) *Crip Theory. Cultural Signs of Queerness and Disability*, New York: New York University Press.

McRuer, R. (2010) Disability nationalism in crip times. *Journal of Literary & Cultural Disability Studies* 4 (3): 163–178.

McRuer, R. (2018) *Crip Times. Disability, Globalization, and Resistance*, New York: New York University Press.

Meekosha, H. (2011) Human rights and the global South: The case of disability. *Third World Quarterly* 32 (8): 1383–1397.

Meruane, L. (2021) *Zona Ciega*, Santiago de Chile: Random House.

Michalko, R. (1998) *The Mystery of the Eye and the Shadow of Blindness*, Toronto: University of Toronto Press.

Mitchell, D. T. y Snyder, S. (2015) *The Biopolitics of Disability. Neoliberalism, Ableationalism, and Peripheral Embodiment*, Ann Arbor, MI: University of Michigan Press.

Pleyers, G. (2022) La vida en contra del neoliberalismo, in R. Ganter et al. (eds.) *El despertar chileno: Revuelta y subjetividad política*, Buenos Aires: CLACSO.

Puar, J. (2017) *The Right to Maim. Debility, Capacity, Disability*, Durham, NC: Duke University Press.

Rodríguez de la Flor, F. (2009) *Giro Visual*, Salamanca: Delirio.

Sanz, M. (2022) Lina Meruane por Marta Sanz: literatura contra el dolor [online]. *Lengua*. Available from: www.penguinlibros.com/ar/revista-lengua/entrevistas/lina-meruane-marta-sanz-zona-ciega [accessed 29 March 2022].

Siebers, T. (2010) *Disability Aesthetics*, Ann Arbor: The University of Michigan Press.

Sontag, S. (2003) *Regarding the Pains of Others*, New York: Picador.

Valverde Gefaell, C. (2015) *De la necropolítica neoliberal a la empatía radical*, Barcelona: Icaria.

PART III

Stage and the Page

Performance, Dramatics, and Literary Representation

12

SIGHTED-BLINDNESS-CONSULTANTS AND THE EVER-LASTING STATION OF BLINDNESS

Devon Healey

Preliminary Discussion: Journeys of and Into Blindness

Cultural stations are integral to human life; all of us move through a plethora of such stations as we live our lives. There are some cultural stations which hold a greater significance in our lives than do others. These are the stations at which ontology and epistemology intersect, constructing distinct routes or lines of movement. Disability, for instance, represents one such cultural station. It conventionally intersects with non-disability generating not only new routes for life-movements but new understandings of ontology and epistemology. Being, knowing and knowledge are transformed in cultural stations where disability and non-disability intersect.

This chapter is concerned with blindness and the cultural stations we, blind people, encounter in our journeys of and into blindness. In Western culture, indeed even globally, medicine, in particular ophthalmology, is one such station. This station is significant in that nearly all blind people stop there. Some remain at this station for quite some time; others move to related cultural stations such as rehabilitation and special education quite quickly; still others barely come to rest on these platforms before discovering and moving to an entirely different cultural station. But, where do these others go? They make a brief stop and then, where? What other stations, other than rehabilitation and special education, are available to blind people as we move through the life of blindness?

There are, as Rod Michalko (1999) says, 'many blindnesses' (180), many cultural assumptions of what blindness is, of what blind people 'look like' and of how we should be moving toward and through the cultural stations of blindness. The word *many* suggests not only several blindnesses but also several destinations of blindness and thus multi-arrival-points. This chapter engages blindness after its departure from the cultural station of ophthalmology and from related stations to arrive at

DOI: 10.4324/9781003275060-16

two less obvious stations than those of ophthalmology, rehabilitation and special education.

The sighted-blindness-consultant and the destination of blindness at which this station arrives is my first of two stops. Through an autoethnographic analysis of an encounter I had as a blind actor with a sighted-blindness-consultant on the set of a popular television show, the assumptions of both the sighted consultant and the notion that blindness requires a consultant in the first place is explored. The social implications of such an encounter on the relation between blindness and sight, a relation that accompanies us in any journey of blindness and greets us at every cultural station, is also explored.

The work of Rod Michalko marks my second cultural station. To know our blindness, we generally consult others – typically sighted others – particularly ophthalmologists, rehabilitators, in a word, experts. These so-called experts often recommend that we consult with blind people, those blind people who have accepted fully the words of these experts and who have not yet left their cultural stations and remain there resting in the version of blindness as requiring experts. Interestingly, blind people who fully adopt a version of blindness presented to them by experts do not have their own cultural station. They do not represent a station at which to stop since they have not left the cultural station of the expert. This means that the journey of blindness ends before it has begun. Before moving with blindness out of the cultural station of ophthalmology and its related stops and entering the cultural station of the work of Rod Michalko, I explore the station of the expert a little further.

The Sighted-Blindness-Consultant: Performing Blindness

'Is this you?' read the subject line of an email from my agent.
Is this you?
My eyes lingered, for a moment, on these words . . .
Is this you?

At first blush, this question seems quite straight forward; the answer could be only one of two options: yes, it is me or no, it is not me. But, the 'this' is rarely, if ever, straight forward, and when it proceeds 'you' the question itself calls for a question. *Is this you?* To which me does this question refer? The email might provide the beginning of a way to respond to this question. It is not as straight forward as it initially appeared since it involves a 'you' and a 'this you' and it involves indirectly a 'me'. There is nothing straight forward about *this*.

A popular sci-fi television show was holding auditions for the role of an assistant-teacher at a school for the blind and, the emailed breakdown went on to say, they 'welcomed' blind actors to submit.[1] 'Is this you?' – my agent wanted to know was I the 'this' they were welcoming.

This question had been one she, my agent, and I had talked around for quite some time. 'If you tell people you are blind', she said, 'then you are really limiting yourself. How would I submit you for auditions?' Was this question asked of non-disabled actors who auditioned for the role of a disabled character, received the part and won an Oscar?[2] What is interesting is that a disability such as blindness is conceived of as negatively influencing the career of an actor whereas a non-disability, for example sight, does not have the same negative influence. This makes reference to the cultural understanding that disability is not only itself negative, but also negative in its consequences. Many of the cultural stations through which blind people travel are dressed with this style of negativity.

'I can memorize the sides[3] that are provided but if, in the audition, they change the lines, show me specific movements or ask me to read anything', I reminded my agent, 'I won't – I mean, I can't – I'm blind'. There was no question that blindness was an aspect of me for my agent and there was also no question, for her, that the 'this you' part of me should not be disclosed. She had to introduce an entirely different 'you' than blindness in order to ask the question 'is this you?' in an email. 'Tell them you're dyslexic', she said, 'no questions asked; all artistic people are dyslexic!'

I did not tell them that I was dyslexic. And yet, knowing I was blind (and not dyslexic) and knowing the role was that of a blind person, my agent was still able to ask, 'is this you?' And, I was equally able to respond, *yes. This is me.* But, what grounds the possibility of asking a blind person whether she is a blind person represented in the question, is this you? The answer lies in the category *blind actor.* My agent knowing that I was blind and that I was an actor still wondered whether the two categories could be combined. Could blindness and actor be combined? And, was I this combination – thus, *is this you?*

I landed the audition and a week later booked the gig.[4]

What was intriguing about the audition (perhaps a foreshadowing of what was to come on set) was that there was no indication that blindness was expected, let alone 'welcome'. The audition was held on the fourth floor of a six-floor walk-up building. No one was present on the fourth floor to greet and/or guide me, or any other blind actors, to the audition room. Moreover, all paperwork was printed in size 11-point font and left on a small table, almost hidden, behind a large plant. Where was blindness? What conceptions of blindness must they have had such that this audition space 'welcomed' blindness? Was this conception of blindness expertly derived? What sort of 'expert in blindness' would suggest such an unwelcoming space to welcome blindness? Clearly, the expertise of this cultural station was understood as beginning with the audition and not with its space. Equally as clear, producing an unwelcoming space for blindness focused more on the cultural aspect of the cultural station of expertise than it did on its physical and built environment. The station platform represented *only* arrival at the cultural station of expertise; getting to the experts was another matter altogether.

After I had completed the audition I lingered in the room for a moment as the casting directors, heads bowed, eyes cast down, silently looked at (presumably reading) the papers in front of them. Were they looking at my resumé? Did they know that I was what they had welcomed and were looking for? Did they know that

I was indeed a blind actor? I waited, hoping for them to say something, anything. *Where was blindness?* As I was about to leave the room, I turned to the casting directors and said, 'I'm blind. I thought you should know'. I could not see if my words jolted their heads up. They may have 'welcomed' blind actors to submit but it was clear they had not expected any of us to appear.

The television show was a supernatural-thriller and, as I said earlier, I landed the part. I played a blind assistant-teacher at a school for the blind. The episode revealed that the students of the school were to be offered as a sacrifice, killed and then reborn as vampires, their blindness making them especially powerful as their other senses were, naturally, heightened. Such an understanding is not restricted to sci-fi television shows. The absence of sight understood as heightening the strength of the remaining senses reflects the cultural understanding of blindness as loss, limit, and lack. This understanding suggests that there is nothing of value to be gleamed or perceived through blindness and so, the other senses must overcompensate with enhanced capacity for the loss of sight. The cultural understanding of blindness as the representation of heightened hearing, taste, touch, and smell removes blindness as having any valuable sensorial perceptions of the world. This sense of blindness made the fate of the young students at the school for the blind seem almost logical.

Blindness was everywhere and yet nowhere on set. There were 25 sighted young actors playing blind students, accompanied by 25 white canes. I watched as they twirled, tapped, and played with the white canes in between filming. Were they asked, as I was, *is this you?* Teaching the cast and crew, including me, how to *be* blind and not only convincingly, but authentically so was the goal of the sighted-blindness-consultant. Did the consultant know I was blind, I wondered. The audition did welcome blind actors, after all, and I had announced my blindness to the casting directors in the audition room. And yet, no one seemed to know that I was blind. Visual gestures as a means of communication dominated on set. I watched as crew members waved their hands to the left or right silently indicating to an actor or fellow crew member where to move. Papers were passed around detailing the daily schedule of filming, breaks, and so on, without any reading out loud. Everyone and everything moved under the assumption that everyone was sighted and that everything was there to be seen. Everyone acted as though this assumption were true. I may have been welcomed in the audition but my presence, my blindness, was not expected to move beyond that audition room. Welcoming blindness in anticipation of it is one thing, expecting its arrival is quite another. The duelling perspectives of welcoming and expecting place blindness in a culturally precarious position on the precipice of being there without quite being there. And, there I was, blind, on the set of a television show playing a blind character learning how to act blind in an authentic and convincing way from a sighted-blindness-consultant.

> 'No, no! A blind person would never do that!' boomed a voice from behind the camera.
> I stopped in my tracks.
> 'Cut!' yelled the director.

Were they talking about me? Was the 'cut' my fault? The answers: 'Blind people don't move that way'. The booming voice belonged to the sighted-blindness-consultant. She moved from behind the camera and walked toward me. 'Trust me, I know. I work with them'. Her tone and confidence radiated with a familiarity, an assumed authority I had heard many times (Bolt, 2021). 'Let's review', her voice continued to boom as she gestured with her hands high in the air indicating to the cast to come close and crowd around her: 'whose got questions?' She began the review.

They all had questions:

How would the blind teacher know that there were students in the room?
How would the students and teacher talk to each other if they can't see? Would they just interrupt each other?
How would a blind teacher find the classroom?
Does the blind teacher walk around the classroom while reading a braille book – is that even possible?
What do blind people see?

These questions represent an attempt to understand and come to know blindness through the expertise of sight. How do blind people talk? How do they speak to one another? How do they read? A group of sighted actors, a sighted-blindness-consultant and me . . . a blind person, and yet not 'seen' as such, all of us, learning how blind people 'do' everyday life. In the midst of all these questions lurked a version of blindness dressed in the sheer curiosity of those who are sighted, a curiosity that cannot imagine doing anything if they were blind. This curiosity generates an interesting understanding of the epistemology of blindness, as, ironically, a lack of knowledge and thus of ability. It generates, too, an ontology of blindness, one that understands it as an inferior way of being. We, blind people, are told we are blind (typically a diagnosis of ophthalmology) and we learn how to act blind (typically through the expertise of disciplines such as rehabilitation and special education) and even through the expertise of sighted-blindness-consultants.

I, a blind person, was there, present; yet, I was not understood as an expert in blindness. After all, I had never worked 'with them'. The sighted-blindness-consultant directed me to have a 'glazed look' in my eyes with my gaze locked just off to the right. She provided me with a very specific choreography; stretch out my right arm in front of me and use the top of my right hand to tap around me as I walked, slowly, around the classroom. 'Remember', she said, 'you are blind. Trust me, I won't let you look silly'. I nodded. She understood my nod to be an indication of trust. It was not. I was now authentically and convincingly blind, according to the sighted-blindness-consultant. This experience reformed the answer to the question, 'is this you?' NO, the answer now must be; nor is it blindness.

As I have already said, the 'sight-as-expert' perspective is a particularly troubling cultural station. It does, after all, remove any valuable epistemological position from blindness. We, blind people, travel through many such stations in our journey into blindness.[5] There are, however, stations not so troubling, ones that do not remove any valuable perception, thus any epistemological positions, from blind people. As Charles Dickens (1861) reminds us, 'But wonders may be done with an eye by hiding it' (Chapter 9, n.p.). I now turn to one such cultural station.

The Ever-Lasting Station of Blindness: Blind Perception

While this cultural station is not troubling in the way of the expert, it is so in another way. This station asks us to understand our blindness and that of others as a phenomenon that is ever-lasting. Try as the experts and the rest of us might, we cannot rid human existence of blindness. This means, among other things, that blindness belongs in human existence and vice versa.

Disability Studies scholar Rod Michalko (1998), puts the matter this way:

> Coming to understand that the story of blindness is not over in one telling is already the beginning of the development of a mature relation to it. We aim not to be through with blindness until it is through with us, and, since it will never be through with us, we must seek to never be through with it. I will be blind for the rest of my life, and blindness will never be through with me. Blindness is present in human existence as a whole, and thus blindness will never be through with humanity. . . . There is no pleasure to be felt in the eye when it sees, and blindness alone certainly does not deprive anyone of the pleasures of education, cultivation, or thought.
>
> *(134, 141)*

The understanding that the story of blindness is not over in one telling, as Michalko suggests, presupposes the understanding that blindness *is* a story. Thus, the beginning of blindness is marked by the stories we tell. The cultural stations I have discussed so far represent a story of blindness; but, they do not represent the end of blindness; it is not over with the telling of these stories and the arrival at these cultural stations. Indeed, the end of any story of blindness is the beginning of a new one.

The difficulty with a new story of blindness, or a new story of anything, is that it troubles the old one. The troubling feature of a new story is that it is typically heard as an undermining of the old one. It is not heard as development, as cultivation or even as education. It is often heard as conflict and when the old story of blindness is told by science, the conflict is oriented to as a rejection of the Truth.

Even though Michalko says blindness is ever-lasting and that we should never be through with it, many, if not most, of the cultural stations demand that we, blind people, be through with blindness. 'You can't dwell on it', 'You've got to keep going, don't let it stop you', and 'You're so much more than blindness' are but a few examples of how we, blind people, are encouraged to avoid our blindness, let alone acknowledge it, so that we may then be through with it. But, what exactly is it that we are not supposed to 'dwell in?' Where is it we are 'going' that blindness is preventing our arrival? And, what 'more' are we than our blindness will allow?

These questions represent a pause or an inhale in the telling of the story of blindness. I have been blind for 14 years and, for the most part, I have been a listener to the stories of blindness. Storytellers such as ophthalmologists have told me the name of my blindness and where it lives in my genetic story; I have been directed by rehabilitation specialists how to get around and do things 'for myself' without relying on sighted others; and I have even been guided as to how I should feel about my blindness by a psychiatrist. I have listened, carefully and intently, to all of these stories with the resolve of being through with my blindness. And yet, I am not. Perhaps I am not a good listener; or, perhaps the stories I have been told end without any satisfaction; or, perhaps blindness is not through with me.

The stories told in the cultural stations of the expert are, indeed, unsatisfactory. They, for instance, end with an implicated contradiction, namely, that the end of the story is what blindness *is*. But, if this is true then I am done not only with blindness, but with *my* blindness. It is difficult to imagine how a part of my life is ended while I am still living it. As Michalko suggests, how can I be through with blindness when blindness is within me, when it mediates my world? How can I be through with blindness when blindness is never quite the same day to day? It constantly takes different forms before my eyes and in my life. Like Michalko, I too, 'will be blind for the rest of my life, and blindness will never be through with me'.

The cultural stations of the expert, along with disability studies, suggest that blindness represents a loss or a lack. Of course, this lack is the lack of sight. Still, a lack or loss on their own does not necessarily represent a problem. The loss needs to be a significant one or the lack needs to be substantial in order for a problem to be a result. The lack of sight, then, must represent a lack of something valuable, even of something essential.

What is valuable about eyesight such that its loss or lack represents a problem? Eyesight, for instance, provides for an ease in navigation, provides for the recognition of people, at a glance and provides, too, for an ease in the accomplishment of innumerable everyday activities. Is the value of sight located solely in the practical activities of everyday life? This suggests that the value of sight is steeped in techné, in a way of doing things. Yet, blind people have ways of accomplishing everyday activities. We have technology and techniques in order to do this. Thus, eyesight must be more than practicality. It is, as Michalko suggests, also pleasurable. We can imagine, for example, the pleasure that comes from watching sunsets or looking at classical works of art such as, the *Mona Lisa*. There is an aesthetic to sight. Is the aesthetic what is most valuable insight, is that what we, blind people, lack? An aesthetic and its subsequent pleasure?

I recall Michalko's (1998) words, 'There is no pleasure to be *felt* in the eye when it sees' (141, emphasis my own). The very act of watching a sunset or of looking at the *Mona Lisa* is not in and of itself pleasurable. There may be a sense of satisfaction found in the act of looking and seeing, a satisfaction Michalko (1998) calls 'a "sensual finality" – a finality that ends, and ironically begins, with the sheer sensual experience of the world' (142). This 'sensual finality' requires that eyes 'liv[e] unthoughtfully . . . a life in, what Kierkegaard calls, the sheer "immediacy" of life. The "immediate person" almost always requires the support of eyes to live in-immediacy' (Michalko, 1998, 142). Such an immediacy is rooted in the act of looking and seeing but such a satisfaction should not be conflated with pleasure. Eyesight is immediate and such immediacy may be understood as satisfying. Blindness, in contrast, does lack immediacy in that it does not provide a sensual finality. A blind relation to the world does not garner an immediate ending in the way looking and seeing does. A blind relation to the world cannot be reduced to the immediate act of looking, seeing, and thus of knowing; blindness is far more perceptive. Indeed, blindness *is* perception.

It is the engagement with what is being perceived that is pleasurable not the eye that sees. Such an engagement requires thought, consideration and creativity. Eyesight itself is not thoughtful, it is not considerate nor is it creative. It lacks a sensual engagement with the world where thought, consideration and creativity are, unending. Perhaps this is why I have been unsatisfied with the stories provided to me by experts. These stories of blindness are couched in an immediacy that ultimately leads to an end whereas the blindness within me, the untold stories of blindness, demands a continuous-storytelling. Perhaps, in these stories of blindness narrated by experts it is not blindness that is rooted in lack or loss but rather, in the idea of the expert itself.

Perception is not restricted to sight, nor is pleasure. There are many pleasures that do not involve sight. Of these pleasures, Michalko (1998) speaks 'of education, cultivated people, the sort of person for whom life means thought: and a Wise [person] rarely needs the support of [their] eyes in order to think' (141). There is a restlessness to blindness in that satisfaction is not immediate. We, blind people, cannot be satiated merely by the sights around us nor should we be satisfied with the stories provided to us by experts and those who live in-immediacy. There is a necessary creativity to blindness that requires a thoughtful engagement with the world and of how we come to know and relate to others. Blindness, as Michalko reminds us, 'certainly does not deprive anyone of the pleasures of education, cultivation, or thought' (141). And yet, it is blindness that is spoken of as lack and loss. As the previous section of this chapter depicts, it is blindness that is understood as limiting one's potential and it is blindness that requires an answer to the question, *is this you?*

The you I once identified myself as, the you for whom being a blind actor was a question, was someone who felt as though their blindness was something to be traversed. The cultural stations to which I had been referred by experts told me that blindness was not something to be explored but rather put aside, ignored even. To be a successful blind person was to do the things that sighted people did, except in a different way. I was meant to feel good when my blindness was not seen by others or incorporated into who I was. I did not dwell in blindness. I keep going. I would not let it stop me. Nor would I allow myself to be blind, I was, after all, told I was so much more. I attempted to live in the immediacy of sight while blind and was left with nothing more than an unsatisfied restlessness. My blindness, despite my efforts, was not through with me and I began to *feel* it.

Concluding Discussion: The Stories We Tell

This chapter engages two integral cultural stations of blindness: first, the sighted-blindness-consultant representing the station of the expert; and second, the ever-lasting station of blindness. The first station is committed to the practicality that blindness engenders. It dedicates its stories to terminating thought on blindness and 'getting on with life'. The second is committed to both listening to the various stories of blindness told in cultural stations and to making something of these stories. It is committed to a continuous telling of the story of blindness. It is committed, too, to a careful telling, to a telling understood as bearing influence. It needs, to borrow from Tanya Titchkosky (2007), to hear its tellings (5). As Indigenous storyteller Thomas King (2003) says:

> For once a story is told, it cannot be called back. Once told, it is loose in the world. So, you have to be careful with the stories you tell. And you have to watch out for the stories that you are told.
>
> *(10)*

The stories we hear of blindness and those we tell must be heard and told with an understanding that our life with blindness is there for 'everyone to see' and will influence greatly how 'everyone sees' blindness.

Notes

1 'Submit' refers to an agent sending the headshot and resume of an actor they represent to a casting director to secure an audition for a specific project.
2 Examples of non-disabled actors who have won an Oscar for their performance of a disabled character include: Patty Duke in, *The Miracle Worker* (1962); Daniel Day-Lewis in, *My Left Foot* (1989); Al Pacino in, *Scent of a Women* (1992); Jamie Foxx in, *Ray* (2004); and Eddie Redmayne in, *The Theory of Everything* (2014).
3 'Sides' refers to the portion of the script (lines) that are sent, in advance, to actors so that they can memorize/prepare.
4 Got the job.
5 For a discussion on the freedom of movement in relation to blindness, see Michalko and Titchkosky (2020) in, *A Cultural History of Disability in the Modern Age* edited by David Mitchell and Sharon Snyder.

References

Bolt, D. (2021) *Metanarratives of Disability: Culture, Assumed Authority, and the Normative Social Order*, Abingdon: Routledge.

Dickens, C. (1861) *Great Expectations*, London: Chapman and Hall.

King, T. (2003) *The Truth About Stories: A Native Narrative*, Toronto: House of Anansi Pres.

Michalko, R. (1998) *The Mystery of the Eye and the Shadow of Blindness*, Toronto: University of Toronto Press.

Michalko, R. (1999) *The Two in One: Walking With Smokie, Walking with Blindness*, Philadelphia: Temple University Press.

Michalko, R. and Titchkosky, T. (2020) Blindness: A cultural history of blindness, in D. Mitchell and S. L. Snyder (eds.) *A Cultural History of Disability in the Modern Age, Volume 6*, London: Bloomsbury Academic. *My Left Foot*. (1989) Film Directed by Jim Sheridan, Ferndale Films.

Ray. (2004) Film Directed by Taylor Hackford, Bristol Bay Productions. *Scent of a Woman*. (1992) Film Directed by Martin Brest, City Light Films.

Titchkosky, T. (2007) *Reading and Writing Disability Differently: The Textured Life of Embodiment*, Toronto: University of Toronto Press. *The Miracle Worker*. (1962) Film Directed by Arthur Penn, Playfilm Productions.

The Theory of Everything. (2014) Fim Directed by James Marsh, Working Title Films.

13

TOUCHING THE ROCK

Masculinity and Macular Degeneration

Declan Kavanagh

Preliminary Discussion: Macula Matters

What is the macula? For some people, the word *macula* will be wholly unfamiliar. Most people are unlikely to have ever heard this word uttered before, or, at least to have noticed and fully registered its meaning. More often than not, people will have encountered the term *macular degeneration*, but not know what exactly it is that is being 'degenerated' – namely, the macula, whose etymological root comes from the Latin: *macula lutea*. When I first heard this word, I was entirely unaware of its meaning. As a scholar of literature, words seldom come to me without my prior knowledge of a history or a connection. I may not understand a word from the outset, but I am usually able to key into a word's possible meanings by think-ing about potential etymologies and by assessing the word's usage and its context. In this case, I distinctly remember the word's meaning escaped me. In that pivotal moment, I did not know what the 'macula' meant nor did I know that I possessed two maculae, one in the retina of each green-blue eye. Up until then, the most exciting thing ever to happen to me in an ocular sense was when I was a young child and my eyes suddenly switched colour. I remember coming home to my mother from a class mate's birthday party and she asked me to stand still and to keep my eyes wide open. As I stood against a wall in the kitchen, she bent down and stared carefully into my eyes, moving her head slightly to the left, and then to the right, as if she were finding an angle that would allow her to dip into my wide inky pupils. 'Your eyes have changed colour', she finally said. Apparently, my eyes had switched from a blue to a green-blue over the course of a friend's afternoon birthday party. I remember feeling concerned at my mother's stark amazement but also strangely powerful, as if, I had made this colour shift occur all by myself. I now stood in my mother's kitchen as a being as curious as an Irish folkloric sprite or changeling; I was, for a time, otherworldly. For weeks, my mother would grab

DOI: 10.4324/9781003275060-17

me so that household visitors could examine my eyes for themselves; 'see, they've changed to green', she would exclaim. In hindsight, I think that most of our neighbours were not too observant when it came to the eye colour of a five-year-old child. Their performances of furrowed brows, gasps, and follow-up questions served to humour her more than anything else.

At 27 years old, when the locum optician in a well-known chain store said to me 'there's something strange in the macula of both eyes', I felt oddly disempowered. Their bafflement and the subsequent rushed nature of the appointment and referral to the local ophthalmology hospital unit served to unsettle me. This time, the change did not seem like a magic trick that I would want to claim as my own. And yet, this was my body, these were my green-blue eyes and, suddenly, within the confines of a regular eye check-up, I was met with the pervasive and weighty sense that I was beginning to lose something very valuable; something that, until now, I was not quite aware that I even possessed. According to the Macular Society, the leading charity in the United Kingdom that advocates on behalf of those with macular conditions, the macula is:

> Part of the retina at the back of the eye. It is only about 5 mm across, but is responsible for our central vision, most of our colour vision and the fine detail of what we see. The macula has a very high concentration of photoreceptor cells – the cells that detect light. They send signals to the brain, which interprets them as images. The rest of the retina processes our peripheral, or side vision.
>
> *(Anon, 2022)*

This definition of the macula was the first that I read in 2014 when I came across the Macular Society's website after my initial eye check-up at the opticians. It was at this point that I began to try to square what I knew about blindness against what I could learn about the function and significance of the macula. Degeneration of the macula would not lead to complete blindness, I was told, but what did this mean? No one would really tell me. Admittedly, what I knew already about blindness was very little. I had, however, an overarching sense of the ideas about blindness that were recurrent within culture and society. As this chapter explores, macular degeneration as a discourse often re-affirms flawed ideas about blindness and the blind, but, in cases like mine, it also can serve to challenge such narratives. In encountering issues with my vision and finding out about macular disease, I was also, on some level, beginning to wade through what David Bolt has termed the metanarrative of blindness. In his book, *The Metanarrative of Blindness: A Re-reading of Twentieth-Century Anglophone Writing* (2014), Bolt defines the metanarrative of blindness as 'the story in relation to which those of us who have visual impairments often find ourselves defined, an overriding narrative that seems to displace agency' (Bolt, 2014, 10). Throughout his analysis, Bolt identifies aspects of the metanarrative of blindness, such as the way in which the figure of 'the blind beggar' often comes to dominate people's perceptions of those with visual impairments: 'there is a recurrent use of tropes such as the blind beggar, which reaches far beyond the literary and indeed cultural imagination' (Bolt, 2014, 10–11). In my own mind, I had not focused so much on the blind beggar, however, I did imagine a 'blind man' and, in doing so, I came to imagine a man who was defined by nothing but his blindness. As will be explored in this chapter, the very ideas that accrue around our own cultural notions of masculinity such as 'independence', 'strength', 'impenetrability', 'productivity', and 'capacity' face erasure in the discursive eddies of the metanarrative of blindness. The ocularnormativism, which Bolt identifies in *The Metanarrative of Blindness*, can also be read as a fetishisation of seeing as power that further extends into the cultural primacy of the cis-gendered male gaze as a founding narrative of male power and privilege. The blind man can gaze but he cannot see and in not 'seeing' he relinquishes his claim to masculinity; normative manliness is, in part, about commanding the gaze.

I return to the metanarrative of blindness throughout this chapter as I explore two cultural stations of blindness, that is, two literary texts that have aided me in my own unpacking of what blindness might *mean*. The first text is John M. Hull's memoir *Notes on Blindness: A Journey Through the Dark* re-issued in 2017 and originally published in 1990 as *Touching the Rock: An Experience of Blindness*. The second is Derek Jarman's book entitled *Chroma: A Book of Colour* (1994). Both Hull's memoir on blindness and Jarman's meditations on the use of colour are roughly contemporaneous as texts that co-emerge in the early 1990s, each with gestation periods of a few years earlier than that. Both are also curiously texts of my childhood that I was blind to at the time. Although inaccessible to me as a child, both Hull's and Jarman's writings on blindness align temporally with my mother noticing the change in my eye colour in the early 1990s. As such, when I found them, each as important as the other, I thought of them as gifts, as parts of a shared history, that lay waiting for me to claim. Similarly, when my husband wanted us to adopt a rescue cat in 2019, I found another surprising gift curled up asleep under a blanket; her name was Belinda, and we were told that she was blind. As I continue to navigate the slow, and sometimes quick degeneration of my maculae, I think of these texts and my cat as gifts. I am reminded that not all gifts are wanted ones. In *Notes on Blindness*, John M. Hull ponders the question of blindness itself as a gift: 'In recent weeks the thought has been in my mind that blindness could be a gift. I cannot quite remember where I got this idea' (Hull, 2017, 182). Hull is at pains to accept blindness as a gift: 'If blindness is a gift, it is not one that I would wish on anybody. It is not a gift I want to receive. It is something which I would rather like to give back, but one which I find I cannot help accepting' (Hull, 2017, 183). Each cultural station that I include here has helped me, even forced me at times, to dislodge the all-encompassing hegemony of the metanarrative of blindness. As I explore in the next section, the methodologies that I have gleaned from disability studies, and from scholars, such as David Bolt, are equally gifts that have been passed on to me as I navigate the varied intellectual, social, political, and cultural questions that attend 'blindness'.

Can a methodology also be a gift? When I was finally diagnosed in 2014 with a macular condition, the timing could not have been worse for me in a professional sense to say little of its personal impact. The week that I went into that opticians on the high-street in Canterbury, was the same week in which I had successfully secured my first permanent job as a lecturer in English literature at the University of Kent. Fresh from being awarded my PhD, I had been working in the School of English since 2013 on a temporary contract. I had never felt so at home, so intellectually rewarded, and so a part of something worthwhile and sustaining as I felt during those first months teaching. That week had been an incredibly stressful one. I was attending to a busy end of term and dealing with a lot of essay marking, whilst also preparing a job presentation that I hoped would put me in the running for the longer-term position. I was hoping against hope, and had already conceded that I would not get the job and that I would have to end my Canterbury tale that summer. When I interviewed, and subsequently got offered the job, I was so elated I fell off my office chair and hid under the table. It was a moment of real accomplishment for me and one of absolute joy. It was that afternoon, when walking home from campus, still brimming with the sense of all that was now possible, that my vision started to change, or at least, when I began to pay attention to it. I remember walking along the high-street and noticing a lamppost suddenly disappearing in my view. If I moved my head slightly, the lamppost would re-appear but at a certain angle and with a dip of my head, the lamppost itself would suddenly wobble or even vanish. I began to panic; as my rational mind failed to account for what it was that I was seeing and not seeing. I thought that the sleepless nights preparing for the interview had made my eyes tire and I went to bed that night hoping that the lamppost trick would not be repeated. Over the next few days, my visual distortions grew more apparent. I was, although I did not know it, experiencing a retinal bleed. Blood vessels behind my retina had leaked and the fluid building up was making it hard for light to reach the fovea, which is the central point of the macula. What unfolded for me then was a long road to a diagnosis. I attended the opticians and got a referral to the local hospital but the wait times were such that I did not get to see a consultant for some months and that was only because I, myself, went through an A&E department. In the case of a retinal bleed, treatment is urgent. As I note at the start of this chapter, the optician told me that there was scarring in my macula, one in each eye. These scars were historic but something had happened to reactivate the scar in my right eye, which was now leaking fluid. None of this was properly relayed to me, and in my encounters with the optician, the GP retinal specialist, and others, I had to piece things together a bit at a time.

It would be impossible to keep narrative accuracy and cohesion when detailing these encounters but in one such appointment, organised by my GP, I was summoned to the office of my surgery's Retinal Specialist. This man was used to diagnosing age-related macular degeneration cases and to helping those with diabetes who needed to be screened for potential problems with their eyes. At this point, I had been living with acute anxiety over my eyes; the anti-depressant medication that the GP had prescribed me was not working for me. I had gained weight, lost weight, gained some more. My personal hygiene was not being maintained. I am sure that I looked like a vulnerable and depressed young man. I remember perceiving, from the outset, that this man was quite perturbed by me being in his office. It was as if he was having to humour me and that my presentation there amounted to nothing more than the machinations of a hypochondriac. He did not make eye contact with me but instead gave me directions to sit down and to put my chin on a ledge that was attached to an apparatus with multiple lenses and a bright light. I do not remember if he dilated my pupils with eye drops. When he looked into my eyes his body language immediately changed. I remember him darting up and then leaning in closer to inspect each eye again. The white light was shining brightly and I can still feel his cold fingers keeping my eye lid up as I went through the motions of looking up, looking down, looking left, looking right. He was completely silent after checking my eyes. He went over to the basin and washed his hands for what seemed like an eternity. I felt like I was trespassing on someone else's funeral. Suddenly, in a brisk movement, the Retinal Specialist came over to me and firmly grasped my arm just above the elbow. As he squeezed it hard he said 'I am very sorry, son'. The interaction happened so fast that the next thing I knew he had opened the door to his office and was standing with one had on the door handle waiting to close it behind me. I remember thinking that he wants me to leave; he wants me to vanish. I began to walk to the door and as I did I asked 'What did you see?'. He averted my gaze and my question by keeping his head turned to the side and by saying once in a clear voice that a hospital referral would be sent immediately. As soon as I had stepped over the threshold the door was closed.

I recount this particular appointment because it has shaped my ideas on blindness more than any that have followed so far. In this moment, I was met with the full force of the metanarrative of blindness; I was treated as a tragic case. The tragedy of blindness as a diagnosis, as something so terrible that it must be avoided, played out in the Retinal Specialist's poor handling of my appointment. He did not take the time to tell me what he had seen. *He did not tell me anything.* He showed me a measure of pity but not empathy. There was nothing in this moment that offered me connection, support, or even hope. The metanarrative of blindness (Bolt, 2014) operates on many discursive levels but one such level is the way in which it narrativises blindness as a tragic affliction that de-subjectivises the person. The person's agency in this situation is rendered less legible than the imposing metanarrative of blindness, which constructs the subject as a reductive stereotype. In this case, I am convinced that I scared this man, or at least, that the ideas about blindness that he held scared him when reviewing me. He was not expecting to find any scarring in my retina as I was not presenting as the usual case. I was a young man. The metanarrative of blindness often manifests the figure of the blind beggar (Bolt, 2014), however, that beggar is also often aged. Within the metanarrative of blindness, age and blindness are frequent bedfellows. As Tobin Siebers identifies when discussing the ideology of ability, 'Disability defines the invisible centre around which our contradictory ideology about human ability revolves' (Siebers, 2008, 8–9). The idea of bodies being capacious is intimately tied to the notion of the youthful and able body. The idea of a young man going blind comes into tension with the metanarrative of blindness, which posits a blind older man as the stereotype. With macular conditions, the association with age is further entrenched, as age-related macular degeneration is the most commonly known type. The Macular Society details how 'there are many forms of macular disease, including age-related macular degeneration (AMD). There are two forms of AMD – dry and wet. Other forms of macular disease affect much younger people, even children' (Anon, 2022). The kind of macular condition that I presented with looks and acts very similarly to wet aged-related macular degeneration. However, by all accounts, at 27 years of age, otherwise healthy, this was not something with which I should have been presenting. The sight condition affecting me was not related to an ageing macula.

As the Retinal Specialist's door was closed, many others opened. Because, perhaps, I had just secured a permanent job, my mind on the road to diagnosis was firmly focused on how I might avoid the scenario of losing my vision and also losing my academic job. Over the course of these months, I reached out to many academics who are visually impaired or blind and who work in various academic posts, many being leaders in their respective fields. Professor Chris Mounsey at the University of Winchester, Professor David Bolt at Liverpool Hope University, and Professor Anna Lawson at the University of Leeds, all took some valuable time out of their busy schedules to talk to me about how they worked with sight loss and what they worked on. Each of these academics opened doors for me, which allowed me to step out of the dark 'tragedy' that befell me since visiting the Retinal Specialist. These individuals, in the performance of their jobs, their lives, their ordinariness, gifted me with other narratives for 'blindness', which still sustain me both professionally and personally. Moreover, finding the disability-studies methods used by scholars like Bolt and Mounsey (two scholars within my field) gave me the necessary coordinates to start the process of re-thinking what I knew about blindness and about disability more capaciously.

In this chapter, I closely follow the autocritical discourse analysis that David Bolt introduced, in his essay in the collection *Metanarratives of Disability: Culture, Assumed Authority, and the Normative Social Order* (2021), as it offers a tool for challenging the ways in which 'the personal narratives of disabled people are often overshadowed by ubiquitous metanarratives of disability' (Bolt, 2021, 215). In his chapter, 'The Metanarrative of Arthritis', Bolt specifies that 'the premise of autocritical discourse analysis is that due consideration of these personal narratives can help to disrupt the overarching assumptions and generalisations by which social encounters are frequently influenced' (Bolt, 2021, 215). In my own academic training, I am more familiar with the historical methods of assessing the eighteenth-century texts that I deal with. I am versed in critical theories and practices and I am attuned to the methods of close reading that provide the bedrock of the broader field of literary studies. As this section shows, the personal narrative of the many times that I was 'not diagnosed' by specialists intertwines and intervenes in my own critical approach to representations of blindness. The method of autocritical discourse empowers me to include, not exclude, those personal experiences that have prompted me to evaluate critically the metanarrative of blindness at those very moments when it most infringed upon my sense of dignity – my very existence. For those of us who are disabled and who work in research, such disability-studies methodologies are intellectually and emotionally life sustaining. Methodological traditions and modalities passed amongst disabled scholars, and those who work within disability studies, certainly are gifts.

Notes on Blindness: 'Show Daddy'

I first encountered John M. Hull's memoir *Notes on Blindness* after I attended a talk at the Wellcome Collection in London, which celebrated the re-issue of the book. It was 2017 and a few years after my diagnosis. I had in the summer of 2014 been diagnosed with 'macular degeneration' and over the course of the next few years had periodically received injections of a drug called Lucentis into the eyeball of each eye. First my right eye was treated and then my left. At one time, both eyes were being injected. Each injection had psychic and physical costs; the anxiety provoking thought of having my eye clamped open, numbing the eye ball with searing drops, before a needle delivered the drug to the back of my eye, left me shaken and unable to work for days. These injections were not a cure but merely a treatment. Lucentis worked to brush the fluid off the sensitive part of the macula, cauterising the breach, and preventing further damage. The leak itself, each one of them, had, however, caused some scarring and so, as a result, my vision slowly deteriorated. I sat in this auditorium waiting for Marilyn Hull to speak and if I closed my right eye I could make her disappear. The scotoma in my left eye acted like a vortex that pulled everything into it. By now, this was a common thing that I used to do at talks to relieve boredom as I waited for them to start and, sometimes, admittedly to amuse myself during them if the talk was not keeping my attention. The so-called tragedy of visual impairment actually became, at times, the stuff of my own amusement. After her talk, I learnt from Marilyn, who had been married to John M. Hull, that not only did he continue to work as an academic in Religious Education but he even went on to become Dean of his faculty. I entered into reading *Notes on Blindness* having already been changed by Marilyn's talk and by her reassurances that John Hull continued to work as an academic and at a time – the 1980s – when there was less accessibility technology to help him do so.

If *Notes on Blindness* reset how I thought about doing academic work as a visually impaired person, it also, in a less predictable way, opened up questions about my own masculinity and blindness. In the opening to his memoir, a book recorded on cassette tapes over a number of years, Hull writes 'I was interested in how my children would gradually discover what it meant to have a blind father' (Hull, 2017, xii). A version of masculinity – heterosexual fatherhood – is intimately tied to Hull's depictions of blind experience. He narrates how his son Thomas provides a marker for his own relationship to blindness: 'My final eye operation took place on 1 August. Thomas was born on 22 August. When I cannot quite remember how long I have been blind, I ask myself how old Thomas is' (Hull, 2017, 1). Hull's experience of blindness is beautifully and carefully interwoven into his experience of parenting as a blind man:

> Thomas was three years old a month ago. He knows that he has to treat me differently. Ever since he was tiny I have trained him in the expression 'Show Daddy'. He knows that this does not mean the same as 'Give it to Daddy', which means 'surrender it up'. By contrast, 'Show Daddy' means 'put whatever you've got in your hand into my hand and you will get it straight back'.
>
> *(Hull, 2017, 23)*

Navigating blindness for Hull is also about navigating parenting and feelings of frustration or inadequacy are often tied to his disability and to the impact he perceives it has upon his parenting: 'Occasionally I feel depressed, and this is worst when I am frustrated in playing with the children. I feel as if I have become nothing, unable to act as a father, impotent, unable to survey, to admire, or to exercise jurisdiction or discrimination' (Hull, 2017, 48–49). This passage, taken as a literary description, links Hull's depression to a perception that he cannot act in the male role of father and husband; the highlighted impotency and inability to 'survey' reconnects us to the sense of manliness being tied to the seeing gaze, which, in his words, has the ability to 'admire, or to exercise jurisdiction'. Hull's meditations on blindness underscore his own vulnerability in the face of a blindness that compromises traditional narrative cornerstones of cis-gendered masculinity. In a tense moment in 1984, Hull records how a male passer-by accosted him for being blind: 'a fierce, harsh, male voice, distorted with anger and malice, shouted, "Are you blind, mate? You're not blind!"' (Hull, 2017, 73). Reading this passage evokes in me strong feelings of minority solidarity. This senseless victimisation on the grounds of disability resonates with my own experiences of being verbally attacked on the streets for being a gay man. In her epilogue, Marilyn Hull notes how, for John M. Hull, 'losing his sight gave a middle-class, well-educated, white male in an élite job a searing experience of falling out of the normative world' (Marilyn Hull, 2017, 202). Whilst reading Hull's *Notes* offered me a valuable experience of blindness that challenged my normative views on academic work and sight loss it also presented an experience of cis-gendered hetero-masculinity that left me inevitably somewhat alienated. In order to connect my sense of my own masculinity to blindness, I sought out a queer forefather, and found Derek Jarman; in particular, I found his thoughts on the colour 'blue'.

Chroma: 'My Retina Is a Distant Planet'

How are we perceived, if we are to be perceived at all? For the most part we are invisible. (Jarman, 2019, 89). In *Chroma* (1994), the artist, gardener, and film maker, Derek Jarman offers an exploration of colour and its meanings, with the chapter 'Into the Blue' coming towards the end of his text. This section also informed Jarman's film *Blue* (1993), which features an extended narrative sequence set to a blue screen. Jarman writes his reflections on colour as he experiences AIDS-related retinal lesions, which affect both his peripheral and central vision in both eyes. Whereas Hull's memoir foregrounds how blindness structures the form of *Notes on Blindness* as the memoir is not 'tightly organised' and has 'no particular ending, because blindness has no ending' (Hull, 2017, xii), Jarman's entry 'Into the Blue' reads as many things: it is a lexicographic exploration of the colour blue; a memoir; an art history of colour; a long prose poem; a tissue of research citations; an account of queer rage; a love letter to sight and sightlessness. Generic associations abound and become confused in this section of *Chroma*. In different ways, the formal complexities of both Hull's and Jarman's writings on vision loss present a structural challenge to the metanarrative of blindness, which, in its de-subjectivisation of the blind man serves to flatten and empty out individual accounts of the experience. If, as Hull attests, 'blindness has no ending', then no single narrative can fully document it and the metanarrative of blindness comes under critical strain. Jarman's relationship to the colour blue is shown to be connected to his eye health:

> The doctor in St Bartholomew's Hospital thought he could detect lesions
>   in my retina – the pupils dilated with belladonna – the torch shone into
>   them with a terrible blinding light.
> Look left
> Look down
> Look up
> Look right.
> Blue flashes in my eyes.
>
> (Jarman, 2019, 84)

The scarring on his retina from burst blood vessels reacts to the light of the doctor's eye examination causing an afterglow in his field of vision. Later in this poetic-memory sequence, Jarman, as speaker, connects blue to profound grief at to the loss of male friends and lovers who have died from AIDS-related illnesses:

> Blue is the universal love in which man bathes – it is the terrestrial paradise.
> I'm walking along the beach in a howling gale –
> Another year is passing
> In the roaring waters
> I hear the voices of dead friends
> Love is life that lasts forever.
> My heart's memory turns to you
> David. Howard. Graham. Terry. Paul . . .
>
> (Jarman, 2019, 85)

In keeping with Jarman's narrative complexity in *Chroma*, blue is associated with love and with pain, or more precisely, it can be at times representative of the pain that springs from the attachments of love. Whereas Hull's grief was most acute when facing blindness as a parent, here, Jarman connects the blue of his sight loss to a blue rolling wave of lost male friends, their shared camaraderie now sunken. Sight-loss, for Jarman, is a consequence of something much broader; it cannot be uncoupled from the AIDS pandemic as: 'the virus rages fierce. I have no friends now who are not dead or dying' (Jarman, 2019, 86). Later on, in a sequence that further connects sight loss to queer masculinity, the speaker returns to the bright lights of an eye-check up at the hospital:

> The camera flash
> Atomic bright
> Photos
> The CMV – a green moon then the world turns magenta.
> My retina
> Is a distant planet
> A red Mars
> From a *Boy's Own* comic
> With yellow infection
> Bubbling at the corner.
> I said this looks like a planet
> The doctor says – 'Oh. I think
> It looks like a pizza'.
>
> (Jarman, 2019, 85)

The 'Atomic bright' of the camera signals that sense of catastrophic destruction that the speaker fears is being uncovered by the examination: the retinal scarring is, 'Bubbling at the corner', is threatening expansion. The line 'My retina | Is a distant planet' communicates the alien nature of sight loss. A retinal scan of the back of the eye does indeed look like a strange heavenly body. Jarman likens his scan to 'A red Mars' and in an effort to articulate this sense of strangeness he says to his doctor, 'this looks like a planet'. The record here of the doctor's reply – 'Oh, I think | It looks like a pizza' – humorously deflates the strange otherworldliness of this sight examination in its brisk exchange of planetary exploration for the mundanity of fast food. More to the point of this chapter, however, is the citing of '*Boy's Own Comic*'. The vision of 'Mars' that the retinal scan reminds Jarman of is not a telescopic image of the planet *per se* but instead a cartoon one from his childhood. The *Boys Own Comic* that Jarman refers to here is most likely one of several British magazines aimed at young boys and teenagers that were in print circulation in the 1960s. Jarman approaches the retinal scan in the spirit of boyish adventure, his eye check-up becoming, for a moment, an opportunity for brave curiosity until the entire simile is crushed by the doctor's likening of his retina to pizza, itself an immature image in the context of a serious ophthalmic appointment. Dead male friends and the fleeting possibility of intra-planetary adventure bring masculinity into the very focus of Jarman's sight loss. The scene of the eye check-up recurs a number of times in this chapter, as he reveals how 'the retina is destroyed, though when the bleeding stops what is left of my sight might improve. I have to come to terms with sightlessness' (Jarman, 2019, 86).

Concluding Discussion: Belinda

Both John M. Hull and Derek Jarman lived in the same country, England, and experienced sight loss, in various degrees, within years of each other. Hull was a professor who researched and taught Religious Education, was married and had children. Jarman was queer, an artist, a film maker, and an LGBT right's activist who had a partner 'HB'. Hull's blindness was connected to a history of cataracts and retinal detachments; Jarman's failing vision was but one symptom within a con-stellation of AIDS-related issues that he was experiencing at a time when effective treatment was not accessible to him. If Hull's account aligns with a cis-gendered heterosexual man's account of vision loss, shocking in part for the vulnerability it exposes in a category that is shielded from such vulnerability culturally, then Jarman offers something of the opposite in his account of sight loss as part of an extended web of debility that was wrought by a pandemic, which disproportion-ately affected gay men in Britain at that time. However different these accounts are, this chapter shows how each narrative positions sight loss as being at the centre of how masculinity is accommodated and performed. In the roles of father, lover, and friend, each author keys into the ways in which sight loss plays on male insecurities and prompts reconsiderations of the very narrative tropes that continue to shape white masculine experience. Both *Notes on Blindness* and *Chroma* speak back to the metanarrative of blindness in their careful and imaginative depictions of experi-ences of blindness, which entrench individuality and personal experience over and above the hegemonic meta-discourse of blindness that serves to flatten out meaning and reduce experience to stereotypical cultural co-ordinates.

As the brief forays into these writings have shown, as well as my own personal testimony, blindness brings into sharp relief questions of masculinity and offers the male-identifying person who faces vision loss an opportunity to re-think the cultural conditions of masculinity anew. Rather than the 'blind man' being defined by his blindness as is the case in the metanarrative's trope of the blind beggar, blind-ness (whatever that means) offers us all an opportunity to define masculinity and, with it, an occasion to re-think and re-new modes of affective connection within communities. In Hull's *Notes on Blindness*, I found the possibility of continuing to research and to teach as an academic. I can still remember Marilyn Hull telling me that her husband not only continued to teach and research but actually excelled and raised up the ladder of his university to become Dean. The stories that the blind tell are the stories that do not often get heard. These are the stories that are sustaining: not a beggar, but a Dean. In Jarman, I find something of myself; I somehow also now live in Kent, not far from Prospect Cottage in Dungeness. I am a gay man. I was born in 1986. My eyes changed colour around the time that Jarman wrote *Chroma*. Decades later, when I experienced retinal bleeding, I read his account of the colour blue. I read 'Into the Blue' as if I am reading a version of myself. I am reading what I feel and what I experience. Yet there are many differences. One difference, for me, is that each day I take a pill, which has a 99% efficacy rate for HIV infection prevention. I also live at time, and in a place in the world, where HIV medication is available to me if I were to become HIV positive. This medication would help me to live a normal life span and taking it would also ensure that levels of the virus would become undetectable in my body meaning that I could not pass the virus on to others (undetectable = untransmissible). Like Jarman, I live with the uncertainty of a scarred retina. As I sit finishing this chapter, I am distracted by the stir of our cat, Belinda. More than any cultural station, she has taught me the most about blindness. She has shown me that blindness is simply another mode, another way of experiencing the richness of the world. I am reminded of this every morning at 5 A.M. when she wakes me up to be let out in the garden to hunt. In those early morning moments, I can clearly see that her sense of curiosity and adventure is never diminished.

References

Anon. (2022) What is the Macula? [online]. *The Macular Society*. Available from: www.macularsociety.org/macular-disease/macula/ [accessed 28 June 2022].

Bolt, D. (2014) *The Metanarrative of Blindness: A Re-Reading of Twentieth-Century Anglophone Writing*, Ann Arbor: The University of Michigan Press.

Bolt, D. (2021) The metanarrative of arthritis: Playing and betraying the endgame, in D. Bolt (ed.) *Metanarratives of Disability: Culture, Assumed Authority, and the Normative Social Order*, London and New York: Routledge.

Hull, J. M. (2017) *Notes on Blindness: A Journey Through the Dark*, London: Wellcome Collection.

Hull, M. (2017) Epilogue, in J. M. Hull (ed.) *Notes on Blindness: A Journey Through the Dark*, London: Wellcome Collection.

Jarman, D. (2019) *Chroma: A Book of Colour – June '93*, London: Penguin Random house.

Siebers, T. (2008) *Disability Theory*, Ann Arbor: The University of Michigan Press.

14

BRINGING A BRICK TO MARKET

Pedagogical Perspectives on the Discordant Interplay Between Critical and Cultural Stations of Blindness

David Feeney

Preliminary Discussion: Weaving Disciplinary Fusions Through a Disidentificatory Impasse

This chapter is volunteered as a prompt to literary disability scholars to reflect on whether any semblance of the literary specificity of literary renderings of blindness might be worth salvaging as we subject these representations to analysis. It is underpinned by two interrelated questions: If, first, as few people engaged in contemporary literary studies would contest, literary criticism falls squarely within the sociocultural purview, is there anything that literary studies might recoup as its own within an interdisciplinary literary disability studies context? What, second, are the acceptable limits of rhetorical, stylistic, and expressive dispositions of artists and creative writers within the sphere of critical disability studies' treatment of characterological virtue? The reflections presented here relate more to the ways in which a literary representation becomes a *cultural station* within the field of disability studies than to the impact that any particular representations have had on my conceptions of blindness. Somewhat narcissistically, the emphasis on autoethnography and autocriticality underpinning this volume is interpreted as an invitation to present formative junctures of my own cross-disciplinary journey from English literature to disability studies as cultural stations, rather than any notably exemplary or counter-exemplary cultural artefacts.

Some of the features of these critical reflections – their emphasis on stereotypes, their treatment of objectionable illustrations of (counter)exemplarity, the unrationalised 'genre-hop' that is an occasional feature of their approach to literary comparison, the implicit expectation that students appreciate metanarrative while bypassing narrative that seems to be a characteristic of their application in practice, their deterministic tracings of attitudes or intentions through fictional representations, and the more recent emergence of a tendency to present taxonomic forms

DOI: 10.4324/9781003275060-18

of ableism-related classification as literary analysis – underpin the reflections on the second of the cultural stations presented here. As core components of 'Disability Studies 101', many of these widely applied strategies and critical constructs have come to represent the 'critical coinage' of the disability studies scholar/educator, which, to adapt Stefan Collini's phrase, have become 'rubbed smooth by being constantly circulated' within the field (Collini, 2013, 19). While instances of some of these approaches are cited within these pages, limitations of space compel me to assume that the process of familiarising themselves with these constructs has already been undertaken by the reader. The attention afforded to these aspects of literary disability studies is not presented primarily as theoretical critique. This chapter amounts, rather, to a series of reflections on how the discontinuity of my disciplinary identity informs an altogether too keenly felt sense of my own pedagogical failings when I bring these forms of analysis into service as a means of engaging my students with literary representations of blindness. As the field of disability studies appears to be replete with scholars whose career trajectory has not been entirely dissimilar to my own, these reflections are shared in the hope that they may have a value beyond that of a confessional account of what I have come, over time, to regard both as personal disidentification with the pedagogical application of certain tenets of literary disability studies, and disability studies' disidentification with my conception of literary value.

The chapter begins by positioning literary disability studies within reflections on the sociology of art and literature. After drawing on work by Janet Wolff, Rita Felski, and others, Mathew Arnold's 'literary touchstone' theory is briefly contrasted with the engagement of more contemporary cultural theory with literature as a means of illustrating the extreme forms of aesthetic essentialism and theoretical reductionism critiqued by these authors. The phenomenon of contextomy is then addressed as a problematic modus operandi shared by both approaches to engagement with literary value, and the limitations inherent in critical tendencies to bring this practice into service as a means of evidencing arguments about the literary canvassing of ableist forms of counter-exemplarity are considered. Attention then shifts to failures of cultural theorists to factor an appreciation of the substantial differences between the modes of persuasion and forms of insight that can secure reflective purchase within theoretical and imaginative domains of expression into their critiques of creative transgressions of their own regulative ideals. The chapter concludes with some suggestions of correctives that might be applied to the pedagogical impact of disability studies' longstanding utilisation of contextomy within its approach to the identification and analysis of cultural stations.

(Inter)Disciplinary Miscreance: The Heretical Legacy of the Grounding of Literary Engagement in the Sociology of Aesthetics

My undergraduate and postgraduate studies focused primarily on English literature and aesthetics. What I learnt during that time from such scholars as Janet Wolff and

Rita Felski about the sociology of aesthetic and literary value exerted a formative impact on my critical disposition that has subsequently registered itself as an influence that tempers my commitment to certain tendencies of literary criticism that prevail within my current field of study. Some of the principles underpinning my grounding in the sociology of aesthetic value are recounted here in the hope that the value of doing so will become clear within the context of my reflections on my second cultural station.

For aestheticians and literary theorists of an essentialist persuasion, the assumption that art and literature are answerable only to internalist representational logics and are the product of epiphanic visitations of inspiration, renders the task of elucidating the values demonstrated by literary representation a largely unproblematic undertaking. Sociologists of a profoundly relativistic disposition, conversely, have tended to reduce literary and artistic value to the sum of the ideological predilections and socioeconomic circumstances that can be traced through imaginative representations. Janet Wolff (1993) deems the perspectives at either polarity of the essentialist/reductionist spectrum to be untenable, suggesting that recognition of the ideological embeddedness and social constructedness of conceptions and criteria of aesthetic and literary value do not necessarily have to entail a wholesale discounting of the specifically literary values of creative literary expression. I suggest that the interdisciplinary field of literary disability studies might do well to heed Wolff's delineation of a potentially instructive reconciliatory path between these antithetical tendencies to account for literary value.

Wolff remains unqualifiedly committed to the 'historical, ideological and contingent nature' of a good deal of aesthetic appraisal, and problematises the historically unqueried rationale underpinning the selection of criteria which have yielded under-considered affirmations of aesthetic or literary value (11). This commitment is clearly manifest in her presentation of art, literature, and aesthetics as 'historically specific products of social relations and practices' (15). While unreservedly conceding the sociological orientation of aesthetic value, however, Wolff also argues that sociology has 'exceeded its own brief in so far as it fails to account for the "aesthetic"' (11). Relating Wolff's insights to literary representations of blindness – or disability more generally – it would appear that a meaningful evaluation of the merits of such representations is as unlikely to be yielded by an exacting restriction of attention to the words on a page, as it is by a coercive presentation of a set of strategically excerpted literary passages as indices of ideological bias.

I am as sceptical as Wolff of aesthetic essentialism which perceives itself as trafficking within a refined domain, positioned at an elevated remove from society and its political concerns. I also share her misgivings, however, about the capacity of critical approaches that are premised on the assumption that ideology and social causality are the exclusive determinants of aesthetic value to do interrogative justice to literary representation. The interdisciplinary nature of our subject renders us well positioned, in theory, to devise forms of critical interrogation that accommodate a considered fusion of socio-political and literary criteria within our interrogations of literary value. Within literary disability studies theory, the former criterion-grouping often appears to me to be applied in isolation.

Rita Felski prefaces her refreshingly brazen reflections on the role attributed to critical constructs within endeavours to account for the significance and value of art and literature with Larry Grossberg's observation that 'for cultural studies context is everything and everything is contextual' (Grossberg, 1997, 255, cited in Felski, 2011, 573). The observation is volunteered in an attempt to epitomise what Felski perceives as the elemental resolve of cultural studies to transcend the perceived depthlessness of the representational guise by positioning it within a wider frame of explicative reference. This theoretical insistence that a focus on text be trumped by a concern for context relates, Felski contends, to the conviction that the role of penetrating critical analysis is to draw attention to representational characteristics that 'the literary text does not see' and that might pass the uncircumspect reader by (574). This weighting of critical concern affords opportunities for the cultural theorist to apply a corrective to the complicity of texts in social conditions that warrant stern disavowal.

Like Wolff, Felski is wary of forms of analysis that begin and end in attention to aesthetic aspects of the experiences yielded by literature. She also shares Wolff's suspicions, however, of approaches to literature that traffic exclusively in terms of cultural symptom. 'The singular disadvantage of the "context concept"', according to Felski, 'is that it inveigles us into endless reiterations of the same dichotomies: test versus context, word versus world, literature versus society and history, internalist versus externalist explanations of works of art' (Felski, 2011, 276). The task of doing justice to the distinctiveness and specificity of artworks remains 'a recurring thorn in [the] flesh' of theorists who reduce creative expression to issues of social causality and subscribe to 'the model of explanation-as-reduction' (581). While acknowledging that artworks do not emerge within a social or historical vacuum, Felski is struck by the 'punitive fashion' in which context is regularly applied as a means of impoverishing and disempowering the artwork within the analytical pursuit of 'some final reduction' (582). Her reflections on the essentialist and reductionist forms of interpretation identified by Wolff culminates in Felski's cautionary reminder that there is 'no zero-sum game in which one side must be conclusively crushed so the other can triumph' (584).

The consequence of reducing literary works to the nexus of social factors underpinning their generation or interpretation in an attempt to reveal the 'hidden laws' and 'subterranean structures' that 'determine them' is, according to Felski, that these works 'dissolve into the cultural assumptions and interpretive frameworks of their audiences' (585–586). As someone who now labours within the field of disability studies, the problematic implications of the hold that Felski's reflections have on my conception of artistic value came to mind a number of years ago when I attended a presentation by a leading scholar in the field of disability studies on the history of painterly renderings of disabled characters. The presentation was punctuated by a series of appeals to the designs on the emotional responses of the viewers of their paintings that the speaker appeared to posit as the driving force behind the artists' endeavours. When reflecting on Antonio Tempesta's 'Christ Cures a Leper' (1593), for example the speaker informed the audience: 'clearly we are supposed to see disgust for the leper'. Shifting attention to Peter Breugel's 'The Cripples' or 'The Beggars' (1568), the speaker asked his audience: '[a]re we supposed to think of it as funny? . . . something obviously is supposed to be grotesque about this. I don't know whether the emotion that we are supposed to regard this with is humour. Are we supposed to laugh at these figures?'. Similarly, after clicking to a slide containing Ribera's 'The Boy with the Club Foot' (1642), the audience was instructed that 'one of the things you want to wonder about this is what are we supposed to think about this?'. The analysis of John Everett Millais's 'The Blind Man (1853) amounted to the insight that 'it's supposed to be a funny thing – the blind man can't see'. 'What is our reaction supposed to be?', we were asked, when introduced to Thomas Faed's, 'Worn Out' (1868). When shown a photograph by Dianne Arbus, the audience was invited to ask themselves: 'what is the emotion that is supposed to be portrayed?' (Davis, 2017)[1].

This succession of reductions of paintings to assumptions about the ableist motivations of the artists who generated them reminded me of Felski's confession to being at a loss to comprehend the critical conviction that 'the texts we study are permanently engaged in coercing, mystifying, and hoodwinking their readers' (Felski, 2011, 589). Felski is equally bewildered by the double standard whereby artistic representations are attributed the capacity to exert a formative influence on social attitudes and forms of understanding, only to be dismissed within all-determining contextual frameworks as the by-product of the 'reflex of systems steering the action behind the scenes' (589). As compelling as I find Felski's insights into the 'double-standard' of the cultural theorist's conception of the agency of artistic or literary representation, they seem to fall short of accounting for the role of context in the elevation of certain representations to the status of cultural stations within a literary disability studies context. For all of its privileging of a certain type of context, the engagement of cultural analysis in literary representation is often characterised by a strategic excerption of illustrative passages of counter-exemplarity from the contexts within which these excerpts originally appear, and a subsequent re-contextualisation of these extracts within a persuasive theoretical framework that is more conducive to the theorist's favoured mode of rational disputation.

My Entry Into Disability Studies: Contextomy and the Role of Stereotypes in Students' Engagement With Literary Representations

I have made a couple of attempts to incorporate such perspectives into an engagement with literary representations of blindness. On one occasion, in an attempt to affirmatively delineate a 'differential aesthetic' that might expose the ableist underpinnings of conceptions of aesthetic value in exclusively visual terms, I attempted to bring the testimony of blind people about their aesthetic experiences into various forms of contact with a history of philosophical accounts of the nature of aesthetic experience. On a later occasion, I attempted to bring the perspectives of the authors of imaginative representations of blindness into contact with those of literary disability studies theorists. On both occasions, I was told that my approaches were not appropriate within the domain of literary disability studies. Later still, when teaching a course on disability and life writing, I found myself relaying to my students David T. Mitchell's (2000) critique of this literary genre that was premised on the argument that the approaches to authorship assumed by autobiographers of disability 'derives from literary conventions' (312). The cumulative impact of the history of my encounters with such attitudes towards literary representation began, some time ago, to register itself on my understanding in the form of a suggestion that one of the primary misgivings towards literary representations of disability within the field of disability studies may be that they are literature. At a loss to know what to do with my longstanding and passionate interest in literature within my field of employment, I subsequently put it into abeyance and turned my attention to other concerns.

Felski's compulsion explicitly to signpost her decision to present her satirical treatment of context under the title 'context stinks' as a deliberate provocation does not seem insignificant. Doing so enables her to summon a defence should a single component of her intricate line of argument be extracted in isolation and used as evidence to attribute to her opinions that are not accurately representative of her critical stance. Morris Engel (1994) and Matthew McGlone (2005a, 2005b) describe such practice as contextomy – the distortion of a source's originally intended meaning as a consequence of a strategically selective excerpting of words by another party from their original linguistic context. Both authors are at pains to emphasise that the infringement is not the unavoidable act of removing a quote from its original context (this is the essence of quotation), but in the quoter's deliberate exclusion from the excerpt of proximal text that might serve to clarify that the extract in question has a significance that may not be exhausted by, or directly aligned with, the significance to which the quoter is attributing it. The transgression, according to Engel, becomes a fallacy when a strategic (mis)appropriation of an original source is brought into evidential service as the premise of an argument. McGlone (2005a) reiterates Engel's observation by positing a connection between contextomy and the 'expository goals' of an author or critic (511).

McGlone (2005a) provides a helpful summary of the history of the employment of contextomy in the service of various forms of socio-political persuasion within the domains of religious and political propaganda, the promotional practices of film studios, and the spin tactics of partisan political journalists (see also Mayer, 1966; Hill and Cheadle, 1996; Warren and Warren, 1996; Broydo, 1997). Michael McDevitt uses the term 'idea rendering' to refer to the 'process in which media actors translate intellectual provocations into deviance, advancing social control through symbolic action' (McDevitt, 2021, 15). 'When a concept, trope, or other rhetorical bit is extracted from a linguistic context', according to McDevitt, 'it is not just de-contextualized but re-contextualized' into a narrative that is often at a multidimensional remove from the one from which it has been appropriated.

A variety of motives might account for engagement in such practice, but they are equally, as McDevitt sees it, intent on administering forms of social control in ways that have a dubious impact on the integrity of the relayed ideas that cannot be justified by means of simplistic appeal to authorial or critical efficiency (15). In what can scarcely be regarded as a methodological coincidence, both polarities of the 'essentialist/reductionist' spectrum identified by Wolff and Felski as radically antagonistic approaches to literary value manifest in tactical applications of contextomy. This can be illustrated by means of a brief comparison of Matthew Arnold's glorification of literary exemplarity, and the cultural theorist's critique of representations of behavioural or attitudinal counter-exemplarity, which regularly assumes the form of 'simply holding up a sample of the objectionable prose in the tweezers of quotation' (Collini, 2013, 24).

The concept of the touchstone has come to be widely understood as a figurative reference to evaluations of quality or authenticity more generally. Matthew Arnold first popularised the term within a literary context by maintaining that the value of a literary text needs to be judged in relation to other texts. The fusion of disinterested engagement with poetic renderings of meritorious sentiments and a pupil's sensibility was central to Arnold's conception of a meaningful education. The testatory approach to comparative literary evaluation introduced by Arnold in his Study of Poetry (1903–1904) identifies 11 concrete examples, by virtue of which we can arrive at a 'real' estimate of the excellence and beauty of a literary work. These works, representing the 'best', serve as touchstones by which the merits of other literary endeavours can be evaluated, and the presence or absence of high poetic quality can be detected. The basing of literary evaluation on exemplification is presented by Arnold as a means of avoiding the manifold fallacies associated with embedding such judgements on extra-literary considerations. The anthologising of judiciously selected literary excerpts as a core element of a humanising education has not, however, been without criticism. Those criticisms which directly addressed the value of Arnold's extraction of concise passages from longer texts are of greatest relevance to our current purposes.

John Shepard Eells (1955) suggests that the passages selected by Arnold 'have no relation whatsoever to the unity of the poem[s]' from which he extracted them (204). If the 'power' of the exemplary passages, and their 'best imaginative values' are to be 'felt and realized', according to Sheppard Eells, when 'they must be read and pondered in their contexts' (205–207). Because these fragments 'demand reference to what has gone before' (208), a 'comprehensive understanding of the touchstones apart from their contexts is clearly impossible' (207). Addressing an audience at Queen's College in 1948, Charles Kingsley critiqued Arnold's method of presenting literary passages in strategically fragmented form as a means of promoting their literary exemplarity in a way that might be instructive for cultural theorists who adopt the same ploy to demonstrate counter-exemplarity:

> The young have been taught to admire the laurels of Parnassus, but only after they have been clipped and pollarded like a Dutch shrubbery. The roots

which connect them with mythic antiquity, and the fresh leaves and flowers of the growing present, have been generally cut off with care, and the middle part only has been allowed to be used – too often, of course, a sufficiently tough and dry stem. . . . 'Extracts' and 'Select Beauties' are about as practical as the worthy in the old story, who, wishing to sell his house, brought one of the bricks to market as a specimen.

(Kingsley, 1890, cited by Altick, 1998, 177)

My induction into the field of literary disability studies was heralded by my reading of the address Kenneth Jernigan (1974) presented at the annual convention of the National Federation of the Blind entitled 'Is literature against us?'. I remember this text as a compilation of utterances of characters extracted from representations of blindness to demonstrate that the domain of literature is replete with negative attitudes towards blind people. Shortly afterwards, I read Jacob Twersky's (1953) more detailed engagement with literary works undertaken in the service of a similar exegetic goal. In my experiences as an educator, it has become clear that existing inventories of literary stereotypes (see, for example Barnes, 1992; Hunt, 1991; Bolt, 2006) remain among the resources that are brought most frequently into pedagogical service to teach undergraduate disability studies students about literary representations of disability. These resources generally take the form of exercises in contextomy, whereby excerpts of attitudinal or behavioural counter-exemplarity are extracted from their wider narrative contexts in order to illustrate the role of literary or media representation in the construction of negative social attitudes towards disabled people. James Kelman's novel *How Late It Was, How Late* (1998) is an illustrative case in point. I encountered disability studies critiques of this literary work long before I read the original text. In two critical interrogations of the novel (Bolt, 2006, 2013), the following passage was excerpted as a means of illustrating that Kelman's development of Sammy, the novel's principal protagonist, was rooted in ableist stereotyping: 'this blind guy could stand on one side of a wall and know what was happening on the other. He could actually pick up what was going on in a different room, whereabouts people were standing and all that' (Kelman, 1998, 101).

Another critical interrogation (Bolt, 2005) of the same work extracts the utterance 'he would be as well parking the head in a gas oven' (Kelman, 1998, 29) as exemplifying a correlation between loss of vision and the contemplation of suicide. In the first of these excerpted passages, Kelman is actually describing a representation of blindness that Sammy recalls watching on television. His unfolding lived experience of blindness might be interpreted as exposing the representation as the myth that it clearly is. In the second of the excerpted passages, Sammy's contemplation of suicide is prompted by a combination of the discomfort generated by the pillow on his prison bed which he compares to a sheet of tissue paper, and which prevented oxygen from reaching his brain, and his suspicion that his partner Helen might leave him. My interpretation of Sammy's attitude towards losing his sight, at least as it manifests at this juncture of the novel, is that it seems closer to ambivalence than to the depression detected by Bolt. The discrepancy between the conception I had harboured of Kelman's novel when relying on second-hand critical accounts of its portrayal of blindness, and the insights that unfolded when I finally read it, seem to me to illustrate both the perils of contextomy when brought into play to evidence a line of critical argument, and the importance of affording time to our students to engage with narrative in advance of engaging with explicatory metanarrative.

It is not uncommon for my undergraduate students to bring the aforementioned preformulated stereotype inventories into play as a component of the game of 'stereotype bingo' that they regularly present as literary analysis. The analysis entails the scanning of a representation of disability (or, as is more often the case, a disability studies scholar's interpretation of such a representation) until they encounter a reference or an utterance that corresponds to a notation on the 'bingo card' of listed stereotypes and then repeat the process until they have exhausted the array of stereotypes detectable within the representation under review. More recently, some of my more adventurous students have been engaging in more sophisticated forms of literary analysis by applying tabularised forms of analysis derived from the tripartite model of disability (Bolt, 2014, 2015, 2016, 2017, 2020) to literary texts. This model represents a valuable means of interrupting simplistic distinctions between negative and affirmative attitudes towards non-normativity and the problematisation of simplistic evaluative correlations between representational affirmation and literary quality. In the context of Janet Wolff's concern for the specificity of literary value, however, it seems significant that the identification of various configurations of normativity and appreciation generated by applications of this model do not always concern themselves with the potential significance of these distinctions within such diverse genres as novels, autobiographies, or works of imaginative literature that are based on psychological case-studies (see Bolt, 2015). In the absence of familiarity with the texts they are critiquing, it is not unknown for students' submissions to assume the form of annotated spreadsheets, with truncated excerpts being entered into particular columns depending on the degree to which they exemplify ableism, disablism or appreciation. I suspect that my reservations about such instances of theoretical construct trumping attentiveness to literary specificity stem from a conception of interdisciplinarity that, forged in advance of my arrival within the field of disability studies, seems to be at odds with the conceptions and applications of interdisciplinarity that appear to prevail throughout the discipline.

An additional feature of the engagement of cultural theorists in representations of blindness is that their tendency to reduce these representations to selections from a pre-delineated range of critical constructs means that aspects of a representation for which there exists no corresponding critical construct tend to remain unremarked upon. The critical reception afforded to Anthony Doerr's *All the Light We Cannot See* (2014) seems interesting in this regard. The novel prompted a substantial volume of negative response, much of which seems eminently warranted (see, for example, Longfellow, 2021; Wells-Jensen, 2016). Critics have highlighted mimetic failings, the infantilisation of Marie-Laure, the blind protagonist, and her over-reliance on the support of others. I have not come across a critical source which attends to a scene in which the blind protagonist and a fully sighted friend collectively savour the 'outrageous sweetness' of the perfume that fills the kitchen when they open their last remaining tin of peaches, which reads to me like an inclusive re-rendering of Proust's celebrated madeleine scene (Doerr, 2014, 470). I have written elsewhere (Feeney, 2007) about a history of fully sighted authors whose vision impedes their ability to render blindness in anything but visually charged terms. Within this context, Doerr's depiction of the relationship that develops between Marie-Laure and a fully sighted German soldier through the medium of radio waves seems to me to be a remarkable contribution. The neglect of attention commanded by these aspects of the novel might be partially accounted for in terms of the challenges associated with identifying the notation on the stereotype bingo card to which they bear the closest correspondence.

It remains the case, I argue, that disability studies students who are not afforded time to read the literary works on which they are encouraged to comment critically find themselves reliant on the testimony of cultural theorists who have interpreted these representations in relation to the critical principles that prevail within their discipline. Say, for the purposes of argument (and it seems quite a stretch) these theorists have managed somehow to select literary extracts that perfectly capture what Arnold might call the 'essence' of the literary works from which the counter-exemplary passages have been extracted. In such a case, students who base their literary evaluations on these strategically excerpted passages might be perceived as volunteering 'accurate' forms of literary appraisal. Doing so, however, does not necessarily demonstrate competence in literary analysis. Of course, this is not necessarily a problem within the field of literary disability studies, and my perception of it as such may be another consequence of the fact that the interdisciplinary framework within which I am inclined to operate was forged in advance of my wholesale entry into disability studies. My misgivings about such an approach might be illustrated in relation to Ernest Sosa's account of what he terms the 'AAA normative structure of performances'.

In his 'Knowing Full Well', Sosa (2011) presents belief and knowledge as performances, and devises a system for gauging epistemological credibility in terms of performative normativity. Sosa's distinction between belief and knowledge entails a classification of belief into three performative levels. As a performance, Sosa suggests, belief secures a particular degree of success if it proves to be accurate, another if it is capably or adroitly arrived at, and a further degree of success if the truth in question is directly or necessarily illustrative of the believer's competence. Sosa distinguishes this latter form of belief by virtue of what he describes as its 'aptness' (Sosa, 2011, 1). Archery and hunting motifs recur throughout Sosa's attempts to demarcate and exemplify a variety of orders of belief and the corresponding classifications of epistemological status that can be meaningfully assigned to them. The success of an archer's shot, for example, can be appraised in relation to the degree of accuracy with which it hits its target. It is conceivable, Sosa suggests, that an archer's shot might be unfailingly accurate without achieving unqualified success as a shot. The arrow might pierce the bullseye by virtue of a sequence of unanticipated gusts of wind that successively generate a deviation from and restoration to the arrow's intended trajectory. In such a case, the shot can be said to be accurate and to demonstrate a degree of skill. But the accuracy of such a shot can arguably be more precisely accounted for in terms of good fortune rather than skill. 'This shot is both accurate and adroit', Sosa suggests, 'yet it is not accurate because adroit, so as to manifest the archer's skill and competence' (Sosa, 2011, 4). Evaluated against the criteria of aptness, the critical verdict volunteered by a student in relation to an unread representation, like the archer's accurate shot, however 'accurate' it may happen to be, fails.

Concluding Discussion: Literature, Society, and Antithetical Forms of Expressive Disposition

As I was preparing this chapter, the Canadian Journal of Disability Studies was in the midst of its 'Worsties' campaign. Readers were presented with categories of disability representation and invited to vote for the ones that they felt were most objectionable:

> In the third week of the Worst Representation of Disability Tournament (henceforth The Worsties) you will be voting for characters in fiction. There are four categories: Children's Literature, Young Adult Literature, Adult Literature, and Comic Books & Graphic Novels. If you haven't read all of the works here that is okay! You may skip questions or vote using other methods (eg., reading a brief summary of the work on the internet).
>
> *(Lorenz, 2022)*

The suggestion appears to be that being unfamiliar with the presentations in response to which readers of the Journal are encouraged to register abhorrence should not be an impediment to participation because a summary of the lowlights of the nominated works have been made available elsewhere. This endeavour, although no doubt undertaken with a degree of levity, seems to me to epitomise several of the misgivings about the engagement of disability studies theorists with imaginative representations of disability expressed throughout these pages.

The history of literature is replete with instances of insights being developed through creative manipulations of counter-exemplarity. Helen Small (2017) illustrates her observations about the axiological interface between the domains of literature and politics by reflecting on Thomas Carlyle's tendency to bring 'bad' or 'counter' exemplarity into service as a literary device, or as a rhetorical strategy, when addressing issues of conventional morality. Marilyn Booth (2008) has reflected on how the texts collected by Julie Peakman under the title *Whore Biographies 1700–1825* play on distinctions between exemplarity and counterexemplarity in their sardonic mockery of the prevailing niceties of polite society. In her review of the publication, Booth suggests that the taking of hyperbolic

liberties with the conventions of exemplarity is one of the many rhetorical strategies employed to optimise the effectiveness and representational edge of the bio-
graphical accounts, which advance purposes of social reform through a literary
strategy of 'mock-solemn counter-exemplarity' (Booth, 2008, 472). Stella Ktenas
(2017) has explored various forms of unlikely alignment between Jonathan Swift's
scatological poetry and the principles of feminist literary criticism. Wojciech Kaftanski (2022) has written about Kierkegaard's tendency towards self-presentation in
counter-exemplary terms as a 'negative prototype' as a means of achieving a number of educational, rhetorical, and moral objectives (Kaftanski, 2022, 158–161).
Each of these creatively controversialist approaches to counter-exemplarity contain
passages which, if excerpted in isolation by a theorist of marginality, would generate unlimited critical affront. Doing so, however, would not constitute the refuta-
tion of an oppositional insight as much as it would the condemnation of a closely
aligned insight on the grounds that it was formulated by means of a stylistic disposition that seems alien to one's own.

What seems to me to be at issue here is the acceptable limits of expressive
dispositions within the sphere of critical disability studies, and the discipline's dis-
inclination to entertain the possibility of anti-normative approaches to potentially
emancipatory insight emerging through deliberately provocative forms of characterisation that take forms other than rational disputation. The critical challenge,
according to Helen Small, lies in telling the difference between modes of discourse
and argument that knowingly break with convention in order to impactfully volunteer an insight, and corresponding forms whose disregard for these conventions
stems from an obliviousness to their existence (Small, 2017, 536). It seems to me
that this distinction is rarely factored into literary disability studies theory. Appreciation of the inevitability of the 'clash of discursive worlds', Collini argues, needs
to be factored into forms of critical engagement that take place at the interface of
literature and society (11). He is wary of the critical disregard demonstrated by
cultural theorists for 'the different literary tactics' and 'modes of argument' that
'may be called for in public debate by contrast to philosophical argument' (Collini, 2013, 12). Thomas Keenan suggests that 'the only good example', the only
one worthy of 'interiorization, and identification that example calls for, is the bad
example' (Keenan, 1995, 121). The provocative incorporation of 'bad' or objectionable exemplarity within a representation can be instructive as a creative sign-
posting of what is best avoided. In the apparent absence of concern for the mode of
representation or wider narrative context within which objectionable exemplarity
is rendered, the default position of the disability studies scholar would appear to be
that the bad example is bad.

Applying Collini's logic to sociologically oriented interrogations of literary
representation, it might be argued that the danger here lies in assuming that the
discourse and expressive dispositions that are afforded critical purchase within
the domains of cultural theory and imaginative representation are 'straightfor-
wardly commensurable', that the process of criticism involves 'recommending
proposition B as a replacement for proposition A, and that this substitution can be

cleanly effected without any strain on the surrounding framework of belief' (Collini, 2013, 13). Collini observes that the writer who deviates from conventional strategies of awareness raising – by 'being deliberately provocative', for example, by 'using weapons of satire or humour', is likely to be wrong-headedly reproved (13–14). Like Brian Friel's *Molly Sweeney*, Kelman's *How Late It Was, How Late* is replete with utterances which, if extracted from their original context, will feed into existing critical perceptions of a direct illustrational relationship between counter-exemplarity and attitudinal or intentional antagonism. In order to avoid having negative attitudes attributed to them, Kelman might have had Sammy state directly that it is not true that blind people have an uncanny sense of what is happening in rooms that adjoin theirs. Friel might have had the protagonists of his play inform the blind protagonist that she had a great deal to lose should she elect to have her vision restored, just as Jonathan Swift might have explicitly stated that women should not be reduced to their outward appearance. My experience of progressing from an indirect to a direct form of engagement with Kelman's novel suggests that it might occasionally be the case that arguments between theorists and artists are needlessly developed, and that the perceived need for resolution is ill-judged, because both parties are in ultimate, albeit regularly inadvert, accord.

In the course of his reflections on the capacity of fact-checking to avoid contextomy, McGlone recalls the resolution of Howard Movshhovitz, a film critic for the Denver Post, who resolved '[i]f I ever write a line I think can be quoted, I change it' (Reiner, 1996, cited in McGlone, 2005a, 514). One wonders whether the generators of literary representations of disability might go to similar lengths to devise a means of avoiding subjection to contextomy. In the absence of such a manoeuvre, I conclude by suggesting two ways in which the issues relating to the dissonant interplay between critical and cultural stations of blindness discussed here might be resolved. The first is to factor sufficient time for the reading of literary representations of disability into the curriculum design of undergraduate disability studies courses, thus making disability studies departments, and universities more generally, slower spaces. Marianna Papastephanou and Michael Alhadeff-Jones have engaged in a discussion of the importance of allocating time to reading within contemporary universities. 'Reading a book involves multiple issues of time', Papastephanou suggests. Time should be afforded to individuals 'to read at a slower pace so as to savour the ideas or to pause for thinking some ideas through to their further implications' (Papastephanou, 2018, 97). 'As we all know it', Alhadeff-Jones responds, 'writing and reading takes time. In the contemporary social and academic context, often shaped by a destabilizing sense of acceleration and urgency, protecting the moments required for such "time-consuming" activities is not something that can be taken for granted anymore' (Alhadeff-Jones, 2018, 103). As institutions, we might get out of the habit of ensuring, on the one hand that our students are well versed in the mechanisms of socially generated disablement, while subjecting them, at the same time, to a degree of temporal disablement that precludes the possibility of reading the literary texts on which we expect them to reflect with authority.

My second suggestion might be presented as the involvement of disability studies students in a reconfigured form of the four-stage strategy of 'ideas rendering (and repair)' which McDevitt (2021) has devised in order to track and directly compare ideas before and after they have been subjected to contextomy in the course of being transposed to a different medium. This would essentially entail the engagement of disability students in a process of reverse engineering the practices of literary contextomy encountered in the secondary sources with which we require them to engage. First, a pre-rendering phase might involve the application of textual analysis to identify themes that recur throughout an entire representation of disability. This phase of the analysis should entail being vigilantly heedful of distinct tendencies for 'the conceptual building blocks of conceptual arguments' (15) to be engaged in their entirety and in synecdochical form in the process of their cross-media translation. Conceptual network analysis might then be applied to document any form of de-contextualisation to which the insights volunteered within the original representation might have been subjected in the course of their theoretical analysis. This step would entail comparing 'the semantic relations of key concepts in an original text' to those that feature within the critical re-rendering of these concepts (*ibid.*). The third step would entail a re-application of textual analysis in order to identify the uses to which extracts from creative representations are put in critical discourse, with particular attention being paid to the strategic utilisation of misrepresentative excerpts for the purposes of the development or illustration of arguments, or the affirmation of pre-established theoretical principles. Finally, students might be asked to reflect on how best to restore the excerpted quotations to their original significance in the name of 'repair' (ibid.).

Note

1   As a core member of the Centre for Culture and Disability Studies, I must add that Lennard Davis has given two of our best attended seminars and both are in the top ten most popular films on our YouTube channel.

References

Alhadeff-Jones, M. (2018) A reply to Marianna Papastephanou's review of time and the rhythms of emancipatory education. *Studies in the Philosophy of Education* 37 (1): 103–107.

Altick, R. D. (1998) *The English Common Reader: A Social History of the Mass Reading Public, 1800–1900 2nd Ed*, Columbus: Ohio State University Press.

Arnold, M. (1903–1904) *The Complete Works of Matthew Arnold, Edition de Luxe, 15 vols*, London: Macmillan.

Barnes, C. (1992) *Disabling Imagery and the Media: An Exploration of the Principles for Media Representations of Disabled People*, Halifax: The British Council of Organisations of Disabled People & Ryburn Publishing Limited.

Bolt, D. (2005) Caught in the chasm: Literary representation and suicide among people with impaired vision. *The British Journal of Visual Impairment* 23 (3): 117–121.

Bolt, D. (2006) Beneficial blindness: Literary representation and the so-called positive stereotyping of people with impaired vision. *New Zealand Journal of Disability Studies* 12 (1): 80–100.

Bolt, D. (2013) *The Metanarrative of Blindness: A Re-reading of Twentieth Century Anglophone Writing*, Ann Arbor: University of Michigan Press.

Bolt, D. (2014) *Beyond Ocularnormativism: Blindness, Happiness, and Other Positivisms* [online]. Minneapolis: The Society for Disability Studies.

Bolt, D. (2015) Not forgetting happiness: The tripartite model of disability and Its application in literary criticism. *Disability & Society* 30 (7): 1103–1117.

Bolt, D. (2016) Negative to the extreme: The problematics of the RNIB's See the need campaign. *Disability and Society* 31 (9): 1161–1174.

Bolt, D. (2017) Enabling the classroom and the curriculum: Higher education, literary studies and disability. *Journal of Further and Higher Education* 41 (4): 556–565.

Bolt, D. (2020) Complex and critical: A methodological application of the tripartite model of disability, in L. Ware (ed.) *Critical Readings in Interdisciplinary Disability Studies. (Dis) Assemblages*, Cham: Springer.

Booth, M. (2008) Julie Peakman, ed. Whore Biographies 1700–1825 (review). *Biography* 31 (3): 466–473.

Broydo, L. (1997) (Not Such a) Thriller! *Mother Jones* 22 (6): 17.

Collini, S. (2013) What, ultimately, for? The elusive goal of cultural criticism. *Raritan* 33 (2): 4–26.

Davis, L. J. (2017) Sorrowless lamentation: Viewer's emotional responses to the disabled poor in Art, 22 November. Available from: www.youtube.com/watch?v=ixIhrNYbaF4 [accessed 13 March 2022].

Doerr, A. (2014) *All the Light We Cannot See*, London: Fourth Estate.

Engel, S. M. (1994) *With Good Reason: An Introduction to Informal Fallacies, 5th Ed*, Bedford: St. Martins.

Feeney, D. (2007) *Toward an Aesthetics of Blindness: An Interdisciplinary Response to Synge, Yeats and Friel*, New York: Peter Lang.

Felski, R. (2011) Context stinks. *New Literary History* 42 (4): 573–591.

Grossberg, L. (1997) *Bringing It All Back Home: Essays on Cultural Studies*, Durham: Duke University Press.

Hill, J. and Cheadle, R. (1996) *The Bible Tells Me So: Uses and Abuses of Holy Scripture*, New York: Anchor Doubleday.

Hunt, P. (1991) Discrimination: Disabled people and the media. *Contact* 70: 45–48.

Jernigan, K. (1974) Is literature against us? 3 July. Available from: https://nfb.org/images/nfb/publications/convent/banque74.htm [accessed 29 April 2022].

Kaftanski, W. (2022) *Kierkegaard, Mimesis, and Modernity: A Study of Imitation, Existence, and Affect*, New York and London: Routledge.

Keenan, T. (1995) Fables of responsibility, in A. Gelley (ed.) *Unruly Examples: On the Rhetoric of Exemplarity*, Stanford: Stanford University Press.

Kelman, J. (1998) *How Late It Was, How Late*, London: Vintage.

Kingsley, C. (1890) *On English Literature, in Literary and General Lectures and Essays*, London and New York: MacMillan.

Ktenas, S. (2017) Such gaudy tulips raised from dung: Gender performance in Jonathan Swift's 'The Lady's Dressing Room'. *Philament* 23: 5–30.

Longfellow, L. (2021) Comparative perspectives with a disability lens all the light we cannot see by Anthony Doerr and selected epistles by Olivia Muscat, 16 June. Available from: https://inclusiveeducationplanning.com.au/uncategorized/comparative-perspectives-with-a-disability-lens-all-the-light-we-cannot-see-by-anthony-doerr-and-selected-epistles-by-olivia-muscat/ [accessed 24 April 2022].

Lorenz, D. (2022) *Announcement of World's Worst Representations of Disability Tournament* (The Worsties), 31 January. Available from: https://m.facebook.com/pg/TheCJDS/posts/ [accessed 24 April 2022].

Mayer, M. (1966) *They Thought They Were Free: The Germans, 1933–45*, Chicago: University of Chicago Press.

McDevitt, M. (2021) Social control of intellect. Four features of the academic-media nexus. *Communication Theory*, 1–22.

McGlone, M. S. (2005a) Contextomy: The art of quoting out of context. Media. *Culture & Society* 27 (4): 511–522.

McGlone, M. S. (2005b) Quoted out of context: Contextomy and its consequences. *Journal of Communication* 55 (2): 330–346.

Mitchell, D. T. (2000) Body solitaire: The singular subject of disability autobiography. *American Quarterly* 52 (2): 311–315.

Papastephanou, M. (2018) Michael Alhadeff-Jones, time and the rhythms of emancipatory education: Rethinking the temporal complexity of self and society. *Studies in the Philosophy of Education* 37 (1): 97–102.

Shepard Eells Jr., J. (1955) *The Touchstones of Matthew Arnold*, New York: Bookman Associates.

Small, H. (2017) Speech beyond toleration: On Carlyle and moral controversialism now. *New Literary History* 48 (3): 531–554.

Sosa, E. (2011) *Knowing Full Well*, Princeton: Princeton University Press.

Twersky, J. (1953) *Blindness in Literature: Examples of Depictions and Attitudes*, New York: American Federation of the Blind.

Warren, D. and Warren, D. (1996) *Radio Priest: Charles Coughlin, the Father of Hate Radio*, New York: Free Press.

Wells-Jensen, S. (2016) Anthony don't: On blindness and the portrayal of Marie-Laure in 'all the light we cannot see'. *LightHouse Interpoint*, 22 March. Available from: https://lighthouse-sf.org/2016/03/22/anthony-dont-on-blindness-and-the-portrayal-of-marie-laure-in-all-the-light-we-cannot-see/ [accessed 24 April 2022].

Wolff, J. (1993) *Aesthetics and the Sociology of Art, 2nd Ed*, London: Macmillan.

15

TO BOLDLY GO WHERE NO ONE (SIGHTED) HAS GONE BEFORE

Positive Portrayals of Blindness in *Star Trek: TNG* and H. G. Wells's 'The Country of the Blind'

Brenda Tyrell

Preliminary Discussion: That 'Worst Ailment' of Blindness

In a 1980 lecture, 'Blindness', Jorges Luis Borges posits 'That slow nightfall, that slow loss of sight, began when I began to see' (1980, 108). With this simple statement, Borges encapsulates the significant fear that sighted people hold toward changes in their vision – albeit, loss or diminishing vision. Indeed, according to a *New York Times* article (Brody, 2017), 'A recent study . . . found that most Americans regard loss of eyesight as the worst ailment that could happen to them, surpassing such conditions as loss of limb, memory, hearing or speech, or having H.I.V./AIDS' (D5). Yet, as Borges's comment indicates, our eyesight begins to change the moment we open our eyes and, outside of actively practicing sight-saving treatments (such as supplements and surgery), there is very little to be done to stop this natural process. To be clear, there are steps to slow or prevent non-age-related loss of vision (diabetic retinopathy, glaucoma, and so forth); however, as Brody (2017) reminds us, macular degeneration, 'a leading cause of vision loss in Americans 60 and older, involves *an irreversible loss of retinal cells* that robs people of the central vision needed to read, watch a TV program or identify a face or object in front of them' (emphasis mine). Here, Brody's explanation highlights an issue with how vision alterations are automatically perceived as a thief in the night, determined to 'rob' people of their most valuable possession (i.e. sight). Moreover, when consulting health and wellness sites such as the Centers for Disease Control and Prevention (CDC, 2020), loss or alterations in vision are portrayed in such a way to influence the way we (especially those who retain their vision) perceive the importance of vision. For example, when consulting the CDC's 'Vision Health Initiative (VHI)', words like 'burden' and 'loss' present a clear societal assumption that living with alterations of vision is not only an individual 'problem', it is a public, national issue – something to be cured, prevented, and avoided at all costs. Ironically, it is one into which I found myself falling.

DOI: 10.4324/9781003275060-19

As a person who has experienced vision impairment since my pre-teen years, not being able to see clearly without corrective lenses is a situation I've come to accept. However, when my eye doctor informed me that they saw the beginnings of macular degeneration, with the blithe comment that 'you'll probably be blind by the time you're sixty' (I was then 40), I immediately panicked. As an avid reader and literature academic, it felt like I had now, to borrow from Borges, entered that 'slow nightfall' (Borges, 1980, 108) until the moment I could no longer read an actual book. What was my reaction? I immediately began stockpiling audio versions of my most beloved books before quickly realising two points: first, this stockpiling was probably not the most financially-lucrative solution to what I perceived as the worst thing that could happen to me; and second, in my view, it is difficult to replace the *experience* of an actual book – the feel, the smell, seeing the words on the page, and so forth. Yes, audio books could serve as a replacement; however, the experience of reading would change in a way I was reluctant to pursue. Interestingly, learning Braille did not even cross my mind, so heightened was my panic. This warped perception leaks into not only societal reactions to vision alterations, but also representations of blindness in popular cultural stations such as literature and television portrayals. It is here where this chapter's work lies.

As a science fiction fan and scholar, I turn towards two cultural stations of blindness from the genre: H. G. Wells's short story 'The Country of the Blind' (2007) and Lieutenant Commander and Chief Engineer Geordi La Forge from the *Star Trek* television series *The Next Generation* (1987–1994). The first section examines the villagers from Wells's short story as a population that adapts and thrives in their isolated world until the sudden appearance of the sighted Nunez, who (mistakenly) understands their blindness to be a means of exploitation. Wells, I argue, subverts the abled/disabled binary and challenges the reader's assumption that it is the *villagers* who are disabled by their ways of seeing. In the second section, I analyse Lieutenant Commander Geordi La Forge from *Star Trek: The Next Generation* and his high-tech VISOR which allows him to experience sight in ways that resist the notion that sight is monolith and there is only one way to see. In all, this chapter proffers an auto critical discourse analysis of two cultural (and highly popular) stations that invite both literary and film audiences to challenge the state of blindness as lack or as in need of a cure.

In this chapter, I draw heavily from Michael Bérubé's (2016) notion of '*ideas about* disability'. Unlike David T. Mitchell and Sharon L. Snyder's narrative prosthesis (discussed later), Bérubé asserts that we can examine texts not for characters identified as disabled, but for 'deployments' or 'ideas' of disability: 'disability in the relation between text and reader *need not involve any character with disabilities at all*. It can involve *ideas about* disability, and ideas about stigma associated with disability, regardless of whether any specific character can be pegged with a specific diagnosis' (19: emphasis in original). The result of this approach, as Bérubé points out, is that it widens the domain of analysis and critique of disability in literature significantly. These deployments of disability 'do not confine themselves to representation. They can be narrative strategies, devices for exploring vast domains of human thought, experience, and action' (2), and analyses of these narratives and strategies requires 'nothing more than the tools of close reading' (3).

In sharp contrast, in Mitchell and Snyder's (2000) genre-defining concept of disability as a narrative prosthesis that 'centers not simply upon the fact that people with disabilities have been the object of representational treatments, but rather that their function in literary discourse is primarily twofold: disability pervades literary narrative, first, as a stock feature of characterisation and, second, as an opportunistic metaphorical device' (47). Mitchell and Snyder also find a consistent 'schematic of narrative structure' (53) throughout the literary texts they analysed. Their formula consists of four steps, beginning with the identification of the non-normative trait and, from there, the narrative shifts to a discovery of how this trait comes into play, as well as any potential consequences, with the trait then becoming the centre of the narrative. Lastly, the non-normative trait is eliminated from the story by one of four ways: cure, rescue, eradication, or overcoming – that is, a 'revaluation of an alternative mode' (53). This design, they argue, haunts nearly every literary text.

Many classic cultural studies theorists (including myself) find value in Mitchell and Snyder's method; however, for this chapter, I choose to utilise Bérubé's '*ideas about* disability' to the cultural stations later. My aim with this approach is to maintain and accentuate the politicised nature and the lived experiences of those who identify and are identified as disabled, whose experiences might be pushed aside for these more fictionalised, non-realist analyses. This is not to say that Mitchell and Snyder's approach is not useful; it is simply to point out that there are other analytical approaches that, as Julia Arvil Minich (2016) urges, work '*with the goal of producing knowledge in support of justice* for people with stigmatised bodies and mind' (no pagination). With that, the first cultural station discussed, I argue, is a prescient and positive example of those characters identified as blind who successfully (for the most part) resist the 'ideas about disability' that a sighted outsider presumes to impose on them.

'The Country of the Blind': Retrofuturised Accessibility

The first cultural station comes from H. G. Wells, often identified as the 'father' of (contemporary) science fiction and the short story/novella 'The Country of the Blind'. The story itself has a complicated history, as I explain in the article 'H. G. Wells's "Country of the Blind": Anticipating the Medical Models of Disability' (2017). Both published versions report the adventures of the sighted Nunez as he stumbles upon a hidden village of people who, as a result of a 'strange disease' (323), slowly lose their sight over the course of 15 generations. In both stories, Nunez eventually becomes acclimated to the village, but it is with great resistance. He truly believes that '[i]n the Country of the Blind, the One-Eyed Man is King' (329); however, the villagers do not cooperate with his grand schemes, leading to the continual power struggle between Nunez and the villagers. In *The Metanarrative of Blindness: A Re-Reading of Twentieth-Century Anglophone Writing*, David Bolt explains that 'many scholars defend the Wellsian classic on the grounds that it reverses the tradition of a blind person in a sighted world' (Bolt, 2017, 84). There is an issue with this approach though, as Bolt asserts, 'people who have visual impairments and people who do not have visual impairments are often represented as though antithetical to one another [thus] [t]he essence of the representational problem, then, is that any strategy of role reversal is predicated on the binary system critiqued throughout this present book' (Bolt, 2017, 84). In other words, although it is important to recognise the role reversal happening in Wells's text, we must not forget that this reversal is supported solely on a societal normative gaze that, as Bolt concurs, 'results in dehumanizing depictions of the blind' (Bolt, 2017, 84). And, this type of depiction certainly happens in 'The Country of the Blind', despite Wells's near-Herculean efforts to avoid it. What my analysis focuses on, however, is not this role reversal, but the accessibility of the village itself.

Early in the story, we learn from Wells's narrator that the one thing that 'marred [the villagers] happiness' (323) is their inability to see. However, from the description provided of the village and its occupants, it is difficult for the reader interested in positive representations of blindness to understand this reported 'marr[ing]'. As Nunez notes as he observes the precision and functionality of the village from above, '[s]heds . . . stood against the boundary wall . . . the irrigation streams ran together into a main channel down the centre of the valley, that debouched into a little lake' (327). Additionally, there are 'a number of paths paved with green, grey, black and white, and each with a curious little kerb [sic] at the side' (327), observing later that, 'Everything . . . had been made to fit their needs; each of the radiating paths [and numbered] of the valley area had a constant angle to the others, and was distinguished by a special notch upon its kerbing; all obstacles and irregularities of path and meadow had long since been cleared away' (335). As for the villagers themselves:

> They led a simple, laborious life, these people, with all the elements of virtue and happiness, as these things can be understood by [people]. They toiled, but not oppressively; they had food and clothing sufficient for their needs; they had days and seasons of rest; they made much of music and singing, and there was love among them, and little children.
>
> *(334)*

In short, the villagers appear to be just fine without sight. Based on these descriptions, one would be hard-pressed not to be convinced that the villagers have not only adapted to blindness, but also rid themselves of the inaccessibility issues imposed on those who experience alterations in vision: crowded, disorganised streets, and inaccessible curbs. Their arrangements only become unusual, yet admirable, when Nunez enters with his imperialistic, normative gaze. So what, exactly, does Nunez object to so stridently concerning the villagers?

To answer this question, we need only look to two passages in the text. In the first passage, Nunez does not seem able to comprehend a world where vision is not a preferred feature, resulting in an increased confidence that, as what he would identify as only able-bodied/minded person in the village, that he, of course, must be the superior being. We see this assumption manifest in a couple of ways: by his language and by his imperialist desires. For example, when he first tries to break free of the villagers, he exclaims, 'You don't understand . . . You are blind, and I can see' (338), as if this simple fact should be self-evident and automatically put him in the dominant (i.e. abled) role. Indeed, the villagers do not comprehend words like 'see' and 'sight', what they call 'unmeaning' (330) and 'wild' (331) words, because they do not experience it (and haven't for 15 generations). When Nunez tries to reason with them using these words, the villagers scoff at him and warn the other villagers that '[h]is senses are still imperfect' (330), which leads Nunez to resist their 'ways of being', which Alison Kafer ascribes in *Feminist, Queer, Crip* (2016) as an 'elsewhere', a place that considers those identified as disabled experience a world that is more 'just' and 'sustainable' (Kafer, 2016, 3).

The second passage reveals Nunez's imperialistic tendencies when he recalls, nearly immediately upon discerning that the villagers are unsighted, that 'this was the Country of the Blind of which the legends told' (329), the country in which that 'the One-Eyed Man is King' (329). As the villagers reveal their 'life and philosophy and religion' (332), however, Nunez quickly realises that 'that his expectation of wonder and reverence at his origin and his gifts was not to be borne out' and, instead, the villagers believed the exact opposite: that Nunez 'must have been specially created to learn and serve the wisdom they had acquired' (333). As they leave him to sleep, he ruminates and festers until he finally bursts out, 'They little know they've been insulting their heaven-sent king and master. I see I must bring them to reason' (333). Ultimately, and most importantly for this chapter, Nunez 'thanked God from the bottom of his heart that the power of sight had been given to him . . . [and] . . . He would show these people once and for all what sight would do for a [person]' (333). Wells's narrator notes that 'the fifth day found the King of the Blind still incognito, as a clumsy and useless stranger among his subjects' (334) – that is, the villagers are having none of Nunez's imperialistic agenda and, in fact, expect Nunez to 'serve [their] wisdom' as he matures and realises the error of his ways.

During his time with the villagers, Nunez eventually falls in love with Medina-Saroté, his 'master['s]' daughter, and, as a result, settles into the routine of the village, as well as considers having the surgery that would remove 'those queer things that are called eyes' (342) and, thus, make him a 'quite admirable citizen' (343). When faced with losing his vision, however, Nunez takes a walk, never to return. In the 1904 version, he leaves Medina-Saroté, who he now considers 'small and remote' (346), climbs up the mountain wall, and 'lay peacefully contented under the cold stars' (347). Conversely, in the 1939 version, Nunez still takes a walk; however, during this walk, he notices a growing fissure in the mountain wall and returns to the village to attempt to warn the villagers of their impending doom (which they do not heed based on their disbelief on Nunez's sight). He and Medina-Saroté escape the disaster and settle with 'Nunez's people' (2007, 44), where they marry and have four *sighted* children. When asked if she consulted the 'oculists' (44) to fix her vision, Medina-Saroté replies, 'The loveliness of *your* world is complicated and fearful loveliness and mine is simple and near. I had rather Nunez saw for me – because he knows nothing of fear' (45). In other words, Medina-Saroté has no desire to see, which is in direct opposition to Nunez's assertion that 'My world is sight' (34). Here, Wells backpedals in his prescient and positive portrayal in two ways: first, he ultimately prefers sight, as evidenced not only by Medina-Saroté's dependence on Nunez, but also in their four sighted children – the 'strange disease' that 'plagued' the villagers for 15 generations magically disappears the moment Medina-Saroté leaves the village. Second, in 1939, the village of blind inhabitants is completely decimated in the landslide, a clear message that, according to Wells, sight is the preferred state. Despite this backpedaling, Wells's positive portrayal of the accessibility issues those identified as blind must overcome is not only prescient of today's disability studies field, but also a unique glimpse into a world that exists just fine without sight.

Lieutenant Commander Geordi La Forge: Reimagined Ways of Seeing

In this section, I analyse Lieutenant Commander Geordi La Forge from *Star Trek: The Next Generation* and his high-tech VISOR (Visual Instrument Sensory Organ Replacement) which allows him to experience sight in ways that resist the notion that sight is monolith and there is only one way to see. Although there are seven seasons and four films in the series, I focus mostly on the first two seasons.[1] The reasons for this limitation are first (and most obvious), one could write several *books* on the series and the sheer amount of time and space involved in that endeavour is simply not possible in this volume. The second reason is because that, after the crew and the fans get to know Geordi, they begin to accept Geordi's VISOR and visual acuity as an assemblage. In other words, the VISOR, Geordi's vision, and Geordi himself cannot be separated and are, indeed, one united entity; thus, the attempts to 'cure' the character fade away from the spotlight, establishing Geordi as just another member of the Enterprise. To be clear, this is not to say that there are no other episodes where Geordi's vision and VISOR appear as a backstory; however, they are more incidental than pivotal in understanding Geordi's character.

At the beginning of the series, Geordi is recognised sometimes solely by his VISOR. For example, during his first visit with ship physician Dr Beverly Crusher, the visor is the first thing seen in the frame ('Encounter at FarPoint, 1987, 00:44:03). Moreover, it is clear by the discussion that Geordi's 'case' and visor are well-known within the Federation of Planets medical community, as evidenced by this comment by Crusher: 'Naturally, I've heard of your case'. Geordi's response indicates his frustration with this popularity, sarcastically finishing Crusher's analysis with '[the VISOR] is a remarkable piece of bioelectronic engineering by which I quote "see much of the EM spectrum ranging from simple heat and infrared through radio waves", et cetera, et cetera and forgive me if I've said and listened to this a thousand times before' ('Encounter at FarPoint, 1987, 00:44:03–0:47:04). However, as the series progresses, an interesting shift occurs: after about the second series, Geordi's high-tech vision and VISOR simply become part of who he is, an assemblage in which one (Geordi) cannot exist without the other (VISOR). In fact, in 'Loud as a Whisper' (1989, S2:E5), Geordi is questioned by Riva, a deaf mediator who is being escorted to peace talks on the Enterprise, about not only his VISOR, but also how he feels about being 'blind as a stump' (Geordi's description) without it. When asked if he 'resents' either the visor or being blind, Geordi responds, 'Well, no, since they're both part of me and, [since] I really like who I am, there's no reason for me to resent either one' ('Loud as a Whisper, 1989, 00:12:50–00:13:39).[2] Even the changes later on in the series, as well as the films, when there is a change in Geordi's appearance (i.e. *sans* visor), the crew accepts these changes either without question or with enthusiasm.

In 'The Naked Now' (1987, S1:E2), a strange virus takes over the Enterprise after a visit to another starship. The 'virus' is spread through touch and Geordi is one of the first to show any symptoms. Notably, while the other crew members lose their inhibitions, Geordi goes into a deep depression, developing a sudden and uncharacteristic yearning to be able to see in the same manner as the rest of the crew. In a particularly poignant moment between Lieutenant Yar and Geordi, the latter pleads with Yar to 'help me not give in to the wild things coming into mind' ('The Naked Now', 1987, 0:11:47). These 'wild things' turn out to be Geordi's desire to 'see like [Yar does]'. Yar immediately responds, 'But you already see better than I can', to which Geordi returns, 'I see more [taking his VISOR off] but more isn't better . . . I want to see in shallow, dim, beautiful human ways' ('The Naked Now', 1987, 00:12:22–0:13:06), inferring that, since Geordi doesn't see in 'human ways', he must not be human (a whole other can of worms in regard to disability). Most alarmingly, the scene is one of the few in which Geordi, *sans* VISOR, must be led by his from the room, in a manner similar to someone being led across a busy intersection.

What is particularly telling here is the assumption that every person who experiences alterations of vision automatically wants to see like every 'normal' sighted person, even in the far, more technically-advanced future (*TNG* takes place in the twenty-fourth century between the years of 2364–2370). Kafer identifies this 'presumption of agreement' as stemming from the normative assumption that 'a future with disability is a future no one wants', adding ' "We" all know this [agreement], and there is no room for "you" to think differently', which generates 'this belief that we all desire the same future' (Kafer, 2016, 2–3). In Geordi's case, because sight is the preferred (i.e. normal) state by those who can see without impairment, Yar, the rest of the crew, and the producers/writers of the episode assume that Geordi prefers to be sighted; and assume that their fans believe the same. Yet, during a conversation between Yar, Picard, and Deanna Troi (ship's counsellor), this yearning is uncharacteristic of Geordi. Yar notes that Geordi is 'not violent [but] very upset. He kept talking about wanting normal vision', to which Troi explains to Picard, that this 'longing for normal sight [is] a sudden yearning' ('The Naked Now', 1987,

00:13:19–00:14:26). Moreover, if we recall from the first episode, Geordi has had multiple opportunities to 'fix' his eyesight and, ultimately, he refuses them.

This refusal is no clearer than in a later episode ('Hide and Q', 1987, S1:E9), in which Commander William Riker, through a series of events, gains the ability to grant what, in his normative view, 'something I know they'd like' ('Hide and Q', 1987, 00:37:18). After trying to grant several other crew members their 'dreams', Riker zeroes in on Geordi, saying, 'I know what you want' ('Hide and Q', 1987, 00:39:33). He then removes Geordi's VISOR and Geordi's usually-milky eyes clear and his vision is instantly restored. After looking around a bit, Riker asks 'then we throw away the VISOR?', to which Geordi responds, 'I don't think so, sir. . . . The price is a little too high for me and I don't like who I'd have to thank. Make me the way I was . . . [imploring] please' ('Hide and Q', 1987, 00:40:15–40:32). If we return to the introductory statements concerning the sighted population's fear of visual alterations, Rikers's assumption that Geordi, as an unsighted person, would naturally dream of having his sight (that he never actually had) returned. Kafer calls this assumption 'compulsory nostalgia' which, she explains, is a 'reimagining of lost pasts [that] can bleed easily into a normalizing nostalgia . . . bound up in a kind of [longing/yearning] for the lost able mind/body, the nostalgic past mind/body that perhaps never was' (Kafer, 2016, 42). Riker assumes that there is another Geordi, one that longs for a return of the sight he never had, hidden deep under the surface of the Geordi standing in front of him. Kafer puts a finer point on this concept when she reveals that there is 'a cultural expectation that the relation between [those] two selves is always one of loss, and of loss that moves in only one direction. (Kafer, 2016, 42–43). Later in the page, Kafer claims that 'this assumption that disability cannot be a desirable location, and that it must always be accompanied by a nostalgia for the lost [vision] is what animates "the cure question" to familiar to disabled people' (Kafer, 2013, 43). Indeed, the Enterprise's medical doctors, be it Crusher or Katherine Pulaski, are consistently offering Geordi ways to improve his VISOR in order to see 'better', when in fact, the VISOR allows him to see as well as he would like. And, although Geordi eventually elects for optical lens much later in the series, for the most part, he is persistent in this refusal.

The last episode discussed is 'Heart of Glory' (1987, S1:E19). In this episode, we learn that Data and Geordi have been developing the 'visual acuity transmitter' (VAT) that transmits what Geordi's VISOR sees to the Enterprise when he is away-missions. When the VAT is switched on, the entire Bridge can see what Geordi sees – although they cannot necessarily interpret it. Picard's first reaction is 'Now, I'm beginning to understand him' ('Heart of Glory ', 1988, 00:07:18–00:10:23), which could be analysed in a more negative way in that Picard's understanding of Geordi is based on what he sees. However, that is exactly the point of this section: Geordi and his VISOR are an *assemblage* and, thus, it makes sense that, if Picard can visualise what Geordi's VISOR sees, he is indeed one step closer to understanding Geordi. An important moment in the scene reflects an understanding on both Picard *and* Geordi's behalf when Picard asks if Geordi can 'filter out the extraneous information' of Riker's outline and Geordi explains that he 'get[s] it all simultaneously'. Geordi further explains that he 'selects what I want and disregards the rest', and challenges Picard, asking 'how, in a noisy room can you select one specific voice or sound'? Notably, when Geordi focuses on Data, Picard asks about the 'aura' surrounding the 'android'; here, *Geordi* assumes that the sighted crew members see the same thing that his VISOR does and also experiences a learning moment in assuming what the sighted see. Although it is late in the first season before viewers get a point-of-view (the first of the series) from Geordi's VISOR, it is this point in the series' portrayal of Geordi that, I argue, viewers begin to see the character as the rest of the crew does – a fully capable human who has no desire to 'cure' what the sighted crew and fans may see as a disability. From this point forward, the series, the fans, and the writers simply accept that Geordi is just an ordinary crew member and, ultimately, create a positive representation of blindness within the franchise.

Concluding Discussion: Altered Vision as (Non) Disability

I recently taught a seminar on *Star Trek* and its portrayal of feminism, disability, and racism throughout the franchise's entire history. Not surprisingly, when we viewed the episodes that featured Geordi and his VISOR, a majority of students identified him as disabled. When I asked them to explain what makes Geordi disabled, they responded with what most people would: he can't see (much like Nunez when confronting the villagers). When I challenged them with 'but he can – he just sees with the VISOR and, later, corrective lenses', I could almost see the wheels turning. I pushed just a bit harder, asking 'how is that different from someone who needs glasses to see'? If we as a class attempted to interpret Geordi's alterations of vision through Mitchell and Snyder's narrative prosthesis, rather than Bérubé's '*ideas* about disability', it is likely that students would not entertain the possibility that Geordi is not a character to be identified simply by what they would consider a disability; or, more surprisingly, attempted to convince their instructor that the *Klingons* might as be considered disabled based on Bérubé's concept.

Conversely, Medina-Saroté emphatically announces at the end of the 1939 version of Wells's 'The Country of the Blind' that 'it must be very terrible to see'. With this statement, she directly addresses the fundamental struggle within the story: lines are drawn between the blind and the sighted, with each side seeing the other as disabled, as the failing part of an otherwise perfect society, as the group that must be oppressed, cured, or destroyed. Either way, this 'plague of blindness' (323) must be avoided at all costs. In the background, however, Wells anticipates an entirely accessible village based solely on what he imagines those experiencing visual alterations would require to thrive. When Wells wrote this story, disability studies as a field did not exist; however, through the story, Wells allows contemporary Wellsian and disability studies scholars a glimpse into a world where no one is solely abled or disabled. Perhaps, this is not such a terrible thing to see.

Notes

1   Throughout this section, I abbreviate the episodes by S# (season): E# (episode)- e.g., S1:E1.
2   Of note, Howie Seago, the man who played Riva, identifies as deaf in reality. According to the 'trivia' content of this scene, Seago 'petitioned the producers to create an episode involving deaf people'.

References

Bérubé, M. (2016) *The Secret Life of Stories: From Don Quixote to Harry Potter, How Understanding Intellectual Disability Transforms the Way We Read*, New York: New York University Press.
Bolt, D. (2017) *The Metanarrative of Blindness: A Re-Reading of Twentieth-Century Anglophone Writing*, Ann Arbor: University of Michigan Press.
Borges, J. L. (1980) *Blindness: Seven Nights*, trans. E. Weinberger, London: Faber and Faber.
Brody, J. E. (2017) The Worst That Could Happen? Going Blind, People Say. *New York Times* [online]. Available from: www.nytimes.com/2017/02/20/well/the-worst-that-could-happen-going-blind-people-say html [accessed 30 June 2022].
Centers for Disease Control and Prevention (CDC). (2020) Basics of vision and eye health [online]. *Centers for Disease Control and Prevention*. Available from: www.cdc.gov/vision-health/basics/index.html [accessed 7 May 2022].
Encounter at FarPoint. (1987) *Star Trek: The Next Generation*. Season One, Episode One and Two. Paramount Pictures, 28 September.
Heart of Glory. (1988) *Star Trek: The Next Generation*. Season One, Episode Nineteen. Paramount Pictures, 21 March.
Hide and Q. (1987) *Star Trek: The Next Generation*. Season One, Episode Nine. Paramount Pictures, 23 November.
Kafer, A. (2013) *Feminist, Queer, Crip*, Bloomington: Indiana University Press.
Loud as a Whisper. (1989) *Star Trek: The Next Generation*. Season Two, Episode Five. Paramount Pictures, 9 January.
Minich, J. A. (2016) Enabling whom? Critical disability studies now. *Lateral: Journal of the Cultural Studies Association* 5 (1) [online]. Available from: https://csalateral.org/issue/5-1/forum-alt-humanities-critical-disability-studies-now-minich/ [accessed 10 May 2022].
Mitchell, D. T. and Snyder, S. L. (2000) *Narrative Prosthesis: Disability and the Dependencies of Discourse*, Ann Arbor: University of Michigan Press.
The Naked Now. (1987) *Star Trek: The Next Generation*. Season One, Episode Two. Paramount Pictures, 5 October.
Tyrell, B. (2017) H. G. Wells's 'country of the blind': Anticipating medical models of disability. *Science Fiction Studies* 44 (2): 396–397.
Wells, H. G. (2007) 'The Country of the Blind', *H.G. Wells: The Complete Short Story Collection*, London: Penguin Books.

16

REVISITING RUINS OF BLINDNESS

A Sketched Out Silhouette

David Bolt

Preliminary Discussion: Self-Portrait of a Blind Man

The cultural stations of blindness on which I focus in this chapter are drawn from a period of my life that started a long transition from unsuccessful singer-songwriter to successful academic. At the end of 1995, I drew an invisible line under my stubborn if not sulky teenage dreams and enrolled onto an access course at Stoke-on-Trent college, the aim being to find a route into Higher Education suitable for someone in their late twenties who had left school in their early teens. The course commenced in February, 1996, and my growing interest in identity politics led me to focus primarily on psychology and sociology. In order to demonstrate and indeed gain broader knowledge, however, I was also required to study other subjects. In fact, it was a couple of these almost supplementary subjects – namely, literature and philosophy – that became central to the subsequent direction of my education. I went on to secure a place on a literary studies degree at the University of Staffordshire, which engaged with identity politics but was based squarely in the humanities. This base felt pertinent to me, for although I had finally left behind most of my musical ambitions I was (and am) still keen to improve my creative writing and of course my writing more broadly.

The first of the cultural stations was signposted during the interim between my access and degree courses. Because the access course finished in February, 1997, and the degree started late September, I had a few months in which to plough through numerous audio books in a naïve panic to supplement my education. It was during that reading spree that a fellow drinker in The Village Tavern, Wolstanton, introduced me to Dylan Thomas's *Under Milk Wood: A Play for Voices* (first published in 1954). I knew woefully little about the famous writer but was aware that, like my father and I, he came from South Wales. More specifically, like my paternal grandfather, he was born in Swansea during the Great War. Indeed,

DOI: 10.4324/9781003275060-20

Mumbles, the birthplace of my grandfather, is named in *Under Milk Wood*. Nevertheless, far from nationality, I knew the actual reason behind the recommendation was that *Under Milk Wood* contained a prominent blind character, Captain Cat. It was for this reason above all that I found an affinity with the work and sought out a few versions in preparation for my degree. As it transpired, *Under Milk Wood* did not feature in the set reading list but I nonetheless made it the primary text in one of my third-year essays.

The second of the cultural stations was signposted during my undergraduate degree in 1999, on the very module that enabled me to write about *Under Milk Wood* – namely, Martin McQuillan's Deconstruction Reading Politics. The module's main set text was Jacques Derrida's *Specters of Marx: The Work of Mourning, the State of the Debt*, and *the New International* (1994). It was in that rich writing that I first read about the 'visor effect', whereby we cannot see the one staring at us (Derrida, 1994, 7), whose influence was later implicit in my own work on the unseen gazer (Bolt, 2014). However, in accordance with the Derridean identification of moments where the apparently proper logic must be overridden by a more powerful variant in order to progress (Kamuf, 1991), which impacts on many lines of argument in the present chapter, I was even more struck by the mass of supplementary reading, most obviously *Memoirs of the Blind: The Self-Portrait and Other ruins* (1993). Thanks to our always encouraging tutor, I was also lucky enough to attend a Deconstruction Reading Politics conference held at the University of Staffordshire in the same year, which included presentations by Peggy Kamuf, Fred Botting, Nicholas Royle, J. Hillis Miller, and so on.[1] What is more, within a couple of years of doing the deconstruction module, as I still announce each year to my Critical Disability Theory MA students (and anyone who will listen), I met Derrida himself.

The two cultural stations of blindness are interrelated to an extent that grounds the autocritical discourse analysis of the chapter. One of my reasons for the very coinage of this research method was to mobilise non-normative personal narratives in the deconstruction of normative metanarratives (Bolt, 2021). It is therefore noteworthy that my application of deconstruction can be traced back a couple of decades to my undergraduate reading of *Under Milk Wood*, although I must admit that much around the deconstructive process still remains rather elusive to me. What I do take from it, in the chapter at least, is that even a prominent portrayal may dissolve when reconsidered in the name of singularity. In keeping with the metanarratives of disability (Bolt, 2012, 2020b, 2021), and the metanarrative of blindness more specifically (Bolt, 2014; Healey and Michalko, 2021; Karah, 2021; Padilla, 2021), autocritical discourse analysis reveals how, encroached by multiple universals, the blind figure of culture is nonetheless framed in silhouette. What is more, this reductive displacement of detail often resonates in society, where the singularity of creativity is paralleled by the novelty of a moment in time: both are done a seemingly irresistible disservice when it comes to the matter of representation.

Under Milk Wood: Play God

Written for the radio, to give it a 'reality' that is 'as disembodied as possible' (Korg, 1965, 177), *Under Milk Wood* introduces the many inhabitants of Llareggub, a fictional seaside town in Wales. More than voice contact, this radio play consists of monologue, song, and multiple narration, which interact to impart dreams, desires, happenings, and memories that build up the poetic and profound sense of a characterful community. In a 'script that demands reading aloud' (Kidder, 1973, 190), the play is also enjoyed via the stage and film. Indeed, it is sometimes argued that a focus on the original radio form can be at the expense of the innovative creativity available to versions that have a visual aspect (Wrigley, 2014). For example, there is said to be an emphasis on visual perception that, in combination with the multiple narrative perspectives, works well with a multi-camera production (Wrigley, 2014). Nevertheless, given the overarching topic of the present book and the point that radio is sometimes described as the blind medium (Starkey, 2012; Whittington, 2014), it is the original form of the work to which this chapter refers.

As written, *Under Milk Wood* begins at a beginning that seems set to disrupt ocularnormativism, whereby visual means are assumed right and proper in all things (Bolt, 2014, 2020a; Houston, 2021; Penketh, 2022), for although knowing is based on seeing, listening is the key to both. From the outset the implied listener is allocated a privileged position, without visual perception but nonetheless omniscient in relation to the characters and their environment, so much so that dreams and waking reality seamlessly interweave with each other (Wrigley, 2014). What is more, as well as the implied listener, the blind character Captain Cat is rendered 'seemingly omniscient' (Wrigley, 2014, 78, 81). To this end, his prominence is indicated in the opening moonless night, while all are sleeping, for he is the principal character mentioned, blind 'in the muffled middle by the pump and the town clock' (Thomas, 1992, 1). He dreams he is with the 'long drowned' Dancing Williams, Tom-Fred the donkeyman, Jonah Jarvis, Alfred Pomeroy Jones, Curly Bevan, and especially 'dead' Rosie Probert, all his 'dead dears' (Thomas, 1992, 3–6). This dream and the underpinning memories, along with his position at the pumping heart of the town, are contrived to situate Captain Cat centrally in the implied listener's imagination.

The disruption of ocularnormativism continues as time passes and morning comes. It is, as the implied listener is promptly informed, Captain Cat at the town clock who takes charge of time and starts the day: 'One by one, the sleepers are rung out of sleep this one morning as every morning' and 'soon you shall see the chimneys' slow upflying snow' as he, 'in sailor's cap and seaboots, announces to-day with his loud get-out-of-bed bell' (Thomas, 1992, 25). In the largely plotless play, 'apart from the town itself and the well-marked progress of the day from morning to nightfall, there are few suggestions of time or place' (Korg, 1965, 177). This being so, Captain Cat's temporal function within the town and thus the play's structure is all the more significant.

More than announcing the new day, Captain Cat is instrumental if not central to its loving description. Through his 'still normal sense of hearing, he continues to be aware of the nature of the community life about him' (Kirtley, 1975, 72). Sat at his open window, he 'hears all the morning of the town' (Thomas, 1992, 40) and provides a 'sensitive commentary' said to make the implied listener 'forget his blindness' (Wrigley, 2014, 81). For example, he hears somebody coming just before he notices the voice contact of the women around the pump fall silent in such a way that the identity of the person can be inferred. He knows by the very 'noise of the hush' that it must be Polly Garter: 'Hullo, Polly, who's there?' he asks and she replies, 'Me, love' (Thomas, 1992, 45). This example may be said to epitomise how Captain Cat's 'language productively confuses the senses of seeing and hearing, and silence and noise' (Wrigley, 2014, 81). Moreover, the exchange is notable as the only instance of voice contact he has in the whole play; the rest of the time he speaks to himself or within his dreams. This being so, a particular significance must be attached to the spoken words in which he is addressed as *love*.

As morning passes, it is Captain Cat's association with love and time that inter-rupts, or perhaps ultimately enhances, his omniscience in relation to the present state of the town. He knows morning school is over when he hears the 'naughty forfeiting children tumble and rhyme on the cobbles' (Thomas, 1992, 59). He sits at his window, flung open to the midday sun, falls asleep, and dreams about his distant past, 'when his eyes were blue and bright' (Thomas, 1992, 71). He 'weeps as he sleeps and sails' far across the years and seas to brawling bars and one-night stands (Thomas, 1992, 71). His dreams are continually focused on memories of Rosie Probert, the 'one love of his sea-life that was sardined with women', who 'clearly and near to him speaks from the bedroom of her dust' (Thomas, 1992, 71–72). As well as her 'little deck hand', 'favourite husband', 'honey', 'pretty sugar sailor', she calls him 'Tom Cat' but he reassures her she was his 'true sweetheart', his 'cosy love' (Thomas, 1992, 72–73). He asks if he can shipwreck in her thighs and she invites him to knock twice at the door of her grave. Devastatingly, as her memory starts to fade from the dream, she reminds him to remember her but adds that she has forgotten him, that she is 'going into the darkness of the darkness for ever', that she has forgotten she 'was ever born' (Thomas, 1992, 73–74). As he awakens, a passing little girl points out to her mother that he is 'crying all over his nose' and the First Voice informs the listener that he is crying out for Rosie to come back from the 'silences and echoes of the passages of the eternal night' (Thomas, 1992, 74). The child's voice in the town's waking state thereby marks the end of Captain Cat's dream work that, in the lament if not search for love, has enabled time to be so fruitfully navigated.

Captain Cat's multiple associations with love and time, as well as his appar-ent omniscience, not to mention the implicit tears of rain that he cries down on the town, enhance his prominent portrayal with connotations of divinity. These connotations are deepened by the fact that the radio play has been said to reflect the conclusion its author reached in 1951, that poetry functions as a celebration of humankind and, by extension, God; that it can be read as the last of Thomas's 'hymns of praise for the world of man's experience and its Creator' (Korg, 1965, 178). Accordingly, as the central personification of this celebration, Captain Cat, at the close of the fateful day, 'climbs into his bunk' and through the 'voyages of his tears he sails to see the dead' (Thomas, 1992, 87). This final dream informs the divine interpretation insofar as it resonates with the notion that, at the end of the day, when people die they meet their maker; they get to be with God. Captain Cat's portrayal is so prominent that it can be read not only as all-knowing but also godlike, ontologically elevated rather than marginalised. He can be interpreted as the play god.

Memoirs of the Blind: Deconstruction Reading the Play for Voices

Much as Dylan Thomas's Under Milk Wood can be thought of as drama, poetry, and/or even fictional documentary (Wrigley, 2014), Jacques Derrida's Memoirs of the Blind rather defies straightforward or proper categorisation. The book can be thought of as an exhibition catalogue supplemented by philosophical writing, a work of philosophy supplemented by artwork, and/or something else entirely. Indeed, whereas Thomas calls Under Milk Wood a play for voices in its very title, Derrida only stresses that Memoirs of the Blind is not the 'journal of an exhibition' (Derrida, 1993, 33). Formalities notwithstanding, the book certainly relates to an art exhibition that Derrida curated at the Louvre in 1990. The Derridean project was therefore realised nearly four decades after Under Milk Wood first aired on the radio but, although the Welsh writer's play is not mentioned by the French philosopher, critical connections can be drawn between the two formally ambiguous works.

The formal blurring of the works is caused in part by the invocation and interruption of memory. Akin to the way in which the dreams of captain Cat are supplemented by his memories, which disrupts plot progression, Derrida's philosophical engagement with artistic portrayal is unexpectedly supplemented by his germane recollections of direct experience. Coincidentally, if not ironically, while working on the blindness exhibition something happens that holds him up and tempts him to reframe it as the 'self-portrait of a blind man' (Derrida, 1993, 32). When the exhibition is 'already envisaged', he has to cancel a meeting in the Department of Drawings due to 'facial paralysis caused by a virus', whereby the left side of his face stiffens, the eye becomes 'transfixed and horrible to behold in a mirror – a real sight for sore eyes – the eyelid no longer closing normally' (Derrida, 1993, 32). If it only lasts for a couple of weeks or so, this experience nonetheless results in a memory of blindness that supplements Memoirs of the Blind – without which, therefore, the proper logic of the work would be notably lacking.

The place of memory within the portraiture of blindness can be problematic. In general, someone who has no visual perception may well draw on memories instinctively and extensively to perform minor and major tasks, the trouble being that, socially and culturally, the noun memory then becomes qualified by adjectives that range from *muscle* to *photographic*. The latter is an obvious example of ocular-normativism that soon deconstructs when the visual rug is pulled from beneath it: 'Standing on his own two feet, a blind man explores by feeling out an area that he must recognize without yet cognizing it' (Derrida, 1993, 4). In practice, cognition gained by touch is not always but often revisited by the same means, a hand, bare or holding a cane, which Derrida extends further to the sharpened pencil that points only to the dead end of depiction. This blind alley, as it might as well be termed, nonetheless provides a space, a moment in time for questions: 'what about the day, then, the rhythm of the days and nights without day or light, the dates and calendars that scan memories and memoirs? How would the memoirs of the blind be written?' (Derrida, 1993, 33). Memories and their very temporality seem to become elusive in this realm of representation.

The place of memories is somewhere alongside those of dreams and auditory perceptions in *Under Milk Wood*, where Captain Cat is portrayed as a blind figure who, far from dropping the beat, leads the rhythm of the day. In keeping with the divine interpretation, the 'blind man can be a seer, and he sometimes has the vocation of a visionary' (Derrida, 1993, 2). Accordingly, Captain Cat is blind but nonetheless celebrated as omniscient, for his voice carries authority that is said to convince the implied listener to 'forget his blindness and trust his knowledge' (Wrigley, 2014, 81). Although manifestly positive, this reading is grounded in ocularnormative epistemology that resonates with the postulation that blindness violates what has become known as nature. Blindness is an 'accident that interrupts the regular course of things or transgresses natural laws', for the 'whole history, the whole semantics of the European idea, in its Greek genealogy, as we know–as we see–relates seeing to knowing' (Derrida, 193, 12). Against this cultural backdrop, a bit like the Derridean portrait of blindness, Captain Cat emerges as a rather radical character, whose omniscience is drawn from memories, dreams, and auditory rather than visual perceptions.

For all that, when read through *Memoirs of the Blind*, Captain Cat's originality as a prominent portrayal of blindness becomes problematised. 'To begin at the beginning', says the first voice in *Under Milk Wood*, with a 'spring, moonless night in the small town, starless and bible-black, the cobblestreets silent' (Thomas, 1992, 1). However, in *Memoirs of the Blind*, to so begin is in itself to ruin: 'At the origin comes ruin; ruin comes to the origin, it is what first comes and happens to the origin, in the beginning' (Derrida, 1993, 65). Captain Cat is the beginning, the play god, the first and foremost of all the characters mentioned in *Under Milk Wood*, who may be said to illustrate the notion of 'a memory of the trait that speculates, as in a dream, about its own possibility' (Derrida, 1993, 3). He has morning, afternoon, and evening dreams populated by love from his sighted past, as though visiting him in his blind present. As a dream within a play, though, this calls to be read antithetically (counter to the apparent reality), so his portrayal comes to exemplify residual existence (Bolt, 2019), whereby blindness defines a faded and degraded version of life, which serves to elevate past sightedness to the level of essential existence. The portrayal of blindness slips from originality into a problematic familiarity.

What *Memoirs of the Blind* helps to reveal is the ruins in the representation, a death within the very portraiture of blindness. The 'staring eye always resembles an eye of the blind', writes Derrida, 'sometimes the eye of the dead, at that precise moment when mourning begins: it is still open, a pious hand should soon come to close it; it would recall a portrait of the dying' (Derrida, 1993, 57). Accordingly, published a couple of decades after *Under Milk Wood*, a classic psychological study identifies a pejorative living death motif in the radio play. From this perspective, Captain Cat is a 'lonely isolate whose sadness is known only to the local children, as they alone have spied him in his solitary weeping' (Kirtley, 1975, 72). His 'modest, if not minimal, assets' are obscured by the 'overpowering burden of his losses', for the 'vision of death, and with it social alienation, and the inexorable despair and impotence of old age and infirmity' are depicted as the 'critical features of blindness' (Kirtley, 1975, 72). The singularity of Captain Cat as an original creation, a poetic or dramatic cultural figure, is denied by the inherent mourning of his recognisable character traits. There are implicit ruins of universality in the play god's accordance with the metanarrative of blindness (Bolt, 2014), wherein life without visual perception is equated with death.

Concluding Discussion: When I Met Derrida

In conclusion, I must add a few metaphorical pencil lines and/or brushstrokes to the self-portrait to which this chapter amounts. If 'what is called a self-portrait depends on the fact' that it is so-called, as Derrida writes, an 'act of naming should allow or entitle me to call just about anything a self-portrait, not only any drawing ('portrait' or not) but anything that happens to me, anything by which I can be affected or let myself be affected' (Derrida, 1993, 65). By definition, the cultural stations of blindness on which I focus here have affected me and so, for argument's sake, can be said to become part of a self-portrait. My metaphorical artwork reflects the ruins within my own representation, where the novelty of a moment in time becomes crowded if not displaced by universals.

As the two cultural stations of blindness are framed within this self-portrait, a moment in time slips from affect to affectation through the clanging of name-dropping, especially the boring boast that I have met Derrida. If and when the ruin of this universalised representation of a meeting is revisited with a search for the remnants of novelty in mind, when I met Derrida I did not meet him insofar as there was no voice contact between the two of us. Rather, in 2001, three fellow Derrida readers and I travelled from the University of Staffordshire to Loughborough University, where he gave a talk.[2] I was transfixed throughout and sat at the next table during lunch and refreshments but did not seize my one opportunity to speak with him. My memory is that the voice contact I wanted to initiate about *Memoirs of the Blind* and *Under Milk Wood* was as thwarted as it was driven by my admiration. In accordance with a metanarrative of intellectualism, I placed myself, an unknown postgraduate student, as other in relation to the eminent philosopher and thought that before getting into any conversations I should at least complete the doctorate I had barely started. Alas, Derrida died just three years later, in 2004, a few months after I graduated but before I had chance to muster the confidence to contact him.

Any endeavour to finish this self-portrait just reveals more mourning in the sense that the pencil is too blunt and the brushstrokes are too wide, as are all the blindness metaphors, literary and philosophical, so I am drawn to render my subject in silhouette. I discovered this technique in my teenage years, when doing an oil painting that looked okay at the moment of creativity but, as my then very variable vision cleared, emerged as a terrible grey that I then chose to darken to the extreme. This quick fix blotted out all of the original character, in a way that foreshadowed so much in my subsequent self-portraiture. When returning from the Loughborough University event, I was told that Derrida had looked over at me at one point, as if to seek the everywhere and evermore essential eye contact, a suggested reason being that, among hundreds of academics, he and I were the only ones wearing ties. Whether or not that was the case, when I share this detail with my students I tend to elicit laughter from the truism that I wore a tie, the only one I possessed at the time, precisely because I was *going to meet* Derrida; whereas he wore a tie because he *was* Derrida. My deeper memory, however, invoked a variant of the visor effect, as I imagined he had looked over, expecting me to meet his eye and smile or nod. When I did neither, he had perhaps realised that I had not seen him – I probably still had some vision at that time but it would have been very minimal and more or less limited to light perception. I wondered if he had thought about his *Memoirs of the Blind* as he glanced at a youngish reader who, naively, imagined or perhaps dreamed he could one day join the 'great tradition of blind writers' (Derrida, 1993, 33). It also went through my mind that he had experienced impaired vision on a temporary basis, that he understood non-normative perception from within, which may have elicited empathy or interest or something on which we could have built a conversation. Did he recall something from his own memory and see us at some level as two blind men? Did he see me as anything other than a blind man? Did anyone else at the event see me as something other than a blind man? How did the novelty of that moment in time resonate as a microcosm of society more broadly? It is this and other such pondering that illustrates the ruin of self-portraiture, for even if I set out to sketch my subject with multiple traits, I am well aware that, be it by myself, someone, or everyone, the end result is likely to become silhouetted as blindness.

Notes

1   Many of the papers presented at this conference were developed and subsequently published in an edited volume – namely, Martin McQuillan's *Deconstruction Reading Politics*, Basingstoke: Palgrave Macmillan, 2007.
2   This event inspired a dramatic representation some two decades later – namely, John Schad and Fred Dalmasso's *Derrida/Benjamin: Two Plays for the Stage*, New York: Springer, 2021.

References

Bolt, D. (2012) Social encounters, cultural representation and critical avoidance, in N. Watson, A. Roulstone, and C. Thomas (eds.) *Routledge Handbook of Disability Studies*, Abingdon: Routledge.

Bolt, D. (2014) *The Metanarrative of Blindness: A Re-Reading of Twentieth-Century Anglophone Writing*, Ann Arbour: University of Michigan Press.

Bolt, D. (2019) *Cultural Disability Studies in Education: Interdisciplinary Navigations of the Normative Divide*, Abingdon: Routledge.

Bolt, D. (2020a) Radio blindness: Interdisciplinarity, ocularnormativity, and young people's preparation for academia. *Journal of Further and Higher Education* 44 (9): 1233–1244.

Bolt, D. (2020b) The metanarrative of disability: Social encounters, cultural representation and critical avoidance, in N. Watson and S. Vehmas (eds.) *Routledge Handbook of Disability Studies, 2nd Ed*, Abingdon: Routledge.

Bolt, D. (2021) *Metanarratives of Disability: Culture, Assumed Authority, and the Normative Social Order*, Abingdon: Routledge.

Derrida, J. (1993) *Memoirs of the Blind: The Self-Portrait and Other Ruins*, trans. Pascale-Anne Brault and Michael Naas, London: University of Chicago Press.

Derrida, J. (1994) *Spectres of Marx: The Work of Mourning, the State of the Debt, and the New International*, trans. Peggy Kamuf, London: Routledge.

Healey, D. and Michalko, R. (2021) The metanarrative of blindness in North America: Meaning, feeling, and feel, in D. Bolt (ed.) *Metanarratives of Disability: Culture, Assumed Authority, and the Normative Social Order*, Abingdon: Routledge.

Houston, E. (2021) Polysemic interpretations: Examining how women with visual impairments incorporate, resist, and subvert advertising content. *Journal of Advertising*, 1–16.

Kamuf, P. (1991) *A Derrida Reader: Between the Blinds*, London: Harvester Wheatsheaf.

Karah, H. (2021) The metanarrative of blindness in India: Special education and assumed knowledge cultures, in D. Bolt (ed.) *Metanarratives of Disability: Culture, Assumed Authority, and the Normative Social Order*, Abingdon: Routledge.

Kidder, R. M. (1973) *Dylan Thomas: The Country of the Spirit*, Princeton, NJ: Princeton University Press.

Kirtley, D. D. (1975) *The Psychology of Blindness*, Chicago: Nelson-Hall.

Korg, J. (1965) *Dylan Thomas*, Boston: Twayne.

Padilla, A. (2021) The metanarrative of blindness in the global South: A LatDisCrit Counterstory to the bittersweet mythology of blindness as giftedness, in D. Bolt (ed.) *Metanarratives of Disability: Culture, Assumed Authority, and the Normative Social Order*, Abingdon: Routledge.

Penketh, C. (2022) Historicizing an ocularnormative future for art education. *Journal of Literary and Cultural Disability Studies* 16 (1): 5–22.

Starkey, G. (2012) Radio studies: The sound and vision of an established medium in the digital age. *Sociology Compass* 6 (11): 845–855.

Thomas, D. (1992) *Under Milk Wood: A Play for Voices*, London: Orion.

Whittington, I. (2014) Radio studies and 20th-century literature: Ethics, aesthetics, and remediation. *Literature Compass* 11 (9): 634–648.

Wrigley, A. (2014) Dylan Thomas' *under milk wood*, 'a play for voices' on radio, stage and television. *Critical Studies in Television* 9 (3): 77–88.

INDEX

Note: Page numbers followed by 'n' indicate a note on the corresponding page.

For Product Safety Concerns and Information please contact our EU
representative GPSR@taylorandfrancis.com
Taylor & Francis Verlag GmbH, Kaufingerstraße 24, 80331 München, Germany

www.ingramcontent.com/pod-product-compliance
Lightning Source LLC
Chambersburg PA
CBHW070331270326
41926CB00017B/3836

* 9 7 8 1 0 3 2 2 2 9 9 2 8 *